Unlocking Literacy

Second Edition

Robert Fisher and Mary Williams

 David Fulton Publishers

David Fulton Publishers Ltd
The Chiswick Centre, 414 Chiswick High Road, London W4 5TF
www.fultonpublishers.co.uk

.

First published in Great Britain in 2006 by David Fulton Publishers.

David Fulton Publishers is a division of Granada Learning Ltd, part of ITV plc.

10 9 8 7 6 5 4 3 2 1

British Library Cataloguing in Publication Data
A catalogue record for this book is available from the British Library.

ISBN 1 84312 386 X

Typeset by Fish Books, London
Printed and bound in Great Britain

Contents

About the contributors

Françoise Allen was first educated in France where she specialised in English Linguistics. She taught languages in multicultural comprehensive schools in west London for ten years, including two years as head of faculty. She is currently course tutor in Modern Foreign Languages in the School of Sport and Education at Brunel University and runs the PGCE in Secondary Education award. Her research interests include bilingualism and the development of literacy through learning a foreign language.

Robert Catt has taught English within 11–18 comprehensive schools. His interests in language and learning have involved research in both the UK and USA. He has also worked abroad with teachers and their teacher educators, most recently in Poland and Uzbekistan. He is Education staff tutor with The Open University in the south of England, working within the Centre for Language and Communication.

Robert Fisher was until recently Professor of Education and Director of the Centre for Research in Teaching Thinking at Brunel University. His research publications on teaching and thinking are internationally recognised and he has published more than twenty books on education. His recent publications include *Teaching Thinking* (Continuum) and the highly acclaimed *Stories for Thinking* series (Nash Pollock). He is involved in research and training with schools and local education authorities, is an adviser to the Department for Education and Skills and is a frequent speaker at national and international conferences on the teaching of literacy, creativity and thinking skills.

Paula Frew currently works as a Primary Strategy Consultant in London. She moved from classroom teaching to working with children with special needs fifteen years ago during which time she trained and worked as a Reading Recovery teacher. She has recently completed research into the effectiveness of the Early Literacy Support Programme which is part of the National Strategy.

John Garvey is a Senior Lecturer in Education at St Mary's University College, Twickenham. Prior to his career in lecturing he was a primary teacher for seven years and a head teacher in the London Borough of Richmond upon Thames. He has particular research interests in the use of interactive whiteboards for learning and teaching, and text manipulation software.

Gerry Gregory taught in inner-London secondary schools for nine years after National Service and in Brazil for three. He was a Senior Lecturer in Education at Shoreditch College of Education and at Brunel University. He has published texts for mature slow readers; articles/chapters on fiction (Iris Murdoch, Aldous Huxley); writing in secondary English; language and technology education; community publishing and education (PhD topic); quality assurance and education; writing in higher education; and on the teaching of grammar. His current focus is on teaching about language change.

Pam Hodson taught in secondary schools for 18 years. From 1989–92, she worked as an advisory teacher on the LINC Project. She was a lecturer in Primary English at Brunel University and is currently head of the Primary English team at Kingston University where she lectures on both postgraduate and undergraduate courses. She has co-authored with Deborah Jones *Teaching Children to Write* (David Fulton Publishers) and her research interests include using digital video to support children's literacy development and the teaching of speaking and listening in the primary classroom.

Colleen Johnson spent several years as an actor in Canada and the UK, working mainly in theatre in education, co-founding two theatre companies. She has a wide range of teaching experience in primary, secondary, further, adult and higher education, specialising in drama, voice production and lecturing skills. She is a Senior Lecturer in Drama in Primary Education at St Mary's University College, Twickenham.

Deborah Jones taught in primary schools in London and Cambridgeshire before joining an LEA advisory and inspection service where she worked first on the LINC project and subsequently co-ordinated assessment for the LEA. She is a senior lecturer in the School of Sport and Education at Brunel University with research interests in language and literacy and gender in education. She has co-authored with Pam Hodson *Teaching Children to Write* (David Fulton Publishers). She teaches at undergraduate, masters and doctoral levels within the University.

Julie Scanlon is a Key Stage 2 class teacher in a rural primary school in north east Wales and a sessional lecturer in Early Childhood and Education Studies at

NEWI, Wrexham. She co-authored *Supporting Reading* in 2004, published by David Fulton Publishers as part of the Helping Hands series and has contributed to other language and literacy publications.

Mary Williams worked for 20 years as a primary school teacher, the last nine as head teacher of a nursery/infant school. She was until recently a senior lecturer at Brunel University and now works as a part-time educational consultant in Brunel's Able Children's Education Centre (BACE). Her research interests include literacy teaching and learning; gifted and talented pupils in the early years, as part of the Department for Education and Skills' 'Nurturing Young Talent' initiative; and metacognition. She is editor and co-editor, respectively, of *Unlocking Writing* and *Unlocking Creativity* (David Fulton Publishers).

Acknowledgements

We would like to thank the many teachers, student teachers and children in west London schools whose work has informed our research.

We are grateful for permission to include the following published poems and extracts:

'I Saw a Jolly Hunter' and 'My Mother Saw a Dancing Bear', from *Collected Poems* by Charles Causley, published by Macmillan, reprinted by permission of David Higham Associates Limited; 'I'm a Parrot', by Grace Nichols, reproduced with permission of Curtis Brown Group Ltd, on behalf of Grace Nichols, copyright Grace Nichols 1988; and material previously published in *First Stories for Thinking* and *First Poems for Thinking* by Robert Fisher, reproduced with permission of Nash Pollock Publishing.

Every effort has been made to obtain permission to include copyright material in this book; in case of failure to obtain permission the editors and publishers undertake to make good any omissions in future printings.

Introduction

Is there a key somewhere that will help me understand what all these words mean?

(Ben, aged 11)

One of the central purposes of education is to help pupils to read and write. For many children like Ben, learning to be literate is a struggle, as they and their teachers search for the key that will unlock the mysteries of learning to read and write. In this book we explore ways to help children like Ben develop their skills in literacy, thinking and learning. In this revised edition of *Unlocking Literacy* we set out to show how literacy teaching, including during the Literacy Hour, can be used creatively and imaginatively to develop reading, writing, speaking and listening with children of all ages and abilities. This book offers a guide for those engaged in teaching literacy and the Literacy Hour in schools, and for all who are interested in improving the quality of reading, writing, speaking and listening of children aged 3 to 14 (*Curriculum Guidance for the Foundation Stage* (DfEE 2000), Key Stages 1–3 in the National Curriculum for England and Wales (DfEE1999)).

With new chapters devoted to 'speaking and listening', the use of the interactive whiteboard and language demands in the age of texting, the book is brought up to date with what it needs to be literate at the beginning of the twenty-first century. All chapters have been revised to incorporate significant new initiatives in teaching and learning, particularly 'Excellence and Enjoyment (DfES 2003a) and 'The Primary Strategy: Speaking, Listening and Learning' (DfES 2003b). The book takes an inclusive stance on most issues relating to language and literacy learning while providing a chapter that specifically deals with children who have special educational needs in terms of their literacy and language development. Essential adaptations to the curriculum for pupils who are learning English as an additional language are suggested throughout the book as appropriate. This book is based on a number of underlying beliefs about the benefits that being literate brings for all pupils irrespective of their individual language backgrounds.

Literacy brings valuable ways of thinking about ourselves and our world. Being able to read enables us to learn from people we do not and cannot personally know. Written language allows us to communicate across space and time. It gives us access to 'the best that is thought and known in the world'.[1] Learning to be literate is more than learning the basic skills of reading and writing. Access to literature helps to shape the personality, enables us to understand ourselves, and others, better and develops emotional intelligence.[2] Being literate helps to facilitate critical and creative thinking and the ability to solve problems. Our underlying belief is that reading and writing are not just mechanical skills but are in their most important functions *thinking* activities.

Not all of human thinking needs words, but language is essential for extending thinking, for extending learning through reading and writing and for communicating with others. If words are the tools for thought, as many psychologists such as Vygotsky claim, then teaching children to be literate is to give them tools for thinking.[3] It will enhance children's cognitive growth and help them get more out of learning and of life. As Charlene, aged 10, put it: 'If you did not have words how would you know what to say? How would you know what to think?'.

Learning to be literate begins with speaking and listening: an ability that has, at last, been fully recognised as important (DfES 2003b). Speech enables us to describe the world, but written speech has a separate linguistic function; it enables us to sustain and order our thinking. Writing allows us to reflect on and shape what is said in systematic and sustained ways. Reading enables us to focus on, to make judgements about and to be critical about what we, and others, have said. As Dean, aged 9, said in explaining the difference between speaking and reading: 'You can go back to a book and see what it says, but once you've said something words fly away and they're gone'.

In this book we have tried to find creative ways of extending children's thinking through their use of language. Language is a social tool used for a wide range of purposes. Our reasons for using language are social, personal and to do with purposes we want to achieve. As Lynette, aged 7, said: 'You have to use words to get what you want'. To help a child become literate means giving them the means to achieve more in learning and in life. Giving children a *purpose* for their reading and writing is another key focus of this book.

Language is the raw material of literature. An aim of literacy teaching is to enable children to experience a wide range of personal, imaginative and functional language. Through literature they learn about the uses of language and the patterns of thought and feeling that language can convey. They learn through literature how the use of language can help create, sustain or destroy relationships. It is through exploring human relationships in literature that moral imagination develops and children acquire, adapt and develop their values. 'You don't understand what it's like until you read about it,' said Joanne, during a class discussion on the value of newspapers. Reading, reflecting on and responding to what is read also provide the essential groundwork for children's own writing.[4]

We live in an age of information overload, in a state that the psychologist William James called a 'buzzing, blooming confusion'. How to deal with the welter of information that surrounds us is one of the major challenges our children face in modern society. They must learn not only how to cope with information but also how to shape, organise and control it for themselves. The computer and communications technology – recently via the mobile telephone – are sources of endless data. Children need the thinking and information-processing skills that will help them to identify what they need to know, how to access that knowledge, judge its value, interpret and communicate it. They need to be able to answer the question asked by Gary, aged 8, when he was trying to locate information on the computer: 'What do you do once you've got it on the screen?'.

Children need to learn through language but also to learn about language. This means learning about the social uses of language as well as the structure of words, sentences and texts. We believe that children's knowledge about language should start from what children can do and from the considerable implicit knowledge about language they already possess. What we suggest in this book are ways of helping them to make this knowledge explicit. Vygotsky argued that there are two stages in the development of literacy: first, its automatic unconscious acquisition (typified when 'natural readers' say they don't know how they learnt to read); and, second, active conscious control over their knowledge (such as when a child shapes writing for an audience and a purpose). The term 'metacognition' refers to this conscious control over one's thinking. A theme of this book is to show how children can gain conscious control over the thinking involved in literacy, and how to develop awareness of the nature of language and of themselves as thinkers and learners.[5] We believe that the key to higher order reading and writing skills is higher order thinking. Such thinking is not easy, as Anna, aged 10, said: 'Thinking about thinking is the hardest kind of thinking'. But we believe such thinking, thinking that helps them to gain conscious control of the processes of literacy, is in the grasp of all children if they are given the right kinds of help.

If language is to do with making meaning, we believe that children's literacy is best developed through meaningful activities both in English lessons and elsewhere across the curriculum. These activities need to be structured, but must also be creative,[6] so that learning to read and write is seen by children to have real purpose. We offer therefore some models of creative literacy teaching that provide challenge within a structured framework, drawn from the research of our own and others' classroom practice. In particular we focus on the structured framework of the Literacy Hour, now used in schools in England and Wales, and aim to show ways in which teaching in the Literacy Hour can be developed in creative and problem-solving ways to add value, variety and interest to the routines of teaching

A new Primary National Strategy in England was launched in 2003. The aims of the new strategy are contained in the recent government publication, *Excellence and Enjoyment* (DfES 2003a). Among its key aims were that schools and teachers should take greater ownership of the curriculum and be more creative in their approaches to teaching and learning. Teachers should be able to plan and develop a rich and exciting curriculum for their children that would develop their capacity to learn. Ofsted (2002) said, in *The Curriculum in Successful Primary Schools,* that good schools adapted the National Curriculum and the national strategies to suit their children, to make learning exciting and giving children a rich experience. Because every school is different the primary strategy does not offer a 'one size fits all' approach. Successful schools are encouraged to plan their own teaching frameworks to provide engaging and effective learning experiences. They try to bring excellence and enjoyment into every lesson. As one teacher put it: 'We need to stop and to ask ourselves – how can I make this lesson special?'.

In this book we attempt to illustrate creative approaches to teaching. It is not a recipe book; we believe there are many kinds of good teacher and many ways to teach literacy, and in our view the best ways are those that rely on the critical and reflective judgement of teachers. These judgements need to be underpinned by research and an awareness of what has proved successful and effective in other classrooms, so what we offer here is not only what has worked for us and for our teacher researchers, but also what is informed by published research and current initiatives in this country and abroad. Sometimes, as the words of Jody, aged 11, remind us: 'It helps you to think if you hear what others say'.

This book is about the development of language and linguistic intelligence[7] and how to create high-quality interaction between teacher and child so as to improve levels of achievement. We aim to show creative ways to teach literacy not only within the Literacy Hour, but beyond it, and to develop critical literacy and higher order reading and writing skills across the curriculum.

In this book you will find chapters on the following topics:

- Chapter 1: 'Stories are for thinking' explores ways stories can be used for developing literacy, through questioning and discussion, reading, writing and other creative activities to help develop thinking across the curriculum. Reading stories is the natural way to unlock and develop the literacy skills of young children. We look at ways of using stories as part of a Literacy Hour lesson and as a stimulus for thinking with individual children, small groups, whole classes or with larger groups of children, as in a school assembly.

- Chapter 2: 'A poem is alive' presents ways of using poetry with young children to develop literacy. It shows how children's questions can be a focus for discussing poems within a shared or guided reading session, and how to encourage children to make expressive and creative responses to poems, as well as ideas for composing. This chapter shows how the poetic voice within any child can be unlocked, and how children can be supported in becoming poets themselves.

- Chapter 3: '"Jolly good," I said' presents a rationale for using poetry with older children, and ways of moving children on from familiar and everyday uses of language towards engagement with more demanding language use. The chapter shows how challenging work with children can involve enjoyment, expression and feeling. Dynamic approaches to teaching poetry provide models that can be adapted for use in any classroom to develop literacy and the kinds of interactive and 'intersubjective' teaching that develops higher order thinking and linguistic awareness.

- Chapter 4: 'Playing with words' presents ways to teach phonic and phonemic awareness, informed by recent research and the ongoing debate about how best to approach the teaching of reading. Ideas are given for effective classroom practice at word level including how to teach phonemes to young children and how to extend phonic knowledge to older children, using both synthetic and analytic approaches. Other features of work at word level are included, such as ways of developing vocabulary knowledge and skills in spelling.

- Chapter 5: 'Teaching grammar and knowledge about language' discusses arguments for and against the teaching of grammar. Drawing on research in schools it presents approaches to teaching grammar within and beyond the Literacy Hour which have been effective in developing children's knowledge about grammar and language. This chapter considers the context of current interest in the teaching and learning of 'grammar' in relation to the National Curriculum and National Literacy Strategy and argues the case for descriptive grammar teaching. It also explores some broad principles and some particular examples of effective grammar teaching and learning.

- Chapter 6: 'Is this write?' considers how children's writing develops from the early years to a growing control over and awareness of the writing process. It sets out to show how children develop as writers, and how they can be encouraged to write in vigorous, committed, honest and interesting styles, in both narrative and non-narrative forms. A key theme in this chapter is to show how children can learn to match their style to an audience and purpose. Various strategies are suggested to help develop creative approaches to teaching writing in the classroom including how to help pupils gain metacognitive understanding of themselves as writers.

- Chapter 7: 'It's good to talk' aims to put into context the guidance offered in *The Primary Strategy: Speaking, Listening and Learning* (DfES 2003b) and discusses how to implement its recommendations in the primary classroom. The chapter celebrates the fact that the importance of speaking and listening for learning has been fully recognised at last. It suggests that whereas standard English is important as the language of power in terms of government and trade, first languages and dialects are also crucial for the social and emotional development of the child.

- Chapter 8: 'Sparks which make learning vivid' focuses on the key role that drama can play in the development of speaking and listening as part of children's literacy learning as acknowledged in *The Primary Strategy: Speaking, Listening and Learning* (ibid), as it is a learning medium through which children can explore concepts and acquire knowledge and understanding. It shows ways in which drama can be developed in the classroom and the important role that it can play in developing not only language skills but also self-esteem, social skills and confidence. Examples of successful classroom work in drama are presented and analysed, showing how drama can be used to enhance learning in English and across the curriculum.

- Chapter 9: 'Where am I going?' places assessment at the heart of effective teaching and learning. Assessing children's literacy is of fundamental importance as it motivates children to see what they have achieved. It also informs them, and their teachers, about what else they need to learn. This chapter also looks at ways of helping teachers to assess their pupils, and for children to set targets for themselves – to raise their self-awareness as readers, writers and users of language and literacy in order to catapult forward their thinking and learning.

- Chapter 10: 'Teaching children with special educational needs (SEN) in the mainstream classroom' presents practical ways to use the classroom environment and specific teaching interventions to help develop literacy in children with special literacy needs. The teaching methods that help children with special needs also work effectively with all children.

- Chapter 11: 'Using the interactive whiteboard' for whole-class teaching of reading and writing examines how teaching can revolutionise with the judicious use of this facility. The chapter sets out to show how the modelling of processes and skills enhances literacy learning as part of shared endeavour with children. The importance of maximising the interactive nature of the medium is emphasised and practical examples of how to do this are shared. The problem for those lacking confidence in ICT of how to get started is considered, with reassurance beings given that it can be a relatively painless process. Many useful websites are also included.

- Chapter 12: 'Literacy for life' shows how the world of signs and symbols has opened up a new language for children to learn. From an early age children are made aware of the visual impact of environmental print. They need to be able to deconstruct these media texts effectively in order to gain meaning from them. This involves understanding how 'authors' use colour, font style and size and choice of image to get their meaning across. Practical ways of introducing this into the classroom are discussed and are shown to have motivated children who have little interest in traditional forms of literacy. This has enabled them to develop confidence and enthusiasm that transcends all four Programmes of Study of the National Curriculum for English.

All of these chapters are aimed at helping teachers to unlock literacy for life for the children they teach. We believe the challenge is to try to retain in our teaching the spirit of the following quotation:

> Language is a system of sounds, meanings and structures with which we make sense of the world around us. It functions as a tool of thought; as a means of social organisation; as the repository and means of transmission of knowledge; as the raw material of literature, and as the creator and sustainer – or destroyer – of human relationships. It changes inevitably over time and, as change is not uniform, from place to place. Because language is a fundamental part of being human, it is an important aspect of a person's sense of self; because it is a fundamental part of any community, it is an important part of a person's sense of social identity.
>
> (DES 1989:6:18)[8]

This book aims to show how this can be achieved, and how answers may be found to the question, summed up in the words of an eleven-year-old struggling reader: 'Is there a key somewhere that will help me understand what these words mean?'.

Notes

1.   Matthew Arnold (1822–88) defined the value of literary criticism as 'a disinterested endeavour to learn and propagate the best that is known and thought in the world' (*The Function of Literary Criticism at the Present Time*).

2.   The Bullock Report, *A Language for Life* (DES 1975:124), is eloquent on the value of literature in helping to shape the personality and sharpen critical intelligence, and the importance of literature to learning and life were also echoed in subsequent reports such as the Kingman Report (DES 1988) and Cox Report (DES 1989).

3.   Lev Vygotsky (1962) *Thought and Language*. Cambridge, MA.: MIT Press.

4.   The Kingman Report (DES 1988) argued that wide and responsive reading was necessary for children to get an ear for language and a store of ideas for use in writing, and that once expressed through writing these structures would in turn add flexibility and power to children's speech. In this way literacy plays an important role in developing spoken language.

5.   For an introduction to metacognition, see Fisher, R. (1998) 'Thinking about thinking: developing metacognition in children', *Early Child Development and Care* 141, 1–13 and Williams, M. (ed.) (2002) *Unlocking Writing*, published by David Fulton Publishers.

6.   See *Unlocking Creativity* edited by Robert Fisher and Mary Williams (2004), published by David Fulton Publishers.

7.   See *Head Start: How to Develop Your Child's Mind*, (1999) by Robert Fisher, London: Souvenir Press, for more on the nature of linguistic intelligence and how it can be developed.

8.   Cox Report – DES (1989:6:18) *English for Ages 5 to 16*. So called after Professor Brian Cox of Manchester University who chaired the working group.

References

Arnold, M. (1864) *The Function of Literary Criticism at the Present Time*.

Bullock, A. (1975) *A Language for Life*. London:HMSO.

DES (1989) *English for Ages 5 to 16* (Cox Report). London: HMSO.

DfEE (1999) *The National Curriculum: Handbook for Primary Teachers in England.* London: DfEE.

DfEE (2000) *Curriculum Guidance for the Foundation Stage.* London: QCA Publications.

DfES (2003a) *Excellence and Enjoyment: A Strategy for Primary Schools.* Nottingham: DfES Publications.

DfES (2003b) *The Primary Strategy*: *Speaking, Listening, Learning: Working with Children in Key Stages 1 and 2.* Norwich: HMSO.

Fisher, R. (1998) 'Thinking about thinking: developing metacognition in children', *Early Child Development and Care*, **141**, 1–13.

Fisher, R. (1999) *Head Start: How to Develop Your Child's Mind.* London: Souvenir Press.

Fisher, R. and Williams, M. (eds) (2004) *Unlocking Creativity.* London: David Fulton Publishers.

Kingman, J. (1988) *Report of the Committee of Inquiry into the Teaching of English Language.* London: HMSO.

Ofsted (2002) *The Curriculum in Successful Primary Schools.* London: HMSO.

Vygotsky, L. (1962) *Thought and Language.* Cambridge, MA.: MIT Press.

Williams, M. (ed.) (2002) *Unlocking Writing.* London: David Fulton Publishers.

'Stories are for thinking': creative ways to share reading

Robert Fisher

Books are not made to be believed, but to be subjected to enquiry. When we consider a book, we must not ask ourselves what it says, but what it means.

(Umberto Eco)

What's the point of a story unless you think about it?

(Karen, aged 6)

Introduction

Literacy begins in thinking about stories. In all cultures there are epic stories that have been handed down through the ages, first spoken or sung and later written, that have fed the human mind. (Literacy in every culture begins in speaking, listening, seeing and thinking.)

A group of eight-year-old children had been listening to the story of Adam and Eve. 'Was there anything,' asked the teacher, 'that was strange, interesting or puzzling about the story?' One child's hand shot up. 'No,' said the teacher. The story was a thinking story so she wanted them all to stop and think about it. She waited a minute or two while the children thought about the story. She then invited questions. This time many hands shot up. 'How did the snake talk?' 'Why did God create Adam and Eve as adults and not as children?' 'How was the snake bad if everything in the garden was good?' 'Why did God make the snake?' 'When Adam and Eve left the garden where did they go?' 'Did Adam and Eve eat the wild animals?' 'Did the wild animals eat each other?' 'What happened to the Garden of Eden after Adam and Eve left it?' 'Did they know what a child was?' Their questioning and discussion went on for some time. At the end, one of the children said: 'I didn't know there was so much to think about in this story!'.

Why stories?

A story is something that might happen to you.

(Anne, aged 7)

In every language, and in every culture, stories are the fundamental way of organising human experience and understanding the world. The use of stories has long been recognised as a valuable means of developing literacy with children. Stories have the advantage of being embedded in human concerns, yet offer the child the chance to 'de-centre' from the immediacy of their personal lives. Stories liberate children from the here-and-now: they are intellectual constructions but they are also life-like. They are intellectually challenging, but also humanly rewarding.

One reason why stories have an affective power is that 'stories have this crucial feature, which life and history lack, that they have beginnings and ends and so can fix meanings to events'.[1] Stories are in a sense 'given' in a way that life, with its messiness and incompleteness, is not. Children live in a mosaic of disconnected bits of experience. Unlike the complexity of everyday events, stories have a completeness and an ending. What makes them stories is that their ending completes (in a rational sense) or satisfies (in an affective sense) whatever was introduced at the beginning and elaborated in the middle. As Abigail, aged 8, said: 'In stories you don't know what will happen until the end, but you know you are going to find out'.

A good story creates a possible world as an object of intellectual enquiry. What makes a story challenging is its polysemic nature, the possible layers of meaning and interpretation it contains. A good story draws us in by engaging the emotions. Rahim, aged 6, explained this by saying: 'In a good story you never know what is going to happen next'. The fantasy element of stories allows children to reflect more clearly on real experiences through powerful imaginary experience. A story is created to be enjoyed, but if it is a good story it challenges us to interpret and understand it. In listening to stories children learn about the features of narrative, and use of language as well as imagined worlds that move them away from the here and now and engage them in what Coleridge called 'a willing suspension of disbelief'.[2] Recognition of the important role of stories infuses the Framework for Teaching the Literacy Hour, at text, sentence and word level.

Children are more likely to develop into thoughtful and critical readers if teachers and parents engage them in discussing what they read. Such discussion is valuable for all children, whatever their age or ability, and is particularly important for boys who are reluctant readers.

Research has shown that children read from a wide range of genres, although adventure stories are the most popular at all ages and for both sexes.[3] The range of reading that children should be introduced to includes:

- traditional stories
- fairy stories
- stories about fantasy worlds
- stories by significant children's authors
- myths, legends and folktales
- fables and animal stories
- adventure stories
- historical stories
- TV adaptations
- stories from a range of cultures

What is critical literacy?

'I know what the words say but I don't know what they mean,' said a seven-year-old struggling with a difficult book. The first task a reader faces is to find out what the words on the page or screen say. To be a reader one must break the code and decipher what Jamie, aged 5, called 'all those funny squiggles, running around like tadpoles on a page'. A reader has first to break the code, decipher the strange marks, to answer the question 'What does it say?'. Being able to say the words is not the most important part of reading, but finding out what they mean is. What motivates a reader is the web of meaning woven by the words. If we try to read a book which makes no meaning for us we soon weary of it. Children need to do more than merely say the words if they want to be good at reading: they must understand the many meanings that words convey. If we want them to be active lifelong readers; they will need to think about and develop a critical response to what they read. They need to answer the question 'What does it mean?'.

Critical readers apply creative thinking to their reading.[4] Helping children to be critical readers means helping them to be more than readers of the plot. They need to be able to interpret the story, to read the lines, but also to read between the lines and beyond the lines. They need the skills to be able to question, rethink and develop their ideas and understanding of what they read. We want them to discover that the reading is not over when a story is finished, but continues through reflection, inferences and deductions, through translating ideas into their own words and making their own interpretations of what they read. We want them to be able to make a personal response to the story, to answer the question, 'What does it mean to me?'. This is a creative act, for no story or text will be responded to in quite the same way by any two readers.

If children are to become critical readers in the fullest sense they also need to be reading-users, and to answer the question, 'What can we do with it?'. Critical readers are able to recreate and respond to texts, and also to use them for their own creative purposes. Any story can be a stimulus for a child's own story-writing (for more on developing story-writing see Chapter 6).

A reader is not the 'author' of the text, as some theorists have claimed, any more than a pianist playing Mozart is the composer. But a reader, like a musician, is engaged in an act of interpretation, which is also an act of self-expression. A piece of music can be played or a story read at a literal level by simply playing the notes or reading the words. But at a deeper level we understand the story (or music) by linking it to our own experience of life. This provides the deeper pleasures in reading and explains why a good story or book can be returned to again and again. As Tracy, aged 8, put it; 'A good story makes you think how would you feel if it happened to you'.

Texts can be used as a means of teaching children to be writers, for example by analysing the structures of texts; to be critical readers, for example by questioning the text; and to be literate thinkers, for example by developing the ability to interrogate what they read, see and hear.

Interrogating the text

'A good story is adventure,' said Ben, aged 6. It is an adventure for the characters involved, but is also an adventure in thinking. It invites the reader to make a leap of imagination. Children need to be helped to make the imaginative leap that expands their thinking. One way of doing this is through questioning. By asking questions, teachers model what good readers do as they try to make sense of what they read. We ask the questions we hope our children will later learn to ask themselves. Such questions help develop the habits of mind of good readers. They practise with us what they will later do by themselves. So what kinds of questions should we be asking?

A story has a setting, so one question we can always ask is 'What kind of world is this?'. All stories occur in a place and at a particular time. Part of the adventure of a story is to be taken on a magic carpet of the mind to other places and other times, to meet other people doing things that might be very similar or very different to what we do. Any story can be explored by asking questions such as those in Figure 1.1.

After reading or hearing the story the first challenge which can be presented to a young child is to ask them to recollect and retell the events of the story in their own words. Young children are, of course, very keen to tell a story in the right way, in the right order. As Lucy, aged 5, said, after hearing some deviation in the retelling of the Cinderella story: 'That's not the right story. You have got to tell it right'.

Once the story is established in their minds, children can enjoy playing with the narrative if they are encouraged to do so. An example of this occurred when Rumpelstiltskin was being used as a story for thinking with five-year-olds. Once the story had been read, reconstructed and discussed some of the children were invited to act out their own version in front of the class. They volunteered to play the different parts, and with a few props began acting the story. The child playing

Key aspect	Some questions to ask
Setting	When is it (now or a long time ago)?
	Where is it (here or somewhere else)?
	What is it like there (how is it like/unlike here)?
Character	Who are the characters in the story (can you name them)?
	How would you describe them (what do they look like)?
	How are the characters related?
Plot	What happens in the story?
	What was/were the key events?
	What might have happened?
Point of view	What does the character think?
	What do the other characters think?
Dialogue	What did the character/s say?
	Why did they say that?
	What might have been said?
Language	What special words are there (what new words)?
	What sound/spelling patterns can you see?
	What punctuation is used? Why?
Themes	What is the story about?
	What is strange, interesting or puzzling about the story?
	What questions or comments do you have about the story?

FIGURE 1.1 Questions to extend children's thinking about a story

the king rode into the village and listened to the mother in the story say how her daughter could spin straw into gold. The king then asked whether the daughter would go with him to the palace to do just that. The mother thought about this request and then said 'No'. The king asked again. The daughter said she would go but the mother refused. The king tried once more but again the mother said no; her daughter could not go with the king, she must stay at home. So the king, not knowing what to do, rode away and that was the end of their version of the story. Afterwards, the girl who played the mother was asked why she had not followed the usual storyline and allowed the king to take her daughter to the palace. She replied: 'Because I knew what would happen if he did!'. (For more on developing literacy through drama see Chapter 8.)

Another kind of personal response is to try to visualise the setting, characters or events in the story. Some children, like adults, are better at seeing with their 'mind's eye' than others. Visual thinking is an important means of learning, remembering and coming to know things. We are all to some extent visual learners. Some children learn best through exercising their visual intelligence.[5] This capacity can be stimulated by asking them to close their eyes and to visualise the story they are reading or hearing in their 'mind's eye', or by taking them for a walk through an imagined scene which you describe while they try to visualise what it looks like. Talk afterwards about what they could see or could not see. One child reported, after a visualisation session, 'It's like you've got a tele inside your head', but another responded, 'The trouble is I don't know how to switch mine on'.

A story is made meaningful by linking it to personal experience and by identifying with the characters. If you were a character in the story, who would you want to be? Why? What would you do, say, think and feel? When a group of six-year-olds was asked which character in the story of Cinderella they would like to be, one child replied, 'A mouse' (the sort that was changed into a horse to pull Cinderella's carriage). When asked why he said, 'Because I like cheese, and so does a mouse'.

Young children often find it difficult to articulate a personal response to a story. As Melanie, aged 7, said, 'It's hard to say what you mean'. But although what they say can seem incoherent, their insights may contain the seeds of a more sophisticated understanding. They often have in their minds more than they can say. Our challenge is to help them to develop and express their intellect: to think for themselves, give voice to their ideas, form their own judgements and personal insights and take pride in having a personal point of view.

One method for achieving this, which has been used successfully across the world, is that of Philosophy for Children. This is a method of using a story as a stimulus for creating what is called a 'community of enquiry' with any group of children.[6] Before looking at ways of using stories in a community of enquiry, as part of a Literacy Hour, we will discuss the kinds of higher order reading skills that can be developed using a 'Stories for Thinking' approach.

Developing higher order reading skills

Oh, I get it, we're not supposed to read the story, we are supposed to think about it.

(James, aged 7)

Once children are able to 'crack' the language code, through being able to read and write at a basic level, they will need to practise their reading with challenging texts and develop the higher order skills that will enable them extend and improve their standard of reading. The following are some of the higher order reading skills that they need to develop:

- skimming
- scanning
- reflective reading: questioning, analysing, predicting
- reasoning: making inferences, deductions and connections
- evaluating.

Skimming is the ability to get the overall gist of a text and to gather the main points. Asking the child to skim through the story before or after you have read it and then to reconstruct it provides practice in skimming. The ability to skim a story or book is important for finding out quickly what the writing is about. This can be done at a superficial level, like Woody Allen who, when asked what Tolstoy's *War and Peace* was about, said 'Russia', or the child, when asked to summarise the story of 'Puss in Boots', said 'a cat'. The value of the use of short stories in the Literacy Hour is that skimming can be carried out relatively easily by both teacher and child. Play the 'Skim a Story' game: speedily skim a story then look away and see how quickly (and accurately) you can tell what the story is about or recall it. Try getting children to practise their skimming skills by this method.

Scanning means looking rapidly but intensely at a text to identify a particular part; for example, the name of a character or when a particular event occurred. Questions to encourage children to scan the text actively include: 'Can you find the part in the story where . . . ?' or, if children are referring to the story, 'Show me where in the story it says . . .'. Play games such as 'Hunt the Word' to help develop their scanning skills by asking them to scan the story to find a particular word, sentence or punctuation mark.

Reflective reading means making a thoughtful response to texts; for example by questioning or analysing what or why something has happened or by making predictions about what is being read. This is important if children are to learn from what they read. Like all skills it develops best when it is practised. A child will learn to question, analyse and make hypotheses about what might happen next by seeing others do it and then doing it themselves. Any text that is read is there to be analysed and questioned. When asked how many questions could be asked about a story, one seven-year-old, who was practised in the art of enquiry, replied, 'More than any of us can think of. You can never run out of questions, because there is always another possible question'.

Reasoning involves making inferences and deductions from text. The trouble with language is that words are not the objects they describe and represent but are all in a sense metaphoric. They stand for things but are not the things themselves, and so must always be incomplete. The words 'old woman', for example, might refer to any one of a number of old women, who might be a range of ages or even of different genders! So it is always possible to ask, 'Who is this old woman?' or 'What is she like?' and draw inferences from clues in the text to help answer the question more fully. Inferences involve using reasons or evidence to reach a conclusion which is more or less likely to be true. During the discussion of one story a child suggested that the woman in the story might be a man dressed up as a woman. This was, of course, possible but the children decided that this was unlikely for there was no evidence in the story to support it. 'What man would want to dress up as a woman?' asked Darren (a question it was decided to leave for another time).

Deductions are inferences from text using reasoning alone. For example, any character referred to as 'she' must be female. This is true by definition, as are other things about her; for instance, if she is a person, then one day she was born and one day she will die. If all humans are mortal and Cinderella is human, then Cinderella must be mortal. A great deal can be deduced from the meanings of words, which is why getting children to explain and define them is so important. 'It depends what you mean by…' is a frequent statement made by philosophers, for they know that many arguments and misunderstandings in life arise because people interpret the meanings of words differently. Inferences and deductions from stories are made by exploring what the words of the story imply. As Jade, aged 5, said, puzzling over a word she did not understand, 'If I knew what the word meant I'd know the story'.

To be a critical reader more is needed than just knowing the tale. A story can be evaluated by being compared with others which means assessing the story critically; for example by judging what we like or do not like about it and by establishing what is good or bad about it. One way to evaluate a story is to compare it with others that have already been read. Every good story:

- has an author (or number of authors)   (Who is telling the story?)
- is a special kind of story (gene)   (What kind of story is this?)
- can be linked to other stories   (Is this story like another story you know? How?)
- is special (or original in some way)   (What is noteworthy about this story?)

Developing moral judgement

A child once said to me (getting her words in the wrong order), 'Every moral has a story'. All stories have a moral dimension if they concern aspects of human behaviour. It is often easier to understand fictional situations than situations in our own lives because we can view stories about others from a distance and a more dispassionate viewpoint. The challenging aspects of life are less threatening in stories than in real life. Stories are therefore an excellent vehicle for discussing moral issues, initiating children into thinking about meanings and values, through asking questions such as:

- How are people (characters) behaving in the story?
- How should they behave?
- How would you behave if you were them?

Other questions which can be used to explore the moral dimensions of any story include those shown in Figure 1.2:

Key question	Moral dimension
• 'Have we thought of...?'	imagination
• 'How would you feel if...?'	empathy
• 'What if everybody did...?'	making a principle universal
• 'What would happen if...?'	anticipating consequences
• 'What alternatives are there...?'	hypothetical reasoning
• 'Is it a good reason...?'	giving good reasons
• 'Is this the sort of person you want to be?'	projecting an ideal self
• 'Is this the sort of world you'd like to live in?'	projecting an ideal world

FIGURE 1.2 Exploring morality through stories

One way to involve children in the exercise of literary and moral judgement through shared reading is by creating a community of enquiry in the classroom. A community of enquiry teaches by example, enabling children to practise both a critical approach to reading and to develop habits of rational behaviour through the experience of being in a group where being reasonable (that is giving reasons for what you say and do) and listening to others are the norm. By encouraging children to think, reason and to make moral judgements about the behaviour of others, they are likely to be more considerate, more reasonable and more thoughtful about their own behaviour. Literature can be a moral force that will help educate a child's mind and emotions. As Liane, aged 7, said, in summing up what she learnt from the shared discussion of a story; 'You should always stop and think first'.

Creating a community of enquiry

You should listen to other people because sometimes they have good ideas.

(Jamie, aged 6)

A community of enquiry occurs where reading is shared in a group and discussed in a safe and stimulating environment, that is a place where children learn to think for themselves and to value the thinking of others. The first task in a community of enquiry is to make children feel comfortable, secure and at ease with their teacher and with each other. Ideally, adult and children should be sitting at the same level, on the floor or on chairs in a circle or horseshoe shape, so that all can see, hear and talk to each other easily. This may not be possible but even so, a sense of community can be achieved in a setting which is not ideal. To overcome the problem of having her session interrupted by visitors one teacher put a sign outside her class saying 'Do not disturb, thinking in progress'.

In a community of enquiry, or thinking circle, the teacher takes responsibility for creating the form of the discussion, but the *content* should be, as far as possible, the responsibility of the children. As with any discussion, certain ground rules may need to be established beforehand or written up for all to see. Some examples are: 'We take turns', 'We speak one at a time', 'We listen to each other', and 'We respect what people say'. It can be helpful to begin by playing a thinking game that embodies the rules and encourages children to listen carefully to each other.[7]

A community of enquiry invites children into the club of critical readers. Children who engage in a community of enquiry acquire habits which reflect their experience in the community. If they listen to each other, express their own opinions, and build on each other's ideas they will grow into adults who are willing to listen, who are confident in saying what they think and who are thoughtful about what others say. They will acquire self-esteem about themselves as thinkers and readers.

In a typical community of enquiry the teacher will:

- read the story;
- invite comments or questions;
- lead a discussion;
- invite children to review the discussion; and
- introduce further group or individual activities.

This is how these elements apply to a Stories for Thinking lesson:

1. Reading the story

If the children are non-readers the teacher will read the story or text. It is helpful with young children to read the story twice. The second time is a 'thinking time', when, as they listen, the children are asked to think about anything that might be strange, interesting or puzzling about the story. Children who are readers take turns in reading part of the story, for example, a paragraph each. Any children in the group who cannot read or who find reading very difficult say 'pass' and the next child continues the reading.

2. Inviting comments or questions

> I have a lot of questions that I haven't yet thought of.
>
> (Cassie, aged 7)

After the story has been read by teacher and children, it is time to think about it. Allow some quiet thinking time, then ask the children if there is anything strange, interesting or puzzling about the story. Prevent quick children (the 'hare brains' in the group) from shouting out the first thing they think of by saying you are going to give everyone time to think. Thinking time encourages more thoughtful responses and allows time for more elaborate thinking and for children to formulate questions.

Once the children have had time to think, ask for their comments or questions and write each one in the child's own words on the board. Add the child's name after the comment or question to acknowledge each contribution. You may need to help children formulate their comment into a question or to express their thoughts fully. Try as much as possible to use the child's own words, and check with them that the changes you propose are what they want to say – as in the following excerpt from a discussion:

Child: *He was a bad man.*

Teacher: *We could turn that into a question, couldn't we – 'Was he a bad man?' or 'Why was he a bad man?'*

Child: *Why was he a bad man? (Teacher now writes this up as a question.)*

Once you have a number of questions or comments on the board, each linked to the name of one or more children (for several children might have the same thought or idea) you will have a number of responses to the story to explore in discussion. Choose one of the questions, or ask the children to choose one by voting which they would like to discuss. When the question has been selected begin the discussion by asking the child whose question it was to say why they asked it, and invite others to respond to what is said.

One advantage of writing questions on a chart is that you have a record of contributions that can be added to later or compared with other lists. A frequent finding is that the more experience children acquire with interrogating texts the better at it they become. As one teacher reported: 'For the first few stories the children gave few comments or questions, after six weeks I got twice as many, and now [after a term] they often ask more questions than I can fit on to the board'. Of her lists of questions another teacher said, 'It provides me with written evidence that this is an enquiring classroom'.

3. Leading a discussion

I like it when we have a 'thinking time' about stories.

(Sonal, aged 6)

One way to facilitate the discussion is to ask who agrees or disagrees with particular comments that have been made. The teacher should aim to lead but not dominate the discussion. Initially, you will need to ask a lot of questions yourself, particularly the key question 'Why?'. As the group gets better at discussing together, the balance of teacher and pupil participation will change, and as the community develops the children should do more of the speaking. As Jemma, aged 8, said; 'A story circle is different because it is our turn to say what we think'.

Using a story for thinking

The story entitled *The Cats and the Chapatti* (Figure 1.3) is appropriate for five–eight-year-olds. Use the questions below to stimulate their thinking about it and a key theme from it.[8] To aid discussion there are two kinds of questions that can be asked about the story (Figure 1.5): they involve children in reading the lines and 'reading between the lines'. First ask questions that challenge children's thinking at the literal level of the story, by probing their knowledge of and ability to draw inferences from the text. The examples listed below show the kinds of questions you could ask to elicit an understanding of the main features of the story (Figure 1.6).

Questions should not be limited to the literal level. We should try, as Vygotsky said, to move children on to more abstract and conceptual modes of thinking.[9] The second kind of questions is at a conceptual rather than literal level and probe a child's personal understanding of a theme or concept drawn from the story. They are about reading beyond the lines and seeking a personal response to an issue in the story. They are open questions that encourage children to consider a variety of viewpoints, ideas and arguments, rather than seek one right answer. They are not about trying to 'guess what is in the teacher's head'; they try to get children to think for themselves.

Once upon a time two cats found a chapatti. A chapatti is a kind of Indian bread, a little like a flat pancake. The cats were greedy and began to quarrel over it.

'It's mine!' said one cat. 'I saw it first!'

'No, it's mine,' said the other cat. 'I saw it before you!'

While the cats were arguing a monkey came by and he looked at the chapatti. He felt hungry and wanted the chapatti for himself.

The monkey thought for a while, then said 'Sisters, why are you quarelling? To be fair you should share the chapatti and split it in two. Let me break it in half for you.'

At first the cats were not sure. Was this a fair thing to do? They soon agreed it was. So the monkey picked up the chapatti and broke it into two pieces. He then held the pieces up for the cats to see.

'Oh dear,' he said, 'look, one piece is larger than the other,' and he broke a bit off the larger piece and ate it. He held the pieces up again.

'Oh dear,' he said, 'they are still not equal,' and he broke off another piece and popped it into his mouth. The two cats watched, not realising what was happening.

Again, the monkey held the pieces up and said 'Oh dear, they are *still* not equal,' and ate another piece off the bigger bit. The clever monkey carried on doing this and the pieces became smaller and smaller. Still the cats could not see his plan.

At last there was only one small piece left. 'Oh dear,' he said, 'It's too small to cut in half,' so he quickly gobbled it up and ran away laughing. The two cats stared at each other and slowly realised that they had been tricked by the clever monkey.

FIGURE 1.3 The Cats and the Chapatti

The following list gives the kinds of questions that could be asked about one theme from the story (Figure 1.4).

These questions only model the kind that might stimulate thinking and discussion. By planning possible questions that are appropriate and challenging for your children beforehand, you will always have something to ask if the discussion flags, and by so doing you will model for the child the intelligent habits of an enquiring reader. But the most important questions are those raised by the children themselves (Figure 1.5).

The following is part of a discussion with six- and seven-year-old children (Year 2) after they had read *The Cats and the Chapatti*. They had chosen to answer Anna's question about the story: 'Why did they quarrel?'.

Child: *There were some animals quarrelling.*

Teacher: *What were they saying?*

Child: *'No you can't', 'Yes you can'...that sort of thing.*

Child: *They were contradicting each other.*

Key question: What does the story mean?

How many cats were there? How do you know?

What did the cats find?

What is a chapatti?

Where was the chapatti? Why was it there?

Why did the cats quarrel?

Why did the monkey want the chapatti?

What was the monkey's plan to get the chapatti for himself?

When did the cats realise they had been tricked?

Do you think the monkey was right when he said the last piece was too small to cut in half?

What do you think the moral of this story is?

FIGURE 1.4 Thinking about the story

Key question: What is a quarrel?

What does it mean to quarrel with someone?

Why do people quarrel? What reasons are there for quarrels?

How many people are there in a quarrel?

Can you quarrel with yourself? Have you ever had a quarrel with yourself?

Have you ever had a quarrel with other people? Give an example.

Do you only quarrel with someone you don't like?

What do you do if your friends start quarrelling?

How could you help them end a quarrel?

What is the best way of keeping out of quarrels?

Is it ever good to havea quarrel? Why or why not?

FIGURE 1.5 Thinking about quarrelling

Teacher:	*So a quarrel is like a contradiction?*
Child:	*[after a pause for thought] Yes.*
Child:	*They were quarrelling with each other.*
Teacher:	*Can you quarrel with yourself?*
Child:	*You can't quarrel with yourself. You need to have more than one person.*
Child:	*You can quarrel with yourself. You could punch yourself. Your brain quarrels with you...if you want to test yourself.*
Child:	*I disagree with Sarah. You can't quarrel with yourself. You haven't done anything to yourself.*
Child:	*If you punch your leg, it can't say 'No'. Your brain says 'No'.*
Teacher:	*Can animals say 'Yes' and 'No'?*
Child:	*No, only people can say 'Yes' and 'No'. That's how we are different from animals.*

At the end of the discussion the children were asked to talk about the story in groups and to report back what they thought was its moral. Here are some of their replies:

- Don't trust anyone. (James)
- Don't fight and quarrel. (Andrew)
- Don't be greedy or someone may take what you've got. (Ryan)
- Share with other people. (Conor)
- Don't fight or quarrel with your friends. (Sarah)
- Be kind to everyone. (Emily)

In the early stages of a community of enquiry, discussions tend to be totally teacher directed, but the aim is to shift the focus away from yourself so that the children will, through working together, become able to take more responsibility for the discussion and for the way the community of enquiry functions. Try to encourage this, once the children are familiar with the process, by asking them to respond to each other and to look at the person to whom they are responding and not at you. Introduce the convention 'I agree with...' or 'I disagree with...' and get the children to say with whom they are agreeing or disagreeing. Sometimes, invite the child who has spoken to nominate the next speaker, if there is more than one other who wishes to speak.

A number of questions have been found useful for injecting intellectual rigour into a discussion with young children. They aim to move it away from a situation where children simply give an answer with an anecdotal comment or unsupported observations, to a style of discussion characterised by the giving of reasons and the formulation of argument. They try to encourage children to take responsibility for their comments and to think about what they are saying. The hope is that such questions, in time, will become internalised and come to be asked by the children themselves.

Questions	Cognitive function of questions
● What do you think... (give child's name)? What is your view/opinion/idea about this?	focusing attention
● Why so you say that? Can you give me a reason?	reasoning
● What do you mean by? Can anyone explain that to us?	defining/analysing/clarifying
● Has anyone got another thought/example? Who else can say something about it?	generating alternative views
● How could we tell it is was true? How do you/we know?	testing for truth
● Who agrees/disagrees with... (child's name)? Why? Can you say who/what you agree/disagree with?	sustaining dialogue/ argument
● Who can remember what we have said? What are the ideas/arguments we have put forward? Which ideas were good?	summarising

FIGURE 1.6 Examples of questions found useful in discussion

Teachers could expect to see evidence of progress after a number of such sessions. The sorts of evidence teachers report include an improvement in the children's abilities as shown in Figure 1.7 (for more on assessing children's progress in literacy see Chapter 10).

The community of enquiry provides the opportunity for systematic, sustained and supportive discussion of texts. The teacher helps pupils to assume responsibility for their own ideas, to think for themselves and to benefit from the suggestions, hypotheses and insights of others. By participating in a community founded on reasoning, freedom of expression and mutual respect the children will experience what it means to be a free citizen in a democracy, with the

Evidence: childen can	Skills: children show
● listen to each other	listening skills
● formulate and ask questions	questioning and enquiry skills
● think of good/new ideas	creative thinking
● translate their thoughts and ideas into words	communication
● communicate their ideas	speaking skills
● respond to others in a discussion	co-operative and social skills
● give reasons for what they think	verbal reasoning skills
● develop their understanding of challenging concepts	concept building
● read and respond critically to texts	critical reading skills

FIGURE 1.7 Evidence of improvement in children's abilities

freedom to question, to challenge and to exercise personal choice. There is no better preparation for being an active citizen in such a country than for a child to participate with others in a community of enquiry. In learning how to interrogate texts they will also be developing the skills and confidence to interrogate all aspects of their world.

A Literacy Hour aims to develop:	Stories for Thinking aims to develop:...
● literacy: reading, writing, speaking and listening	● literacy: critical and creative thinking, questioning and reasoning as well as reading, writing, speak and listening
● reading and reflecting at text level, with emphasis on teacher questioning	● reading and reflecting on text, with emphasis on pupil comprehension
● sentence level work to improve comphrehension	● sentence level work in creating questions and comments
● word level work to improve phonics, spelling and vocabulary	● word level work in defining meanings of words and developing concepts
● a plenary session for sharing and reviewing work	● review of the discussion, as well as review or work

FIGURE 1.8 Similarities and differences between the Literacy Hour and Stories for Thinking

Stories for Thinking and the Literacy Hour

The teacher demonstrates reading strategies with a shared text. The class reads the text together and discusses ideas and textual features, engaging in a high level of interaction with the teacher.

(National Literacy Strategy, DfEE 1998)

When we are talking about stories I like to have enough time to do it.

(Kate, aged 6)

During shared reading in the Literacy Hour the teacher demonstrates reading strategies using a shared text. As in a community of enquiry the class reads the story together, discusses ideas and textual features, engaging in a high level of interaction with the teacher. The aim is to engage all children in the sorts of thoughtful reading habits that are characteristic of good readers. Research has found that 'poor readers are not nearly as adept as older children and good readers, respectively, in engaging in planful activities either to make cognitive progress or to monitor it'.[10] The Stories for Thinking method can add value to a Literacy Hour through its planned approach to pupil questioning, reasoning and critical thinking about texts. Some of the similarities and differences between a Stories for Thinking/community of enquiry approach and the Literacy Hour, as outlined in the National Literacy Strategy (DfEE 1998), are shown in Figure 1.8.

The Literacy Hour and Stories for Thinking share some common features. Both emphasise the importance of discussing the text to identify themes, ideas and implicit meanings. Both aim to develop critical reading skills. Stories for Thinking emphasises the importance of children formulating their own questions and aims to add philosophical depth to the discussion. Stories are, of course, not the only source of literary stimulus for thinking: poetry and information texts can also be used. The Literacy Hour emphasises the importance of work at word and sentence level, as well as at text level.[11]

Many teachers are exercising their professional judgement in adapting the Literacy Hour to benefit from a Stories for Thinking approach. Others prefer to find time, usually once a week, for more extended story discussion than the Literacy Hour allows. Stories for Thinking offers a flexible model that can be used in ways which suit the teacher and the children. It will develop literacy but is about more than that: it is also about teaching children to think, in particular to think philosophically about stories and about themselves and the world. This will be as true for children with English as their home language as it is for those for whom English is an additional language (EAL).[12]

Key principles that apply to EAL children also apply to all children in using Stories for Thinking. These principles have been summarised as:

- paying attention to meaning and relevance in context;
- using modelling which combines repetition with variation;
- involving learners in cognitive challenge and interaction;
- helping learners link verbalisation and visualisation.

(Cortazzi and Jin, in Williams 2002)

The principle of linking verbalisation with visualisation is especially important. Seeing supports saying, so we use pictures, tables and charts to support the development of speaking, listening, reading and writing. We also need to encourage visualisation (mental images and imagination) – what we might call 'seeing in the mind's eye'. All children have a rich inner world that they often find difficult to put into words. As Omar, aged 7 put it: 'I can see it in my mind but it is hard to say it'.

A Stories for Thinking lesson may have different names, such as Thinking Circle, Literacy Hour or even Philosophy for Children. Whatever it is called, children are often quick to see the value of having time set aside to think about and through stories. Kirandeep, aged 8, says such discussions are important because 'thinking is what we are here for'. Karen, aged 8, says she likes Stories for Thinking lessons because they makes stories 'a kind of puzzle'. This puzzling quest, once begun, can lead to a lifelong absorption in reading and making meaning from stories.

Conclusion

If we want our pupils to be active and literate citizens engaged in lifelong learning and enquiry, we need to provide opportunities to develop these skills in school. We need to engage their interest and imagination through the use of stories. What is essential to literacy is not just the ability to read and write but to learn to interrogate what they read and to do so with critical understanding. Higher order reading skills are developed through reasoned discussion in groups or 'communities of enquiry'. In creating communities of enquiry in the classroom we also develop the skills and dispositions of active citizenship. In developing the habits of intelligent behaviour through thoughtful discussion we are not just engaged in 'stories for thinking' but also in lessons for life.

Notes

1. Kieran Egan (1986) *Teaching as Story Telling*. London: Methuen.
2. 'That willing suspension of disbelief for the moment, which constitutes poetic faith.' (Coleridge 1827, *Biographia Literaria*, Ch. 14).
3. For more on children's reading choices see M. Coles and C. Hall (1999) *Children's Reading Choices*. London: Routledge.
4. See Fisher R. and Williams M. (eds) (2004) *Unlocking Creativity*. London: David Fulton Publishers.

5. See R. Fisher (1999b) *Head Start: How to Develop Your Child's Mind* (Souvenir Press) for a discussion of children's multiple intelligences, including visual intelligence and ways of developing them.

6. See R. Fisher (1998) *Teaching Thinking: Philosophical Enquiry in the Classroom* (London: Cassell) for an introduction to the theory and practice of philosophy with children. For further information contact: SAPERE (Society for the Advancement of Philosophical Enquiry and Reflection in Education) (www.sapere.net).

7. See R. Fisher (1997) *Games for Thinking* (Oxford: Nash Pollock) for some thinking games.

8. The story and questions appear in *First Stories for Thinking* by R. Fisher (1999a:56).

9. Lev Vygotsky (1978) argued that if you limit learners to literal or 'concrete' thinking you 'suppress the rudiments of abstract thought such children have...school should make every effort to push them to develop in them what is intrinsically lacking in their own development' (p. 89).

10. R. Garner (1987) *Metacognition and Reading Comprehension.* Norwood, NJ: Ablex.

11. See *The National Literacy Strategy: Framework for Teaching* (DfEE 1998) for more on the importance of text-, sentence- and word-level work with texts.

12 See Cortazzi, M. and Jin, L. (2002), in Williams, M. *Unlocking Writing* (London: David Fulton Publishers), pp. 119–21.

References

Coleridge, S.T. (1827) *Biographia Literaria.*

Coles, M. and Hall, C. (1999) *Children's Reading Choices.* London: Routledge.

DfEE (1998) *The National Literacy Strategy: Framework for Teaching.* London: HMSO.

DfEE (1999) *The National Curriculum: Handbook for Primary Teachers in England.* London: HMSO.

DfES (2003a) *The Primary Strategy: Speaking, Listening, Learning: Working with Children in Key Stages 1 and 2.* Norwich: HMSO.

DfES (2003b) *Excellence and Enjoyment: A Strategy for Primary Schools.* Nottingham: DfES Publications.

Egan, K. (1986) *Teaching as Story Telling.* London: Methuen.

Fisher R. (1997) *Games for Thinking.* Oxford: Nash Pollock.

Fisher R. (2003) *Teaching Thinking: Philosophical Enquiry in the Classroom* (2nd edn). London: Continuum.

Fisher, R. (1999b) *Head Start: How to Develop Your Child's Mind.* London: Souvenir Press.

Fisher, R. and Williams M. (eds) (2004) *Unlocking Creativity.* London: David Fulton Publishers.

Garner, R. (1987) *Metacognition and Reading Comprehension.* Norwood, NJ: Ablex.

Vygotsky, L. (1978) *Mind in Society.* Cambridge, MA: Harvard University Press.

Williams M. (ed.) (2002) *Unlocking Writing.* London: David Fulton Publishers.

Further reading

Fisher, R. (1996) *Stories for Thinking.* Oxford: Nash Pollock.

Fisher, R. (1997) *Poems for Thinking.* Oxford: Nash Pollock.

Fisher, R. (1999a) *First Stories for Thinking.* Oxford: Nash Pollock.

Fisher, R. (2000) *First Poems for Thinking.* Oxford: Nash Pollock.

Fisher, R. (2005) *Teaching Children to Think* (2nd edn). Cheltenham: Stanley Thornes.

Hodson, P. and Jones, D. (eds) (2006) *Unlocking Speaking and Listening.* London: David Fulton Publishers.

QCA (2003) *New Perspectives on Spoken English in the Classroom.* London: QCA.

'A poem is alive': using poetry with young children

Robert Fisher

Poetry comes from playing the best game of words which has ever been invented.

(Geoffrey Grigson)[1]

Poems say things better than you can.

(Sarah, aged 7)

Introduction

Every child is born with the poetic ability to respond to words and ideas in a playful way. From their earliest days young children respond and revel in verbal play through the syllabic rhythm of first words such as 'ma-ma' or 'da-da-da-da'. The babbling speech of a young child is an early expression of the poetic capacity to play with sounds. As they grow older, children will use words to play with ideas, like the three-year-old who said one autumn, 'Look, the tree is snowing leaves'.

Poetry begins with a fascination for words and with enjoyment of word games. The following example of rhyming words were strung together by a group of four-year-olds: 'sad dad had a bad lad', 'may play today stay' and 'vet in a jet sent me a wet pet'. How do we build on this early wordplay with rhymes and rhythms and extend it to an enjoyment and understanding of poetry?

Poetry begins by feeding the ear. Children like to listen to poems. They delight in word-sounds and wordplay. They will read old favourites over and over again and enjoy learning a favourite poem by heart. Children have a natural ear for rhyme and rhythm, and poetry feeds this innate response to the patterns of spoken language. The love of poetry begins in the delight of shared wordplay.[2] The gift of words, wrapped in riddles, rhymes and poetry is an enduring gift. 'A poem is,' as Anne, aged 10, says, 'like a present in words.'

Research shows that a rich diet of nursery rhymes is an important factor in subsequent success in learning to read.[3] Children's experience of rhyme and rhythm should be extended to an enjoyment of poetry, to appreciate how it sounds, what it says and the ways it uses language for literary effect. The Framework for teaching the Literacy Hour lays stress on the interplay of listening to, reading and writing poetry. It encourages teachers to share a range of poetry with children including:

- informal wordplay and word games;
- action rhymes and chants;
- nursery and traditional rhymes;
- poems by significant children's authors; and
- riddles, tongue-twisters and shape poems.

Our task as teachers is to help children move on from a love of simple rhyme to an appreciation of poetry that will feed the eye and mind as well as the ear. Both understanding and enjoyment are needed to fully appreciate a poem.[4] A poem is written to contain a distilled essence of meaning, what Ted Hughes (1967) calls the 'spirit' of the poem. As Hughes says, the meaning or spirit of a poem is made up of its living parts, its words, images and rhythms. Helping children to discover the spirit and to make sense of a poem can be one of the most rewarding aspects of teaching English. Teaching then becomes a shared literary adventure when children and teacher meet to enjoy and understand better what is written. 'I don't like poems I don't understand,' says Henry, aged 6, 'so you need someone to read with you.'

The secret of introducing children to poetry is simple. Like learning a language, the best way is immersion. Simply plunge in and share the poetry you like with children and do it often. Teaching poetry turns out to be simpler once one is doing it. 'A poem a day' is an uncomplicated recipe, but reading just one poem a day to a class or a child will create a rich resource of language experience (see Figure 2.1). Giving children a varied range of poetry books to look at and discuss and asking them to choose their favourites to have read out will help begin that process of learning to be discerning readers, writers, listeners and speakers.

What young children need is a rich range of poetry to read and to hear. Hearing particular poems and rhymes a number of times will help them internalise the words and sounds, and they will begin to memorise spontaneously their favourite rhymes. What parents and teachers can do is to help children both to hear and to understand poems. They can explain what to expect from a poem or poetry book, help them through questioning and discussion to make meaning from poems, and show them how they too can communicate through poetry and help them to create their own poems. But what is a poem?

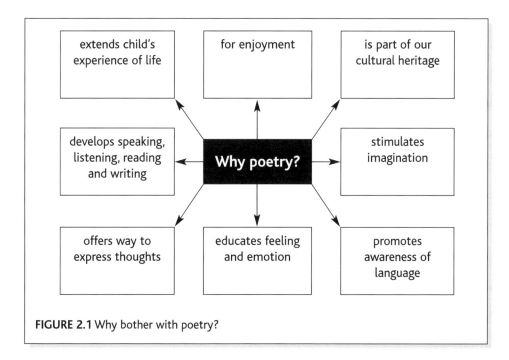

FIGURE 2.1 Why bother with poetry?

It takes time to absorb a poem, to explore the world it creates, its language, its sounds and the message or story it conveys. Dylan Thomas once said poetry 'makes you laugh, cry, prickle, be silent, makes your toenails twinkle'. The purposes of poetry are wider than any other kind of writing; poems can be used to tell stories, play games with language, record experience or reflect thoughts and feelings. A poem might be about the real world or an invented world of the imagination, or both. A poem can transform the ordinary into the extraordinary. It can give voice to an inner world of dreams and imaginings. Like philosophy, poetry often begins in wonder about the world and the ways in which words can reflect, distort and transform the world. As Theseus says in Shakespeare's *A Midsummer Night's Dream:*[5]

> The poet's eye in a fine frenzy rolling,
> Doth glance from heaven to earth, from earth to heaven;
> And as imagination bodes forth
> The forms of things unknown, the poet's pen
> Turns them into shapes, and gives to airy nothing
> A local habitation and a name.

Every poem is about something, and uses words in a special way. It uses 'the best words in the best order', as Coleridge said,[6] to tell its story.

How can children be helped to respond to poetry? A poem may lead to many kinds of thoughts, feelings and ideas. There is no one way but many to experience or appreciate a poem, and some ways of using poems to help young children enjoy poetry and become more able readers will now be explored. The literary roles we seek to develop through poetry can be summed up as: code-breaker, meaning-maker, reading-responder and reading-user, and each role is associated with a key question that can be asked about any poem (see Figure 2.2).

Ways of working with a poem	Roles of the child	Key questions
Speaking and listening Reading	Code-breaker	What does it say?
Questioning Discussing	Meaning-breaker	What does it mean?
Expressing Composing	Reading-responder	What does it mean to me? What can we do with it?

FIGURE 2.2 Literary roles in poetry

We will now look more closely at these ways of working with poetry.

Speaking and listening

Poetry is made for speaking. The earliest poetry was spoken or sung. The first poems that children hear are often the half-remembered nursery rhymes recited to them by parents. These early rhymes may be much repeated, and there is good reason for this. According to W. H. Auden, what makes a poem special is that it is 'memorable speech'.[7] A poem lays down a track in the memory that can be travelled over again and again, so that language becomes rooted in experience. The words and phrases of a much-loved poem or nursery rhyme become not merely items of knowledge, but are given life and meaning by being embedded in an original poem which becomes part of us when laid down in long-term memory. When learning by heart in the natural way, through repeated opportunities to speak and listen, children are connected to their literary inheritance. When they share the words and thoughts of a poem, they are given a poetic voice through which to speak, and words which will echo in the memory. Later, having listened to and expressed the voices of others, they will come to create poetry using their own words and ideas.

A love of poetry begins with listening. Lucky is the child who has poetry read to him/her each week by a parent or teacher. Some teachers try to read a poem a day to their class, with maybe a 'favourite poem' session on Friday. Children can also be encouraged to listen on their own, or with others, to poetry tapes. Listening to poems can become a regular part of classroom activity. A section of the classroom can be turned into a listening corner with a ready supply of tapes. Children can record their favourites and listen to poems recorded by others. Teachers or parents can create their own tapes of spoken poetry to share with children.

In preparing to share poetry with children it is a good idea to practise reading the poem or poems first. Try to add part of yourself to the reading, through emphasising key words or adding humour or passion to your favourite bits. It is even better if the children have the words or book to follow as they listen. Encourage your children to recite favourite poems to each other; ultimately the aim is to inspire children to read poetry for themselves, and to want to do so they must first have appreciated hearing poetry spoken to them. They must have savoured the sounds of poems, and enjoyed entering into other people's word worlds. The initial sharing of a poem could involve many kinds of speaking: for example, whispering, chanting, reading slowly or quickly, or reading with added sound effects. A good poem has its own musical voice and this voice is the musical instrument through which the poem is expressed. No wonder Carlyle defined poetry as 'musical thoughts'.

Children should not only listen to the music of poetry; they should also speak poetry regularly. After your first reading of a poem children can be encouraged to 'read along' with you. This may simply mean asking them to repeat words in the poem that they remember. These will often be rhyming words. Learning to say poetry is as important as learning to hear it. Invite a child to say a word or line for you during the re-reading. A different child's voice could be used for each line or the children could be encouraged to repeat parts of the poem in pairs or groups. The sequence used in presenting a poem to children might include:

- practising reading the poem to yourself (perhaps tape this for the child to hear later)
- showing children what the poem looks like (the words on a page)
- reading the poem to the children (repeating this if necessary)
- inviting children to read or say parts of the poem with you
- encouraging them to say the poem in pairs, or as a group.

Children can be invited to call out the rhyming words of simple poems, for example the rhymes in the following limerick:

> There was a young man from Dunoon,
> Who always ate soup with a...

He said, 'As I eat
Neither fish, fowl or...,
I should finish my dinner quite...'

Young children often find little difficulty in supplying the rhymes 'spoon', 'meat' and 'soon'. What does surprise children is that the original rhymes in this poem actually are 'fork', 'flesh' and 'quick'. This shows that you need not be restricted to given rhyme patterns, but can create interesting effects by supplying your own, possibly bizarre, rhyming words. In this way rhyming poetry can be an ideal means of developing children's phonic skills.

It is a shame, however, if children are limited to a diet of sing-song rhymes. They need to hear a rich repertoire of different kinds of poems, including those written in free verse. Poems need not simply be spoken, but can also be enlivened by other expressive means, including hand movements and actions, the use of puppets, musical instruments and so on (for more on creative ways of performing poetry see 'Expressing' below). A question to ask yourself before you present a poem to children is 'How can I add interest to my reading?'. It may be through use of voice or gesture that added colour is given to a spoken poem. Remember that, for you as well as for the children what is loved enough is not easily forgotten. A teacher described her own approach thus: 'I try my best to memorise the poem beforehand so I can give my children full attention while "reading" it to them. This adds to the drama of the situation both for them and me!' But if you don't love the poem, follow the advice of Ted Hughes,[8] and don't try to learn it.

Reading

According to James, aged 6, a poem 'is a kind of picture in words'. A poem consists of both sounds in the air as well as words pictured on a page. The shared reading of a poem which could take place during the Literacy Hour means getting children to both listen to the sound and see the words of the poem shaped on a page. The use of poems in 'big books', or copied on large sheets of paper, overhead transparencies or whiteboards, means groups of children can share the verbal and visual presence of a poem.

A poem is encoded in language. Helping children to crack the code, and therefore to be able to read the words and release the poem from the page, is a challenging task. This means helping young children to focus on the sounds of words (for more on phonics see Chapter 4), and also to think about what words mean. The importance of reading to young children has been emphasised in many studies, as has the value of learning nursery rhymes and performing other kinds of wordplay. Studies show that young children's sensitivity to rhyme is particularly important in predicting later success in reading. That is why singing and chanting rhymes can be so important in developing early literacy.

Reading aloud to children has a positive effect on developing early reading ability through helping children to differentiate and recognise different sounds (phonemes) in words, but so does getting children to see the words as you read to them. There is a problem in sharing normal-sized books with large groups of children, hence the use of 'big books' in teaching literacy in schools. Of course, you do not need 'big books', nor coloured pictures, to teach literacy. Indeed many of the 'big books' used in schools today are of poor literary quality and the illustrations encourage teachers and children to rely too much on gaining meaning from simple visual images. A poem is a text made up of words; it does not involve pictures on the page but encourages pictures in the mind. It is better, if possible, to rely on text alone, since this forces the child to engage in decoding the words and not to rely on picture cues. It also encourages the creation of mental images. If you want a group of children to share the words of a poem, you can simply print them in bold on a large sheet of paper or digital whiteboard for all to see.

The following is a summary of the key principles involved in sharing the reading of poetry with young children:

- Choose poems to share which children enjoy.
- Present the poem with wholehearted enjoyment.
- Involve the children if possible in the reading, e.g. by chanting some of the words.
- Repeat the reading for children to gain more from the poem.
- Follow up the reading with discussion and further activities involving the poem.

Young children find poetry easier to read if it is rhythmic, and rhymes help the text to be predictable. Nursery rhymes and the kinds of 'kids' verse' that are their modern equivalents, such as the *Dr Seuss* books, help develop phonemic awareness. The trouble is that if phonic or rhyming content is all a teacher is after then any piece of doggerel will do. As one child said of poems after, listening to a nonsense rhyme, 'I like the way they sound but they don't mean anything'. Another young child said when his teacher was beginning a familiar rhyme, 'I know the tune of that', but the tune for that child had no meaning.

Children should be engaged in trying to understand the meaning of poems as well as enjoying the sounds they make, for, after all, it is the meaning derived from a poem that gives it significance. Children should attempt to seek meaning from a wide variety of poems. Reading poetry with children can be a significant urce of growth in vocabulary and comprehension if it is followed up by questioning and discussion. As Nikki, aged 5, says, 'Sometimes you don't know what the words mean until you talk about it'.

Questioning

After reading the poem two or three times, begin the discussion by asking some questions. Most young children do not know a poem is there to be questioned until they are shown how. The function of questions is to focus attention on the poem and engage the mind in trying to construct a message from the poem. If children are to read for meaning the general question they should be encouraged to answer is 'What does it mean?'.

This is best done as a follow-up to shared reading. The main purpose of this activity is to encourage children to think hard about what they have read or heard. This questioning of a text in a group is known by many names – adults engaged in this process might call it a Literary Circle, the Literacy Hour guidelines call it shared reading, and other teachers refer to it as a Thinking Circle or community of enquiry (see Chapter 1). In this shared activity teachers question children about the text, so that they, in turn, will learn how to interrogate the text for themselves. This kind of interactive reading is what good readers do who do not simply read the words in their mind but are actively engaged in taking meaning from the text. The questioning we do with children we hope later they will learn to do for themselves. But what kinds of questions should be asked?

Children might be asked closed or open questions, or a combination of both. Closed questions are those which seek a single answer, for example 'What is the title of the poem?' 'Does it rhyme?' 'Who wrote the poem?'. Such questions probe knowledge about the poem and are either right or wrong. Open questions probe understanding of the poem and are open to a range of possible replies. The value of such questioning in a group is that children are exposed to a variety of viewpoints. They get to hear ideas they would never have thought of themselves. They learn that many interpretations and opinions are possible, and that differences of view are acceptable if supported by suitable reasons or evidence from the text. It is through open questions that children's minds are expanded.

Better than questions asked by the teacher are questions asked by the children themselves. This is because the aim is self-directed, not teacher-directed, learning. Children are being taught not only about a particular poem but are also being shown how to question, discuss and evaluate poetry in general. They are being helped not just to understand a particular piece, but how to interrogate and make meaning from any text. To do this they need to be encouraged to think about, question and comment on what has been read.

> - What is the poem about?
>
> - Did you like the poem? Why, or why not?
>
> - Can you pick out a bit you like and tell us why?
>
> - Do you think this is a good poem? Why do/don't, you think so?
>
> - Is there anything in the poem you don't understand?
>
> **FIGURE 2.3** Open questions that can be asked of any poem

After reading the poem, and perhaps asking some relevant questions, invite the children to share any of their own thoughts or queries about it. One way of valuing their comments is to record them on a board, adding the name of the child to their question or statement to show you value their contribution. This list of children's comments and questions can form the agenda for later discussion.

What is clear from research into this way of working is that children who are used to asking questions, in a classroom that encourages questioning, will tend to ask more and better questions and come to think of reading as a process of active enquiry. Or, as Natalie, aged 7, put it, 'When you think about it there are always some questions to ask'.

The following is an example of a poem, together with some examples of closed and open questions that can be asked about the poem, as well as some queries posed by children.[9]

Why?

Why is grass always green?
What holds up the sky?
Why is hair upon my head?
Why, oh why, oh why?

Why does rain go down, not up?
Why is salt in every sea?
Why is there a sun and moon?
Why is there only one me?

Why do bees buzz and birds sing?
Why do nails grow on my toes?
How long is a piece of string?
Why is it no-one knows?

Why is night so full of dreams?
Why do we have one nose, two eyes?
Why do questions never end?
Why are there so many whys?

(Robert Fisher)

Some closed questions about the poem:

- What is the title of this poem?
- Why does the poem have that title?
- How many verses does the poem have?
- How many questions are there in the poem?
- Can you answer any of the questions in the poem?

Some open questions about this poem:

- What is a question?
- Why do people ask questions?
- Who asks you questions? Can you remember a question you have been asked?
- Do you ask yourself questions? Can you remember a question you have asked yourself?
- Is it good to ask questions? Why, or why not?

Some questions about the poem from a group of six-year-olds:

- What does 'why' mean? (William)
- Why does every line begin with 'why'? (Rosie)
- Why are there so many questions? (Nicola)
- Can't you find all the answers in books? (Paul)
- Doesn't a teacher know? (Sunil)

Discussing

When you hear a poem you don't always get it, but when you talk about it it helps.

(Katie, aged 7)

Usually, the meaning of a poem is distilled in the fewest words. If children are to understand what Ted Hughes calls the 'spirit' of a poem they must integrate the meaning of the words with images and rhythms.[10] In this way they create their own mental model of what the poem describes, and for this to happen they need to have some idea of the main point of the poem, and be sensitive to the relationships between the poem's living parts. Because a poem is so concise, its meanings are often enigmatic. Inference and deduction are needed to make sense of what is suggested and to forge links between what is said and what is implied. Even the simplest poems create ambiguities. Where exactly were Jack and Jill going? When did it take place? Why were they fetching a pail of water? How did they fall down? What happened then?

Discussion with others can help to deepen understanding through the sharing of ideas, creative insights and critical responses to the poem. This is not to spoil the mutual enjoyment of it, but to enrich that pleasure through a deeper understanding of what the poem means to the individual and to others who have read it. Many teachers find discussing poems with children some of their most rewarding teaching experiences. Young children are just at the beginning of the participative process. To get them to listen to the poem, share their ideas and pay attention to what others have to say is quite an achievement in itself. A poem will spark off more interesting discussion with a group of children at some times than at other times.

---

1. Divide the class into groups of four or five who are able to work together.

2. A scribe is chosen or appointed (this may be an adult helper) to write out ideas discussed by the group.

3. Children are given a poem to read together, then silently by themselves, or they may hear it on tape.

4. They pause to think about the poem (thinking time).

5. Each child is invited to say one thing, or ask one question about the poem, which the scribe writes down.

6. Children in the group discuss each comment/question which has been written down.

7. In the plenary session, each group shares what they have written and discussed.

FIGURE 2.4 Organising group reading and discussion of a poem

The advantage of the conventional Literacy Hour is that it can include time for shared reading of a poem; the disadvantage is that there may not be enough time for all the points and issues about the poem to be discussed. The trouble with teaching at pace, for a limited amount of time, is that it may suit the 'hares' but not the 'tortoises'. A creative teacher will not feel constrained by the clock, and will use his or her professional judgement in orchestrating classroom discussion reading time. The oral groundwork of discussion, if it can be sustained, will ance understanding and the quality of children's reading and writing. Discussion can take place in the open forum of shared reading with the class, through group discussion or discussion with individual children.

Topics for discussion with individuals or groups of children include finding words that rhyme, comparing and contrasting two poems (which do they prefer and why?), categorising poems (do they know/can they find another poem like this one?), ways to memorise a poem, sound patterns within a poem (e.g. alliteration), favourite rhymes, poems and poets, and their own chosen titles for poems. Any poem can be discussed and analysed in terms of its form and content. Here are some elements to discuss about any poem:

Form

- words (What does this word mean?)
- lines (What is your favourite line?)
- verses (favourite verse?)
- chorus (repeated words?)
- images (pictures in the mind?)
- metaphors (pictures in words?)
- sounds (sounds of words?)

Content

- story (What is the poem about?)
- feelings (Is it a happy or sad poem?)
- thoughts (What does it make you think of?)
- title (What title would you give this poem?)

William Blake once said, 'What is most poetic is also most private'. What discussion seeks to do is to help children articulate their private thoughts and feelings and to benefit from what others, including the teacher, have to say. But discussing a poem is only one way of responding to it; there are other ways to express what we think and feel.

Expressing

> I like dance poems.
>
> (Kate, aged 6)

A child has many forms of intelligence through which to make a creative response to a poem.[11] Dance, drama, art, craft and music all provide ways to express and recreate aspects of poetry. Invite the children to perform a poem in their own way, illustrated with their own actions, pictures, drawings, models or musical accompaniment. Through any of the expressive arts children can enter the poet's world, and manifest the ideas and images of a poem.

The following are some ways of extending a child's experience of a poem through creative responses:

Twenty creative ways to respond to a poem:

1. Illustrate a poem by drawing, painting or making a three-dimensional model.
2. Tape-record the group reading a poem and share this later.
3. Get the children to close their eyes during a reading to 'see' the poem in their 'mind's eye'.
4. Express the poem through movement and mime.
5. Create a collage of words, quotations and/or pictures about a theme or poet.
6. Make a mask or masks linked to the theme or poem.
7. Write a letter to the poet with any questions you have about the poem.
8. Visit a library to review, survey and choose poetry books.
9. Invite guests to discuss and share their favourite poems and yours.
10. Learn a chosen poem by heart and discuss the best ways of learning poetry.
11. Create and discuss your own title for a given untitled poem.
12. Predict the words missing in a copy of a poem which has some words deleted (cloze).
13. Reconstruct the line or verse order of a poem which has had lines or verses jumbled.
14. Put into poetic form a nursery rhyme that has been written as prose.
15. Create music or sound effects to accompany a spoken poem.
16. Listen to taped readings of a poem.
17. Put some 'wrong' words in a poem and get the children to decide which these are and to propose alternatives.
18. Hunt for special words or letters in a poem, underlining them in different colours.
19. Ask children to choose 'my favourite line' from a poem, to share, display and discuss.

Invite poets to share, discuss and answer questions about their poetry. See also Fisher and Williams (2004).

Composing

Who alive can say,
Thou art not a poet – mayest not tell thy dreams?

(John Keats)[12]

What inspires someone to write poetry? Many poets would say that it is not nature nor the need to express their own feelings that most inspires them, but reading poetry. One of the problems encountered by young children brought up solely on a diet of rhymes is that when it comes to writing poetry this narrow experience becomes an obstacle. It is little wonder that many children say they can't write poetry, and when they concentrate on making rhymes they often abandon the effort to make meaning. This is a pity, since poetry is an ideal medium for emergent writers.

In poetry writing, children need not be bound by the narrow rules which govern nursery rhymes, and are free from the grammatical constraints of prose. They need not write whole sentences with finite verbs, nor use capital letters and full stops, all of which emergent writers find difficult to remember even when they know the rules.

In poetry, meaning can be expressed in the fewest words, provided they are the 'important' ones – nouns, adjectives, verbs and adverbs – and not the repetitive connecting words such as participles, which correct prose demands. For a young writer for whom forming every letter is an effort, poetry writing can provide an important freedom.

The easiest way into composing poetry with young children is through shared writing, where the teacher takes the children's words and ideas and shapes them into a shared piece. A good deal of research points to the value of teachers in modelling the writing process with their children (see Chapter 8), a process which is often called 'scribing', which includes not only writing children's ideas for them but also talking through the process, discussing choices of words and phrases, cutting out unnecessary words, creating poetic effects and so on. Shared or guided writing gives beginning writers the support they need. What they do as a group, with the guiding help of a teacher, they will later be able to do on their own.

One teacher reports an example of this process in action with her class of 5–6-year-olds. Here is one of the poems:

Autumn Leaf

My autumn leaf
is red and brown
it has tiny specks
all over it
like a banana
it has a pointed end
like a star.

(Anna, aged 5)

We had read and discussed a poem about autumn leaves (in *First Poems for Thinking* by R. Fisher). We collected our own autumn leaves, and as the chldren described the leaves they had brought in, I wrote their words and phrases on the board. At first, their descriptions were fairly simple: red, yellow, round, pointed, and so on. I encouraged them to say what they were like and to make comparisons, and I got expressions such as 'thin as tissue paper', 'yellow as the sun' and 'crunchy as Rice Krispies'. I made a point of emphasising that this was their poem, using their words and ideas.

They went on to write a poem in pairs about their chosen leaf, with me focusing my help on one writer's group. We shared and displayed the children's writing in class, together with drawings of their leaves, and read the 'class' and 'individual' poems in assembly that week. None of the poems was brilliant, but the children had begun to see themselves as writers (or 'real poets' as I called them). They had learned about the process of composing poetry, through jotting ideas, drafting, choosing best words, editing, proofreading and sharing with an audience. It was exciting to see five-year-olds acting as real writers, and to see the pride they took in their finished poems.

FIGURE 2.5 Autumn leaves: first poems with five-year-olds

Conclusion

Reading, responding to and writing poems can enable children to voice thoughts and feelings that might otherwise remain trapped, inarticulate and unspoken. Poetry can empower children by offering them many voices, many messages and many tongues – echoed in the words of Whitman:[13]

> Give me the song of a sound unsung,
> Give me the heart of a child that is young,
> Give me friends I can stretch among,
> Give me the words and give me the tongue.

Giving children the voice to express and share their experiences can be one of the most rewarding aspects of teaching literacy. The following is an imple of a five-year-old sharing thoughts about his special pet.[14] First he wrote it as prose, then he was shown how to write it in lines, as poetry, by choosing his best words and putting them in the best order:

> I have a pet koala
> he is all fluffy and grey
> and he is missing an eye
> when mummy put him
> in the washing machine
> he has only one black eye
> it is a pity
> he's stuffed
>
> (Tom, aged 5)

Ted Hughes described the act of writing poetry as 'all outflowing exertion for a short concentrated period, in a particular direction'.[15] What the teacher does is to provide the direction, introduce children to interesting poems and support them in drafting their own. Once created, they can be communicated through publication to provide purpose and an audience, first in the writing group or class, then beyond the class in the school, local library or public space, or to a potentially limitless audience on the internet.

Notes

1. Quoted in *The Poetry Book for Primary Schools* (edited by Anthony Wilson) (1998, London: Poetry Society), p. 5.
2. The Kingman Report (DES 1988) argued that children's fascination with word games was an important foundation for the development of literacy. The importance of word sounds and word play is also stressed in the Curriculum Guidance for the Foundation Stage (QCA 2000).
3. One of the most influential research studies in this area was by L. Bradley and P. Bryant (1983) who found that children's sensitivity to rhyme was an important predictor of subsequent success in reading. Goswami and Bryant (1990) also found a link between the phonological skills developed by awareness of rhyme and alliteration and learning to read. For more on research that underpins the National Literacy Strategy see Beard (1999).
4. The Bullock Report (DES 1975:136) argued that understanding and enjoyment of poetry are essential to one another, and this dual focus is reflected in the *National Literacy Strategy: Framework for Teaching* (DfEE 1998) and in *Excellence and Enjoyment: Learning and Teaching in the Primary Years* (QCA 2004).
5. From *A Midsummer Night's Dream*, by William Shakespeare, Act V, Scene 1.
6. Samuel Taylor Coleridge's *Biographia Liberaria* (1827) defined prose and poetry as follows: 'Prose is derived from words in their best order; poetry is derived from the *best* words in the best order.'
7. In the introduction to their classic anthology, *The Poet's Tongue*, W. H. Auden and John Garrett said: 'Of the many definitions of poetry, the simplest is still the best: "memorable speech". That is to say, it must move our emotions, or excite our intellect, for only that which is moving or exciting is memorable.'

8. In his anthology *By Heart* (1998, London: Faber), Ted Hughes argues that learning by rote succeeds only in creating an aversion to poetry. The heart, he says, is an organ of memory and what is loved by the heart will be learnt.

9. This poem appears in *First Poems for Thinking*, by R. Fisher (2000, Oxford: Nash Pollock), with further questions for use with children. Many issues discussed in this chapter also appear in the introductions to *Poems for Thinking* (Fisher 1997) and *First Poems for Thinking* (Fisher 2000).

10. Ted Hughes (1967) *Poetry in the Making*. London: Faber.

11. For ways of developing the multiple intelligences of a young child see R. Fisher *Head Start: How to Develop Your Child's Mind* (1999, London: Souvenir Press). See also Fisher and Williams (eds) (2004) *Unlocking Creativity*. London: David Fulton Publishers.

12. 'Who alive can say, / Thou art not a poet – mayest not tell thy dreams? / Since every man whose soul is not a clod / Hath visions, and would speak, if he had loved / And been well nurtured in his mother tongue.' (John Keats, 'The Fall of Hyperion', Canto 1.) For more on composing, see Williams, M. (ed.) (2002) *Unlocking Writing*. London: David Fulton Publishers.

13. From Walt Whitman's 'Song of Myself', published in *Leaves of Grass*.

14. This poem is reprinted in *Pet Poems* (edited by R. Fisher) (1989, London: Faber and Faber).

15. Ted Hughes (1967 *op. cit.*).

References

Beard, R. (1999) *National Literacy Strategy: Review of Research and Other Related Evidence*. London: HMSO/DfES.

Bradley, L. and Bryant, P. (1983) 'Categorising sounds and learning to read: a causal connection'. *Native,* **310**, 419–21.

Coleridge, S. T. (1827) *Biographia Liberaria*.

DES (1975) *The Bullock Report*. London: HMSO.

DES (1988) *Kingman Report*. London: HMSO.

DfEE (1998) *National Literacy Strategy: Framework for Teaching*. London: HMSO.

Fisher R. (1997) *Poems for Thinking*. Oxford: Nash Pollock.

Fisher R. (1999) *Head Start: How to Develop Your Child's Mind*. London: Souvenir Press.

Fisher R. (2000) *First Poems for Thinking*. Oxford: Nash Pollock.

Fisher, R. and Williams M. (eds) (2004) *Unlocking Creativity*. London: David Fulton Publishers.

Goswami, U. and Bryant, P. (1990) *Phonological Skills and Learning to Read*. Hove and Hillsdale, NJ: Lawrence Erlbaum Associates.

Hughes, T. (1967) *Poetry in the Making*. London: Faber.

Hughes, T. (ed.) (1998) *By Heart*. London: Faber.

QCA (2000) *Curriculum Guidance for the Foundation Stage*. London: HMSO/DfES.

QCA (2004) *Excellence and Enjoyment: Learning and Teaching in the Primary Years*. London: HMSO/DfES.

Whitman, W. *Selected Poems*. London: Penguin.

Williams, M. (ed.) (2002) *Unlocking Writing*. London: David Fulton Publishers.

Wilson, A. (ed.) (1998) *The Poetry Book for Primary Schools*. London: Poetry Society.

Further reading

Brownjohn, S. (1994) *To Rhyme or Not to Rhyme?* London: Hodder.

Corbett, P. (2002) *How to Teach Poetry Writing at KS3*. London: David Fulton Publishers.

Morgan, M. (2001) *How to Teach Poetry Writing at KS2*. London: David Fulton Publishers.

Morgan, M. (2002) *How to Teach Poetry Writing at KS1*. London: David Fulton Publishers.

'"Jolly good," I said': using poetry with older children

Robert Catt

For tamed and shabby tigers,
And dancing dogs and bears,
And wretched, blind pit ponies,
And little hunted hares.

(Ralph Hodgson, 'The Bells of Heaven')

Introduction

Few teachers require a rationale for the use of poetry in the classroom. Children, especially younger children, generally enjoy reading, memorising, reciting, writing and listening to verse and often express an enviable and uninhibited delight in the play of rhyme and rhythm. Such enjoyment provides a firm basis for the kinds of learning set out within the Programmes of Study for English at Key Stage 2 in the National Curriculum for English (DfEE 1999).

Poetry in the classroom provides some very specific learning opportunities within the Literacy Hour because it draws attention to language itself in these ways:

- Children become quickly aware of poetic form: the shape upon the page, the structure of verses and the auditory appeal of rhyme and rhythm.
- Ideas in poems are often compressed: they sometimes need to be teased out, can even be expressed ambiguously and can create meaning on many levels.

As teachers are aware, however, poetry can also seem to be difficult and often there is a reliance in the classroom upon verse which, in being immediately accessible, offers very few of those opportunities for re-reading and subsequent reflection and discussion which, for many, are an essential appeal of an engagement with poetic language. Teachers need to be encouraged to make an incremental shift towards an increasing variety of more demanding verse in the classroom. In so doing there need be no loss of that essential enjoyment but, rather, a gain in literacy skills as indicated in the *National Literacy Strategy: Framework for Teaching*: 'When pupils read familiar and predictable texts, they can easily become over-reliant on their knowledge of context and grammar' (DfEE 1998:4).

The selected use of verse can extend this knowledge.[1] In working with the demands of verse, children will need to tease out such meaning by giving attention to language features exemplified by meaning, verse form, syntax and diction: 'As pupils gain fluency the forms of teaching should shift to emphasise advanced reading and composition skills at text level' (ibid:5). Such skills demand an *interrogation* of the text. This is often best achieved through dialogue – exploratory talk – often prompted and supported by teachers' questions. Advanced literacy skills will acknowledge difficulty as children begin to realise that poetry can yield easily more than a single, correct meaning and that response and enjoyment are sometimes limitless. Here, though, they will be in the elevated company of one of the most highly regarded poets and critics of the twentieth century. T. S. Eliot wrote, in 1933, that difficulty may be encountered when a reader has been told, or has thought for him or herself, that a poem is going to be difficult. Eliot was aware that some of the poetry to which he was most devoted he did not understand at first reading.

Poetry, then, provides an opportunity to move pupils from a use of language that is everyday and familiar towards an engagement with compressed ideas, connotation (the ways in which words and phrases resonate with associated meanings) and ambiguity. Engagement with verse at text level demands that children draw upon their wider knowledge and experience as they learn to tease out contextual clues and ask appropriate questions. Such engagement will involve children in the four language modes of reading, writing, speaking and listening and will also depend upon what might be termed a 'social literacy' (the ability to 'read' the needs and views of others in the classroom that makes a community of enquiry possible). There is no reason at all why such literacy activities should become divorced from that world of enjoyment, expression and feeling with which those who use poetry in their teaching will already be familiar.

Animals in verse

Hi my name is Cheryl I like really dishy boys. I like doing a lot of sport, table tennis, golf, gymlastics...I am quiet good at art. I think that cutting down the rain forest and killing whales should not be done. I don't like animal circus's because animal's should not be made to do trick's that they don't want to do.

(Cheryl, aged 10)

39

Much of the poetry I have used with children in the Key Stage 2 classroom has been concerned in some way with animals, and, more specifically, our relationship with animals. Why? Because it works. The extract from Cheryl's autobiography, above, has some rich potential for the Literacy Hour including work on apostrophes, homophones ('quite/quiet' might be called near-homo-phone) and neologisms – 'gymlastics' seems a delightfully appropriate inventive noun for what, to the creaking bones of this writer, appears to be a mystifyingly elastic sporting activity. The interest here, however, is in Cheryl's concern regarding the treatment of animals. Evidence of what, for many children, is a major preoccupation can be found in classroom displays, the media and the marketing strategies of those many companies creating consumer interest in the young through association with animals and the preservation of exotic environ-ments. To frame this rationale more sharply, however, it can be argued that engagement with the 'meaning' of such selected poetry provides an introduction to the cultivation of feeling – a compassionate understanding and concern for others – which, surely, is a principal aim of a liberal education.

Tasks

A sequence of activities will now be described using incrementally more demand-ing poems. Although the poems are introduced to children as texts, that is as printed words on the page, the following activities encourage exploration and are presented here to suggest dynamic ways of working within the Literacy Hour.

Ice-breaking: the introductory name game

A class of Year 6 pupils sit on chairs in a large circle within a drama space created by moving tables to the side of the room. I give my name – Robert – and ask each child to do the same. I ask children to stand and I explain the rules for the name game. I will start by looking across the circle at a selected child – I choose Sunita. I will call out her name and walk towards her. As I do so, Sunita will look around the circle, will select a colleague – Jo – call her name and walk towards her. I will sit in Sunita's chair, Sunita will sit in Jo's chair as Jo goes on to select another member of the circle, and so on until all the children have swapped places and are sitting down. Before beginning I ask for a prediction of the time it will take for us all to change places. Richard suggests 15 minutes; Manisha offers 32 seconds. There are some other guesses within these two extremes. I ask if someone could time us and Hamid, who has something resembling a deep sea diver's chronometer strapped to his wrist, volunteers. Our first go at the name game is a little hesitant. Some children forget to call out the name of the friend towards whom they are walking; others need to be reminded to sit down when they have changed places. It takes us one minute and 40 seconds, and Richard has to put up with a little gentle teasing.

I now ask each child to name the person sitting on their right, and this, obviously, works easily, although I have forgotten the name of the boy now sitting next to me. I suggest that it would help my memory to hear each name again but this time tagged with the name of a favourite animal beginning with the same letter as our forename. To provide thinking time,[2] I use myself as an example: 'My name is Robert and I like rhinoceroses'.

The group is now asked to stand again and the name game is repeated with participants urged to improve our time. Hamid acts as starter and time-keeper and, after the final child is seated, is pleased to announce that we have reduced the time to one minute and eight seconds. By way of a memory test I ask each child to name the person now on their right, together with the name of their favourite animal. There has been a good deal of forgetting. I tell the class that some of the work we will be doing will involve the use of memory.

Sequencing

1. Height

The sequencing activity is a useful prelude to subsequent textual exploration; it is also a useful control strategy. Pupils are asked to arrange themselves around the circle in ascending height order, without any speaking: gesture only is allowed. Teachers and children can find some fun in this activity with fine judgements being made between children of the same height and allowances being made for shoes, hair styles and so forth.

2. Birthdays

A more challenging sequencing activity is for pupils to arrange themselves according to their date of birth. The circle begins with the child born nearest to 1 January and ends with the one born nearest to 31 December. Again, only gesture is allowed.

3. Verse

For this activity the teacher needs to have prepared a series of cut-up lines (part or whole verses, see below) from complete poems. On this occasion, teaching a group of 25 pupils, I had prepared fragments of text for each child. On other occasions I have asked two or three children, equipped with complete poems, to act as helpers. Obviously, the choice of verse will depend upon both the teacher's judgement and the number of children participating. The activity can be varied with pupils given either a whole verse or just a single, short line or title where difficulties are anticipated. Each seated child is now given a piece of paper upon which is a fragment from the selected texts. (Although these are, seemingly, distributed at random, the teacher will obviously use her judgement in distributing the slips of paper.) Children are asked not to show their piece of paper to others and are challenged to see if they are able to memorise the words they have received. To facilitate this they are asked to walk quietly around the room repeating the words to themselves. At this stage the teacher can intervene bearing a waste bin. Is anyone confident enough to throw away their piece of paper?

After two or three minutes pupils are asked to stop and listen. They are now told that they are each a part of a poem and are asked to find the rest of their text. A version of the previous sequencing rule is employed here: children are only allowed to speak the words they have memorised. Slowly, three groups will be formed, each comprising one of the three poems, and this process can be facilitated by the teachers and any teaching assistants.

The children are next asked – again, only using the words they have memorised – to sequence themselves in order. If played strictly to the rules, this is a demanding problem-solving activity in which children must listen to and pick up clues from each other. It is, however, an activity within which the teacher and pupil assistants, acting as directors and giving prompts and clues, can play a crucial role.

Chosen text

Choose animal poems to display as a text. There is a wealth of animal verse available, for example *Pet Poems,* edited by R. Fisher. For the occasion described above I chose 'I'm a Parrot' by Grace Nichols, 'The Ballad of Red Fox' by Melvin La Follette, and 'I Saw a Jolly Hunter' by Charles Causley (for poems see below).

Choral speaking

Children are now given rehearsal time and are asked to work in three groups to provide a dramatic presentation of their poem in which readings are enlivened and illustrated through movement, gesture and intonation.

Following my directorial suggestions, members of the 'parrot' group use their bodies to form the bars of a cage for the enraged parrot, each bar turning out to speak a line – using shrill parrotty voices – then turning back to enclose the bird. As the poem concludes, the 'bars' fall back to release the bird with a chorally spoken, 'Can't you understand!'.

The 'jolly hunter' group takes a narrative approach incorporating hunter/ animal mimetic actions, including the collapse of the idiotic hunter and the escape of a gleeful hare.

The 'red fox' group provides a sober contrast with a serious, mystical and prophetic tone in which gesture and sequenced chorus are used to warn the fox of its fate.

Reflective discussion

The structure of the Literacy Hour provides opportunities for reflective discussion in evaluating the performance.[3] Repetition is a feature of each of the three selected poems and teacher-led discussion is likely to give attention to the cumulative effect subsequently created in performance. The children with whom I have worked are quick to respond to the emphatic capitalised conclusion to 'I'm a Parrot'.

I'm a Parrot

I'm a parrot
I live in a cage
I'm nearly always
in a vex-up rage

I used to fly
all light and free
in the luscious
green forest canopy

I'm a parrot
I live in a cage
I'm nearly always
in a vex-up rage

I miss the wind
against my wing
I miss the nut
and the fruit picking

I'm a parrot
I live in a cage
I'm nearly always
in a vex-up rage

(Grace Nichols)

However, on first reading, the Caribbean dialect words – 'vex-up' for 'vexed' (angry) and the elided 'pickyou' for 'peck you' – tend to be missed. Do they make a difference to the effect of the piece? I think so: 'It makes him,' observed one girl of the parrot group, 'sound a bit of a character'. Again, less immediately obvious, but deserving reflective attention, is the phonic contrast between the taut and factual 'I'm a parrot / I live in a cage' and the airy cadence of 'all light and free / in the luscious / green forest canopy'. Awareness of this contrast is an implicit feature of the performed reading but, in my experience, explicit awareness needs to be prompted.

'The Ballad of Red Fox' is altogether more mysterious and elusive:

The Ballad of Red Fox

Yellow sun yellow
Sun yellow sun,
When, oh, when
Will red fox run?

When the hollow horn shall sound,
When the hunter lifts his gun
And liberates the wicked hound,
Then, oh, then shall red fox run.

Yellow sun yellow
Sun yellow sun,
Where, oh, where
Will red fox run?

Through meadows hot as sulphur,
Through forests cool as clay,
Through hedges crisp as morning
And grasses limp as day.

Yellow sky yellow
Sky yellow sky,
How, oh, how
Will red fox die?

With a bullet in his belly,
A dagger in his eye,
And blood upon his red red brush
Shall red fox die.

(Melvin La Follette)

Who is speaking here? Why is the sky yellow? The 'hollow horn' and 'wicked hound' suggest a traditional hunt with which the 'gun', 'bullet' and 'dagger' seem to sit awkwardly. The strange central similes – 'grasses limp as day' – give the piece a surreal emphasis: 'Spooky,' said one child. 'It's death speaking,' suggested another, 'and he doesn't want the fox to die because he keeps saying "oh" and we say that when we don't want something to happen, like "Oh, please don't do it!"' Not all reflective discussion, of course, proceeds as smoothly as this. In discussing the similes I asked one group (and I should have seen it coming) why they thought the 'hedges' were 'crisp as morning'. 'Well, I eat crisps in the morning,' volunteered one boy.

Attention is now given to Causley's 'I Saw a Jolly Hunter'.

I Saw a Jolly Hunter

I saw a jolly hunter
With a jolly gun
Walking in the country
In the jolly sun.

In the jolly meadow
Sat a jolly hare.
Saw the jolly hunter.
Took jolly care.

Hunter jolly eager –
Sight of jolly prey
Forgot gun pointing
Wrong jolly way.

Jolly hunter jolly head
Over heels gone.
Jolly old safety catch
Not jolly on.

Bang went the jolly gun.
Hunter jolly dead.
Jolly hare got clean away.
Jolly good, I said.

(Charles Causley)

'Jolly' is redolent of a caricatured social dialect and, again, quickly prompts the evocation of character. It is also something of a euphemism and it is interesting to ask children to find synonyms. Suggestions included 'silly' and 'funny', but these were quickly rejected by children because 'they don't work'. There seemed to be no substitute because 'it's hard to say what "jolly" means but you sort of know it anyway'. Certainly, it's an adjective with which children enjoy playing. Impressive about Causley's poem is the narrative economy. The over-excitement and clumsiness of the hunter are succinctly conveyed in a way that demands children's attention.

Brainstorm

The class is divided into five groups and each group is given a copy of the poem which all have seen 'performed'. Children are given a few moments to 'brainstorm' some ideas about the character of the hunter in the poem in relation to age, gender, occupation, name and personality. Interestingly, response to this task is varied. Children generally tend towards stereotypical colonial or military personae; but some deliberately work against such obvious characterisation in more inventive ways. One group created an accident-prone cartoon character; another provided a more historical slant with a musket-bearing poacher hunting on the king's land.

Freeze-frame

Groups are then asked to prepare two snapshots or still images:

- a picture of the hunter at work, pursuing, trapping or shooting an animal; and
- a picture of the hunter at leisure, possibly boasting about an exploit.

The still image is a useful and probably very familiar dramatic device and it is worth reflecting for a moment upon its value in relation to problem-solving and extension activities. Under pressure of time (three to four minutes is generally sufficient) children must work together for maximum involvement and with an awareness of their audience. When the still images are being presented, the teacher can encourage speculative questions from the audience: 'Daniel, you don't look very happy; are you a dead or a live animal?'.

Extension possibilities include:

- the idea that this is a video *freeze-frame* from which the teacher, or a selected member of the class (and this is an opportunity to give responsibility to a diffident or shy pupil), can move backwards or forwards in slow motion to illustrate preceding and consequential action;
- the use of a narrator or explainer who, either in or out of role, describes the scene; and
- the incorporation, in the second freeze-frame, of part or all of the hunter's boastful tall story.

I am consistently impressed by the inventive quality of children's work with still images (for more on these see Chapter 8). One group, with seemingly little prior discussion, moved fluently into a pose in which a pompous hunter, equipped with a drink and cigar, sat with his feet upon a prostrate animal rug, frozen in the act of delivering a hunting story to a listener, his long-suffering wife, perhaps, who drooped with boredom, watched by antlered animal trophies on the wall.

Moving on to more difficult poems

Children are each given a copy of 'The Gallows' by Edward Thomas.

The Gallows

There was a weasel lived in the sun
With all his family,
Till a keeper shot him with his gun
And hung him up on a tree,
Where he swings in the wind and rain,
In the sun and in the snow,
Without pleasure, without pain,
On the dead oak tree bough.

There was a crow who was no sleeper,
But a thief and a murderer
Till a very late hour; and this keeper
Made him one of the things that were,
To hang and flap in rain and wind,
In the sun and in the snow.
There are no more sins to be sinned
On the dead oak tree bough.

There was a magpie, too,
Had a long tongue and a long tail;
He could talk and do –
But what did that avail?
He, too, flaps in the wind and rain
Alongside weasel and crow,
Without pleasure, without pain,
On the dead oak tree bough.

And many other beasts
And birds, skin, bone, and feather,
Have been taken from their feasts
And hung up there together,
To swing and have endless leisure
In the sun and in the snow,
Without pain, without pleasure,
On the dead oak tree bough.

(Edward Thomas)

This is a considerably more difficult poem which makes some interrelated investigative demands with regard to rhythm, diction and meaning.

The reading of the poem in itself provides a challenge – should the teacher undertake the first reading? An inevitable difficulty, if children read the text, is the end-stopping of lines which tends to work against fluency, rhythm and understanding. This is a feature of reading that needs discussion. Unwarranted end-stopping can render a poem like 'The Ballad of Red Fox' almost nonsensical. The auditory sense demands the repetition of 'Yellow sun, yellow sun, yellow sun…' and not the syntatic confusion of 'Yellow sun yellow [pause] Sun yellow sun'. In reading for meaning, children should be directed away from end-stopping to pursue sense by reading to the punctuation. One way to achieve this is to read around the circle, each pupil stopping at a punctuation mark. This is a technique that keeps the participants alert, as they await their cues and learn to run lines on. There are also, of course, opportunities for reflective commentary. What counts as a punctuation mark and what kind of weight or intonation does it signal? Thomas's 'The Gallows' provides particularly worthwhile material for such a reading. This is a text worth exploring in some detail both in terms of content and form. The anachronistic appearance and pronunciation of 'bough' is likely to cause some difficulty and comment. As one child astutely pointed out, the similar spelling c-o-u-g-h is pronounced 'coff' and 'this should be said like "boff"'. Another, aware of Thomas's strong rhyme scheme, pointed out that 'bough' should rhyme with 'now' and not 'snow' which would make it 'bo'. (Again, this invites a discussion of homophones.)

The animals' revenge

A lively extension activity to which teachers might be drawn, where they have a confident relationship with a responsive class, is the use of a free reading. Members of such a group were encouraged to think themselves into the situation of a twilight gathering of forest animals moved to some collaborative discussion (see Chapter 7) of the oppression they were suffering at the hands of an intrusive gamekeeper. I find this works best when I begin the reading in a conspiratorial whisper, encouraging children to join in with words, phrases or whole lines echoing the concerns of the animals. Such a free reading allows the verse to be spoken by various voices and from various points in the reading circle. Some elements are voiced singly, others in chorus, others in shadow or repetition. After two or three rehearsed readings, clear characters begin to emerge as voices are raised in agreement or counterpoint. These disparate voices – assertive, timorous, plaintive – raised in common grievance in the refrain 'on the dead oak tree bough' and repeated at the end of each of the four stanzas, provide a device for an ascendant tone of strident injustice. These animals, victims of the hunter's terror, are now militant and angry.

Another still image

Children are asked to present another still image, this time depicting the animals' revenge upon the hunter. Images depicted are likely to range from the predictable (the hunter hoist with his own petard with his leg caught in savage trap) through the surreal (the hunter waking in terror to find the animals of his nightmare palpable and revengeful at the foot of his bed) to the topical and inventive (the hunter tried for his crimes at the international court of animal rights, a badger as prosecutor and a black-capped owl serving the death sentence).

This is a useful and potentially powerful pre-writing activity.

A listening activity

Causley's 'I Saw a Jolly Hunter' is a deceptively simple and succinct piece of verse. Hidden from us is the 'work' – the idea, planning, drafting and rewriting – behind a sophisticated narrative. Causley has talked about his writing, much of which was written in and about his beloved West Country environment. With the aim of making something of the writing process visible, I have read a prose account, taken from an interview with Causley, to Year 6 children. It makes for a good listening activity.[4]

My mother saw...

I come from a little town in Cornwall called Launceston where I was born and have lived all my life. My mum and dad come from there too. My mum went to one particular little school called St Stephen's School. She used to tell me a story about that school that I've certainly never forgotten.

The headmaster of the school was rather a fierce fellow called Mr Davis. He wore a beard and had a cane hanging on a nail at the side of his stand-up desk. One afternoon in summer, and this must have been 80 or 90 years ago, they were all working away at their long oak and iron desks, all those children. There suddenly came a great knock on the schoolroom door. That was the one that opened onto the playground. It was a door almost big enough for a church. It had big studs all over it and a big iron latch.

Anyway, over went Mr Davis to open it, and to everybody's amazement, there in a big white-hot blaze of summer light, framed by the doorway, just like a picture, was a man. He had a coloured silk handkerchief tied round his head and a kind of flute or whistle-pipe stuck in his belt. On the ground beside him was a heavy lump of metal – 'A bit like a cannonball' my mum used to say – with a length of very strong chain attached to it. At the other end of the chain from the cannonball was, what do you think?

Here I pause, then repeat 'What do you think?'. Children are quick to suggest answers but I am anxious to give the activity some structure and I ask them to work in small groups of three or four. First, I try to emphasise the importance of deduction. The answer to my question should be based upon the text which, although giving little definitive information, has some powerful clues: the flute, the chain, the location, the time of year, the period, which is probably late Victorian. Discussion should, then, be based upon insight and evidence rather than mere hurried reaction: 'A monkey…', 'a skeleton…', 'a ghost' have been uninvited and excitedly shouted responses in the past. I also ask that the answer to my question should be presented as a still image to include the man with the flute, the amazed head teacher, Mr Davis, who has opened the school door, possibly a startled peeping child and, certainly, whatever is at the end of the chain. Having presented their images, children are asked to provide under-pinning justification.

A dancing bear

As with the poetry, the text allows for multiple answers. Here is what Causley's mother saw:

> A huge, ragged, dusty bear. A performing bear. 'Bruin', my mother used to call him.
>
> The children fairly gasped with surprise, I can tell you. I think the headmaster did too, but I don't suppose he showed it. Anyway, the keeper asked if the children would like to see the bear do his tricks. So out they all trooped into the playground. At a safe distance they all lined up for the performance, and the keeper began to play his whistle-pipe.
>
> 'Oh,' my mother used to say, 'that bear was a splendid creature.' It had thick fur and strong teeth and claws and great massive limbs and it did everything the keeper told it to do perfectly. It rolled and it tumbled and it marched on its hind legs up and down like one of the red-coated soldiers of those days. And it lay down and pretended to have died in battle for the Queen. It even did a kind of little dance or jig when the keeper played a particularly merry and lively tune. There was no doubt about it, the children enjoyed the show.
>
> Yet, you know, as Mother used to tell me this story…I could tell that the effect on her and all the other children was rather different from the one the keeper had intended. You see, there was something about that bear…that huge, rather shabby, powerful, frightened creature, hot and filthy with dust, its feet torn by tramping the rough roads, its spirit half-broken. You see, that bear was so far, so very far from where it might have been, living naturally, wandering about in great cold northern forests, and free. And I thought to myself, 'One day, you know, I really ought to write a poem about that,' and so I did. And I called it 'My Mother Saw a Dancing Bear'.

What Causley's mother saw was, indubitably, a dancing bear. Rather than dismissing alternative answers as 'wrong', teachers are more likely to examine them for plausibility. The period, location and appearance of the visitor suggest to many children the idea of a pirate, seaman or escaped convict.

Children are now given a copy of Causley's ballad 'My Mother Saw a Dancing Bear'.

My Mother Saw a Dancing Bear

My mother saw a dancing bear
By the schoolyard, a day in June.
The keeper stood with chain and bar
And whistle-pipe, and played a tune.

And bruin lifted up its head
And lifted up its dusty feet,
And all the children laughed to see
It caper in the summer heat.

They watched as for the Queen it died.
They watched it march. They watched it halt.
They heard the keeper as he cried,
'Now, roly-poly! Somersault!'

And then, my mother said, there came
The keeper with a begging-cup,
The bear with burning coat of fur,
Shaming the laughter to a stop.

They paid a penny for the dance,
But what they saw was not the show;
Only, in bruin's aching eyes,
Far-distant forests, and the snow.
'...bruin's aching eyes'.

(Charles Causley)

Evident in Causley's poem is the effect of the compression of an elaborated prose description – the maltreated bear, far from its native land and climate – into a powerful poetic image: the children *read* the source of the creature's misery in its eyes. Within the framework of the Literacy Hour there are a number of complementary strands that can be investigated:

- stylistic analysis – the ways in which the poet's use of language works to particular effect, e.g. the immediacy of the keeper's voice conveyed through direct speech;
- the sense of gawping audience conveyed by the repeated verbs – they *watched*, they *heard*, they *paid*, they *saw*;
- comparisons with the prose piece, itself a written version of Causley's oral account, e.g. what has been omitted, what has been developed?
- the ballad form which not only facilitates reading but has such narrative appeal.

As has been shown, readers bring knowledge to the text and such knowledge can be both consolidated and developed by the teacher's contributions and questions. Embedded within Causley's piece is a succinct historical snapshot of what, at the end of the nineteenth century, would have been a feature of provincial entertainment. But such a historical account has strong topical resonance. Most of the children to whom I introduced the poem had seen television programmes about the maltreatment of bears, dragged from the mountains to entertain tourists in city squares in Greece and Turkey. Many were keen to provide accounts of similar scenes they had observed when visiting other countries. A complementary feature here is the education of the affective sensibility which, as I have indicated here, allows for the shared expression of compassion.

Conclusion

Good textual materials combined with carefully planned activities can provide for a form of learning within what this book refers to as a 'community of enquiry'. Those classroom activities suggested above can, of course, be adapted and extended. Such learning is powerful because it is genuine, as it both builds upon and develops pupils' experience and knowledge. Such learning is also powerful because it is both interactive and what Bruner (1996:161–2) calls 'intersubjective':

> It is through principally interacting with others that children find out what the culture is about and how it conceives the world. Unlike any other species, human beings deliberately teach each other in settings outside the ones in which the knowledge being taught will be used...It is customary to say that this specialization rests upon the gift of language. But perhaps more to the point, it also rests upon our astonishingly well-developed talent for intersubjectivity – the human ability to understand the minds of others, whether through language, gesture, or other means. It is not just words that make this possible, but our capacity to grasp the role of the settings in which words, acts and gestures occur. We are the intersubjective species *par excellence*. It is this that permits us to 'negotiate' meanings when words go astray.
>
> Our Western pedagogical tradition hardly does justice to the importance of intersubjectivity in transmitting culture...teaching is fitted into a mold in which a single, presumably omniscient teacher explicitly tells or shows presumably unknowing learners something they presumably know nothing about... I believe that one of the most important gifts that a cultural psychology can give to education is a reformulation of this impoverished conception. For only a very small part of educating takes place on such a one-way street – and it is probably one of the least successful parts.

I have tried in this chapter to show ways of approaching the teaching of literacy that can develop such intersubjectivity and which, in a period of increasingly top-down curriculum prescription respond to Bruner's significant, timely challenge.

Notes

1. From the *National Literacy Strategy: Framework for Teaching* (1998:4) (London: HMSO) where it is suggested that 'as [pupils] learn...basic decoding skills they should also be taught to check their reading for sense by reference to the grammar and meaning of the text'.
2. See Chapter 1 of Fisher and Williams (eds) (2004) *Unlocking Creativity* (London: David Fulton Publishers) for more on the usefulness of a gestation period for thinking during which creative ideas have time to emerge.
3. See DfES (2003) *Speaking, Listening, Learning: Working with Children in Key Stages 1 and 2*, for an overview of how group discussion and drama can be used to encourage children to be reflective.
4. Now appropriately emphasised in the DfES (2003) *Speaking, Listening, Learning: Working with Children in Key Stages 1 and 2*, QCA teaching objectives.

References

Bruner, J. (1996) 'Culture, mind and education', in Moon, B. and Murphy, P. (eds) *Curriculum in Context*. London: Paul Chapman Publishing/Open University.

DfEE (1998) *National Literacy Strategy: Framework for Teaching*. London: HMSO.

DfEE (1999) *English in the National Curriculum*. London: HMSO.

DfES (2003*) Speaking, Listening, Learning: Working with Children in Key Stages 1 and 2*. London: QCA.

Eliot, T. S. (1933) *The Use of Poetry and the Use of Criticism*. London: Faber.

Fisher, R. and Williams, M. (eds) (2004) *Unlocking Creativity*. London: David Fulton Publishers.

Children's literature

Causley, C. (1983) 'I Saw a Jolly Hunter'. *Collected Poems*. London: Macmillan.

Causley, C. (1983) 'My Mother Saw a Dancing Bear'. *Collected Poems*. London: Macmillan.

Fisher, R. (ed.) (1989) *Pet Poems*. London: Faber & Faber.

Nichols, G. (1988) 'I'm a Parrot'. *Come On Into My Tropical Garden*. London: A&C Black.

Hodgson, R. (1920) 'The Bells of Heaven'. *Modern British Poetry* (ed. Untermeyer, L.). New York: Harcourt Brace & Howe.

La Follette, M. (1923) 'The Ballad of the Red Fox'. New York.

Thomas, E. (1920) 'The Gallows'. *Collected Poems*. London: Selwyn & Blount.

Further reading

Barrs, M. and Rosen, M. (1997) *A Year with Poetry*. London: Centre for Language in Primary Education.

Brownjohn, S. (1994) *To Rhyme or Not to Rhyme?* London: Hodder & Stoughton.

Carter D. (1998) *Teaching Poetry in the Primary School*. London: David Fulton Publishers.

Dymoke, S. (2003) *Drafting and Assessing Poetry*. London: Paul Chapman.

Rosen, M. (1989) *Did I Hear You Write?* London: André Deutsch.

Wilson, A. (ed.) (1998) *The Poetry Book for Primary Schools*. London: The Poetry Society.

'Playing with words': word level work including phonics, vocabulary and spelling

Mary Williams

'Reading would be alright if it weren't for the words!'

(Gary, aged 8)

Introduction

What can be done to ensure that children have easy access to words from an early age so that they don't see them as barriers to reading, as Gary did when he reached Key Stage 2? Reading involves a complicated range of decoding strategies, including sight, sound and context. For example, Andrew, a Year 1 child, read a passage with interest and confidence from an information book about cowboys. However, there was one word that he got consistently wrongly. Each time he met the word 'cattle' he read it as 'kettle', showing that what he read was not making sense to him. Most worryingly, he did not seem to think this mattered. Why could Andrew not decode the word 'cattle'? One reason could be that he was relying on sight recognition of words, and confusing two visually similar words that he already knew: 'cattle' and 'kettle'. He might have looked at the endings '-ettle' and '-attle', thinking incorrectly that these were the same. Or he may have been concentrating on the initial phonemes – 'k' and 'c' – knowing that these make the same sound in certain words, but choosing the wrong word. In this case the syntax was unlikely to help him as the two words were interchangeable, both being nouns. Above all, Andrew did not seem to be using the context to help him confirm or confound his choice of word.

So how could he be helped to read words correctly and with under-standing? The answer lies in helping him to use *all* the key skills of reading: phonic (sound), graphic and word recognition (sight), syntax (grammatical knowledge), and semantic (contextual understanding) in harmony. This presents a considerable challenge to the developing reader. Therefore, it is important for teachers to be aware of the underlying principles that govern this complex process so that children like Gary and Andrew are able to solve problems they encounter when reading. This chapter outlines some suggestions for teaching the reading of words in an interesting and problem-solving way – during 'word level work' in the Literacy Hour (if applicable) – through the teaching of phonics, vocabulary and spelling.

Why teach phonics?

Research in both America and the United Kingdom has shown that it is essential for children to acquire phonic knowledge when learning to read and that 'awareness that spoken language is composed of phonemes is an extremely important predictor of success in learning to read'.[1]

Children learn to recognise and read certain words simply through meeting them over and over again in their personal environment: for example, their own names, 'mummy' and 'daddy', labels on packaging, familiar café signs such as McDonald's or the names of characters from current television programmes such as *Teletubbies* or *Ballamory* (see Chapter 12 for more on environmental print). This ability is linked to memory that facilitates the instant recall of familiar words. The process that enables children to recognise words they have seen in printed form as complete units and to retrieve them from memory is called the 'lexical route' to whole word recognition.[2] This accounts for the success of visual teaching strategies such as 'look-and-say' using flashcards, the *Breakthrough to Literacy* materials[3] and other strategies for learning 'high frequency' words as advocated in the National Literacy Strategy (DfEE 1998).

However, word recognition skills alone will not be enough to enable children to process all the new words they will meet in their reading. As they become more fluent and read a wider range of texts, the number of new words encountered soon outstrips the ability to remember them on sight. In addition to sight vocabulary, young readers need knowledge of the sounds that make up spoken words, in particular phonemes (the smallest units of sound in words) to help them decode unknown words. Phonic knowledge is essential for processing unknown printed words and lack of it causes many of the problems encountered by pupils who experience difficulty in reading at Key Stage 2 (as with Gary above).

In the past many teachers have been sceptical about the effectiveness of phonics taught in isolation from the books children are reading – or when taught using unchallenging work sheets – because successful readers need to orchestrate a full range of strategies in order to become fluent.[4] The 'combined model' in

Figure 4.1 reflects the 'Searchlights' model of the National Literacy Strategy. In the combined model, teaching time should be given to at least one, but preferably more, of the key skills simultaneously, as phonemes are combined into words, words into sentences, sentences into paragraphs etc.[5]

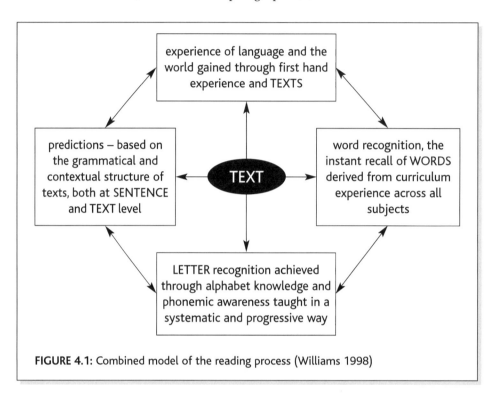

FIGURE 4.1: Combined model of the reading process (Williams 1998)

The effective use of direct teaching, as envisaged within 'shared' and guided group teaching in the Literacy Hour, offers one way that reading strategies and skills can be taught in an integrated and systematic way. However, individual reading encounters between pupil and teacher also play an important role in motivating, as well as assessing, progress[6] (see Chapter 10). As Kate, aged 6, said: 'Sometimes I like to talk to someone about what I've read'.

How should phonemic awareness be taught?

Phonic knowledge is important for unlocking literacy but how should it be taught? First it is important to identify what children need to know in terms of phonic knowledge. Taking the words 'sat' and 'flower' as examples, pupils need to learn that these words are composed of a number of phonemes that comprise the onset (initial phoneme) and rime (end phoneme) and syllable sounds, as follows:

Word	Phoneme(s)	Onset/rime	Syllables
sat	s-a-t	s-at	sat
flower	*fl-ow-e-r	fl-ower	fl-ow-er

*Note: 'fl' is a blend

FIGURE 4.2 Word, phonemes, onset/rime and syllables

In developing 'phonemic awareness' emphasis should be placed on children hearing the phonemes in words. Children between the ages of 2 and 4 enjoy inventing rhymes, as is evidenced in their pre-sleep talking, when they sing to themselves, and by the way they pick up 'jingles' from television advertisements or the meaningless, repetitive sounds made by some TV cartoon characters. There is evidence that 'rhyming ability is present in preschool children, and that children can solve rhyme detection tasks by at least 4 years of age'.[7]

For instance, four-year-olds are able to *hear* and identify which is the odd word out from 'pin; bun; gun',[8] this is essential if they are to recognise these phonemes in their printed form (graphemes) at a later stage. It is important, therefore, to give young children experience of rhyme and alliteration, through songs and poems in nursery and reception classes, to help them hear both onset and rime phonemes (DfEE 2000).

Phonic games based on multi-sensory approaches include:

- I Spy – 'I spy with my little eye something beginning / ending with…'
- Hunt the Thimble – hunt objects which began with a particular sound
- Twenty Questions – for example, 'I'm thinking of something which begins with "t". Can you guess what it is?'

Once children are conversant with the game, they can choose onsets themselves but with adult support to make sure they are correct, e.g. 'Everything in my basket begins with "buh"; everything in my sock starts with "suh". As an alternative; 'Which is the odd one out in my basket: "bag", "peg", "ball" …?'

FIGURE 4.3 Ideas for teaching initial phonemes/onsets

Children also need to practise making analogies from one word to another, through being able to suggest similar onsets and rimes in other words. A survey in 1975 showed that the 500 most frequently used words in primary reading books were reliant on 37 rimes.[9] Although the range of interesting and attractive books available for use in the classroom has increased significantly – replacing the often dull 'key word' series of the 1970s – the focus has remained, rightly, on repetitive vocabulary in the early stages of learning to read. Hence, attention to rime can reduce significantly the amount of learning needed by encouraging the child to make analogies from a known word to an unknown one – for example from *light* to *right*.

Based on multi-sensory approaches:

- I Spy something which rhymes with –at; –en; –igh etc.
- Changing nursery rhymes and poems – Little Bo-Peep has lost her car
- Feely bag game: all the objects in a bag rhyme with, for example, ox. Children guess by feeling objects.
- Odd one out: all the objects on a tray end with a particular rime – except for one.
- Snap – spotting the same rime on a set of cards in picture of word form.
- Suggesting and collecting rhyming, humorous phrases, for example, a *cat* in a *hat* ate a *rat*.
- Rhyming pairs – could be an oral or a written activity, for example, say 'top / hop'. What can children give for 'tap/–'?

FIGURE 4.4 Ideas for teaching rimes

To return to Andrew's problems with the word 'cattle', children's attention also needs to be drawn to the sounds in the middle of words, the medial phonemes. Frequently they look no further than the beginning of the word, giving the ending no more than a cursory glance, but completely overlooking, or failing to appreciate, the importance of the middle. For instance, in the example cited, the all-important 'a' in the middle of 'cattle' has been read as the 'e' in 'kettle'. This is where an ability to segment the word is needed and attention to the middle part of the word is essential. In other words, pupils need to be able to work from the whole word to each of its parts.[10] (See Figure 4.5)

Finally, as it is known that 'awareness of onsets and rimes precedes awareness of phonemes in the development of phonological skills',[11] it is important that a developmental approach to the introduction of phonemic/phonic knowledge is adopted, such as that suggested below.

Suggested progression for teaching phonemic awareness:

- using preschool games and rhyming activities based on *hearing* onset and rimes in words;

- recognising initial phonemes in their written form and using these to spell simple consonant, vowel, consonant words;
- recognising rimes in their written form and using these to spell words;
- recognising consonant digraphs (two consonants which make a phoneme) and blends – that is two or three consonant phonemes said rapidly one after the other, represented by two or three graphemes (for example, 'bl' or 'str'), which in some cases might also be a digraph (as in 'ch');
- hearing the medial sounds in words;
- recognising medial sounds including single vowels and vowel digraphs in their written form and using these to spell words.

- Choose a medial sound, e.g. 'a', as in hat. What other real words can be made using this phoneme? Examples are: mat, sat, cat.
- Odd one out: either in picture or word form, or both, for example: hot, pot, hit, cot.
- Listening game: which of the following have the same phonemes in the middle? Give a starter word, for example 'feet'. Then ask the children if 'leaf', 'health', 'brief', 'heath', 'teeth' conform. This could turn into the sort of investigation suggested for Key Stage 2 pupils in the National Literacy Strategy (see below).
- What if? For example, what happens if the medial phoneme of 'dog' is changed to an 'i'? What new word is made?
- Looking for words within words: *toffee*, *coffee*, *boffin*. Also discuss strategies for dealing with this task; for example, going through the alphabet in order to see if real words can be made. This promotes metacognitive awareness.

FIGURE 4.5 Ideas for teaching medial phonemes

In the National Literacy Strategy it is suggested that the learning sequence should be as follows:

1. initial consonants and short vowel sounds;
2. final sounds in simple words;
3. medial short vowel sounds.

It is vital that phonemic awareness be taught systematically with an emphasis on enjoyment through play (Drifte 2003) drawing on increasing familiarity with published texts and through a child's own writing. This is envisaged in the Literacy Hour, where the focus should be on 'decoding' during 'shared and guided reading' and 'encoding' during 'shared and guided writing'.

Extending phonemic awareness with older children

Children's phonic knowledge needs to be developed and extended at Key Stage 2 where they face the challenge of reading an ever-increasing number of new words in all subjects of the curriculum. Poor phonic knowledge, combined with an over-reliance on word recognition, can cause reading problems in older children. Research has shown that 'children who have good rhyming skills become better readers, and children who have reading difficulties tend to have a rhyming deficit'.[12]

If older children need to extend and develop their understanding of phonics, how should it be taught? There is an ongoing debate, still raging, between those who advocate 'synthetic' as opposed to 'analytic' teaching methods, with the former believing that phonic knowledge should precede learning to read and the latter thinking that phonemic understanding develops alongside practice in reading through analysis of what is read.[13] The National Literacy Strategy advocates a mixture of methods, with the emphasis on synthetic teaching strategies in the Early Years and on analytical learning in Key Stage 2, as older children often understand the significance of analysing the phonemes in words more easily than younger children. As Ravi, a struggling older reader explained, 'You have to think about what the different parts of a word sound like, then put them together to read the word. It's a bit like Lego.' Whatever the teaching approach, it is important that learning phonics is made interesting and motivating, as failure to achieve this is one of the reasons why some children, particularly boys, find learning to read unrewarding and boring.

The following are some ideas for teaching phonemic awareness with older children:

Onsets

- *Invent alliterative noun phrases*, providing opportunities for work on adjectives. Examples are:
  - names in the class or group, e.g. 'attractive Anne', 'energetic Edward'
  - disgusting food, e.g. 'putrid porridge', 'slimy spaghetti'
  - animals, e.g. 'bashful bears', 'coy crocodiles'
  - packaging, e.g. 'a jar of jam', 'a hunk of ham'.
- *Create alliterative sentences* providing opportunities for work on adjectives, adverbs, the apostrophe, subject and predicate etc. An example is: 'Silly Sally suddenly spilled the soup on Susie's smart suit'.
- *Adapt 'parlour games'*, for example, 'The parson's cat is an adorable cat, bashful cat...'; 'I Spy'; 'Hunt the Thimble'; finding objects beginning with a particular onset.[14]

Rimes

- *Rhyme to a theme*, for example, food is crunchy, munchy, chewy, slurpy.
- *Rhyming pairs* (including dictionary work), to be given to groups of children to work out from a given clue, for example:
  - clue – obese feline = fat cat
  - clue – ailing hen = sick chick

  Children then think up one each for themselves and challenge others to find the answer.
- *Consequence limericks*

  Children need to be familiar with the genre, through shared reading, and the creation of a class limerick during shared writing. Use a familiar theme – such as those derived from fairy stories, for example:

  > When Goldilocks saw the three bears,
  > She ran as fast as she could down the stairs,
  > Thank goodness I'm free,
  > She shouted with glee,
  > But I'm sorry I broke all their chairs.

Once the children are familiar with the genre they can play a consequences game in which each child in a group writes a line and then passes it on to the next person who reads it and then adds another line. The funnier the better!

Medial phonemes

Children should be encouraged to collect lists of words that conform to the same grapho-phonic medial patterns, e.g. : tail, mail, rail, over the course of a week, drawing on texts currently being read. The middle phoneme of words can be removed so children work out what the word might be by drawing on phonic and contextual clues to help them, e.g. 'm—l', 'r—l'.

Children may find the more complex aspects of phonic knowledge difficult to grasp, for example hearing consonant digraphs where two letters are represented by one phoneme, such as 'sh' in 'shoe'. The challenge is to extend their phonic and graphic knowledge to include more complex patterns and irregularities, via interesting and absorbing activities. Through analytical word investigations, children can explore the variety of ways in which phonemes are represented as graphemes in words; a problem-solving approach endorsed in *Excellence and Enjoyment* (DfES 2003). Pupils can be asked to make collections of words which subscribe to the particular pattern, then analyse their collections in terms of the frequency of occurrence of each written form, e.g. the vowel, vowel/vowel or vowel/consonant digraph (grapheme) for the 'ee' sound (phoneme) in words, as in 'h*e*', 'm*ee*t', 'l*ea*f', 'monk*ey*'.

Vocabulary

Preschool children begin to be aware of the printed word as they become interested in the signage around them, for example on labels, posters, shop signs and street names. Adults looking after them should bring such print to their attention in as fun a way as possible. In school they should be provided with a print-rich learning environment through the medium of written notices, displays of writing and the giving of routine information in printed form, such as, 'Only four children can play in the home corner'. Children's vocabulary is gradually broadened through teaching and learning of high-frequency words in the National Literacy Strategy and through reading fiction and non-fiction books specifically chosen to challenge their understanding and to increase their repertoire of words. They can be encouraged to 'play with words' through a variety of games and activities including board games, audiotape games, use of computer software and phonic games. They should be asked to collect words which relate to a particular theme within the subject of English itself, for example by compiling a list of words which relate to 'TALK' – like 'whisper', 'shout', 'mutter' or 'bellow' or which refer to a cross-curricular topic such as 'foods from other countries', which might include such words as 'spaghetti', 'curry' or 'baguettes'.

As they get older children need to learn the technical terms of the subject of English itself so that they can be precise when discussing it, as in Table 4.1.

Table 4.1 Examples of the technical vocabulary of English

Phonic knowledge	Poetry	Writing	Linguistic language
onset	assonance	imagery	etymology
rime	blank verse	metaphor	morphology
digraph	calligram	simile	phonology
phoneme	cinquain	onomatopoeia	graphology
syllable	clerihew	palindrome	accent
segmentation	couplet	parody	dialect

Children enjoy learning about etymology, which is the study of the sources and development of words. This includes finding out about the impact of other cultures on the growth of English in the form of words derived from Greek, Latin and French, or, more recently, from the continents of America and Asia that may have a positive affect on the self-esteem of those learning English as an additional language. Through this they acquire an understanding that language is dynamic. You only have to think of the changes to the meaning of the words 'chip' and 'gay' over the last 50 years to appreciate this fully. See if you can guess the meaning of the sixteenth- and seventeenth-century terms below (not intended for use with children!):

- a lip clap
- a bed swerver
- gutfoundered
- pingle
- hippotomonstrosesquipedalian.

(Answers in order: a kiss; someone who is unfaithful to the marital bed; ravenously hungry; to pick at food; an extremely long word!)

An understanding of morphology is also integral to vocabulary extension work. A morpheme is the smallest unit of meaning in a word, for example 'car' is one morpheme; in 'housewife' there are two morphemes: 'house' and 'wife'. Of particular significance is the effect that prefixes and suffixes can have on the meaning of words: for example, adding the prefixes 'post' or 'pre' to the word 'date' makes the interpretation of them very different. Analysing and investigating the structure of words can help children as they learn to spell. Being able to do this is essential if targets for future learning (see Chapter 12) are to be clearly set and fully understood by the pupils themselves.[15]

Spelling

Spelling and handwriting are inextricably linked. They are a skill of the mind and hand. Even relatively competent spellers revert to pen-and-paper trials whenever they are unsure that a spelling is correct, and may write several versions of a word to see which *looks* right, as 'spelling is best remembered from the finger tips'.[16] An example of this is shown in the following draft of a letter written by a Year 4 child as part of a local studies project in which he makes several attempts to spell the word 'could' correctly:

Dear Sir or Madam,

We think you cold improve your buses by putting in a play room for little boys and girls and we think you should put in a TV. You code put a sofa bed in and you code have bed and breakfast. You coude have a computer and you code have a toilet and you coud put a guard dog on the bus becos evry one will want to jump on.

Yours sinserly,
Craig

Craig should be praised for the content of his letter in terms of its ability to persuade the reader to his point of view, and then his attention should be drawn to the spelling of 'could' through his attempt at 'coud' that was nearly correct. If he is unable to correct it for himself he should be shown how to spell the word properly. He needs to *see* the word in its written form and then learn it in one of the ways suggested below. In addition, he should be asked to collect – as a possible homework activity, as many words as he can that have the same ending; for example 'should', 'would'.

Children gradually develop a full understanding of the spelling of a particular word as they experiment with it through trial and error, as the ability to write adopting the correct conventions of transcription of which spelling is a part emerges over a period of time (see Chapter 6).

Stages through which spelling ability may develop[17]

- pre-communicative – when any letters or letter-like shapes will do;
- pre-phonetic – when a word is thought to consist of three letters, e.g. 'prd' for 'purred';
- phonetic – when phonetically accurate, but not correct, e.g. 'luvinglee';
- transitional – when there is a mixture of phonetic and correct spellings in a passage of writing, or within a word; and
- correct – when spelling is mainly accurate but any pupil can revert to a previous stage when faced with new or complex vocabulary, e.g. 'queuemunication', (written by a Year 6 child).

Recent research has shown that children do not progress through these stages in a linear fashion but use them simultaneously (O'Sullivan and Thomas 2000):[18]

Spelling is linked to visual memory and is made challenging by the many irregularities which occur in English; consequently there is a need to learn the high-frequency and medium-frequency words as listed in the National Literacy Strategy. Pupils should be taught how to tackle problematic spellings (see below) such as the following, which many adults still find difficult: sentence, because, February, beautiful, decisive, independent, separate, dyslexia, psychology, accommodation.

The question that any failed speller, whether child or adult, needs to ask is: 'How can I learn to spell a word effectively?'.

Ways to teach spelling

When teaching children to spell, aim to teach a few spellings at a time, perhaps three to four words that are connected in some way. Examples are: words having the same root – as in 'remind', 'reminisce' and 'reminiscent'; or relating to a particular focus of work – such as the days of the week; or as part of the technical vocabulary of a particular subject – for example, in science, words relating to magnetism. New spellings should be taught on a 'little but often' basis with perhaps no more than ten minutes spent on the work every day. Similarly, children are more successful if tested little and often, e.g. a small number each day, rather than by means of longer, weekly tests. To lodge a spelling in the child's visual memory the well-known LOOK, COVER, THINK, WRITE, CHECK routine should be adopted in combination with teaching children to use, as appropriate, the following repertoire of strategies:

- Segment words into chunks and learn each syllable separately, for example, 'com-fort-able'.
- Look at the words within words, for example 'straight/forward'.
- Teach words in the same 'family' (with the same pattern) established through a known spelling whenever possible, for example, '-ea-' words such as 'leaf' and 'each'.
- Offer children spelling rules, for example, 'i before e except after c', when the sound is 'ee', while reminding them that there are occasional exceptions to any rule.
- When possible, teach spelling and handwriting together.

Children should be reassured that everyone makes spelling mistakes from time to time as English has an irregular spelling system. However, anyone can improve their spelling ability if they try, and to help them do this children should be encouraged to set their own targets for themselves in order to take responsibility for their own learning. Once this has been achieved they should be supported in developing their own strategies for spelling unknown or difficult words using the suggestions made above. Above all they should be motivated and challenged to learn in creative and interesting ways (Fisher and Williams 2004). As Susie said of the self-selected list of words she was trying to learn, 'I have a book of secret words I am learning to spell. It's great...it's my own book of spells!'. Susie may not get all her words right, but she has learnt one of the most important lessons in developing literacy, that words matter and can be fun.

Conclusion

Word level work continues to be a controversial aspect of literacy teaching. In April 2005, in an article in *The Guardian* entitled 'War of Words', Wendy Berliner summarised evidence presented to a House of Commons Education

Select Committee on the teaching of reading in which synthetic methods were praised. This led some politicians to call for their immediate introduction into all primary schools in England.[19] Few would disagree that phonic knowledge should be taught systematically but it is equally important that children are taught in creative, investigative ways. Synthetic approaches may be useful to start with, but as children get older they are able to be analytical in the way they learn. There is a danger that over-dependence on phonics, crucial though this is, will not be enough to unlock the wealth of meaning that can be derived from reading fiction and non-fiction texts. Children need to use a range of strategies to decode texts, including phonics, but above all they need to know that being able to read gives them access to a world of novel and exciting ideas.

Notes

1. M. Adams (1990:123), as the result of extensive research carried out in America.
2. E. Funnell and M. Stuart (1995) who suggest that children need access to two routes for processing text when reading: a lexical route, as well as a sub-lexical route.
3. The learning of whole words as relevant to the child, and as suggested by him or her, as in the *Breakthrough to Literacy* language experience approach of D. McKay (1970) that has recently been updated.
4. E. Ashworth in C. Harrison and M. Coles (1992) developed this useful analogy of seeing each strategy needed for successful reading as a section of an orchestra, sometimes playing solo, but frequently needing to be in harmony.
5. Unpublished PhD research (1998) by the author in which a combined model of the reading process derived from K. Stanovich (1980) and the Searchlight model (1998) was suggested as a way forward in terms of increasing understanding of the interrelated nature of strategy/key skill teaching in reading.
6. A timely reminder from P. Guppy and M. Hughes (1999) that individual reading encounters between pupil and teacher can be extremely profitable in terms of motivation and assessment.
7. U. Goswami in R. Beard (1995:64) *RHYME: Reading and Writing* (London: Hodder & Stoughton).
8. Research by L. Bradley and P. Bryant (1983) that led to a reassessment of young children's ability to hear the sounds in words.
9. U. Goswami in R. Beard (1995) *op. cit.*
10. H. Dombey (1998), derived from work undertaken by M. Moustafa in the United States.
11. U. Goswami in R. Beard (1995:37) *op. cit.*
12. U. Goswami in R. Beard (1995:76) *op. cit.*
13. Those advocating synthetic approaches are Sue Lloyd through 'Jolly Phonics', Diana McGuinness, Carmen McGuinness and Geoffrey McGuinness through 'Phono-Graphix' and, for older children, Alan Davies with 'THRASS'. Detractors include Henrietta Dombey of Brighton University (cited in 10 above).
14. See materials produced by Sue Palmer (1995) for the Longman Book Project.
15. QCA (1999) *Target Setting and Assessment in the National Literacy Strategy.* Sudbury: QCA Publications.
16. This quotation comes from Charles Cripps (1989). For further reading about the teaching of spelling refer to M. Peters (1985) and N. Mudd (1994).

17. Proposed by R. Gentry in 1982, drawing on G. Bissex's case study (1980) GNYS AT WRK, of her own child's emergent understanding of the spelling process, but as only one child was observed, some caution is needed in making claims on the basis of these findings.
18. O'Sullivan draws on her research with Thomas (2005) that showed that young children approach spelling in different ways and fluent readers were often competent spellers, although fairly fluent readers did not 'pick up' spelling from their reading.
19. 'Matthew Taylor [*The Guardian* (3.06.2005)] reports that last night the government announced a large-scale review of the way children are taught to read. This is to be carried out by an "independent review panel" that will report in January 2006. As part of their investigations the panel have been asked to examine the merits of "synthetic phonics". In announcing the review, Ruth Kelly, Secretary of State for Education, pointed out that "the debate now centres on not whether to teach phonics but how" so the debate continues.'

References

Adams, M. (1990) *Beginning to Read*. London: Heinemann.

Beard, R. (1995) *RHYME: Reading and Writing*. London: Hodder & Stoughton.

Berliner, W. (2005) 'War of Words'. *Education Guardian,* 5 April.

Bradley, L. and Bryant, P. (1983) 'Categorising sounds and learning to read: a causal connection'. *Nature* **310**, 419–21.

Cripps, C. (1989) 'The Teaching of Spellings'. *Links* **24** (2).

Davies, A. (1996) *THRASS Primary Special Needs Pack*. London: Collins.

DfEE (1998) *The National Literacy Strategy: Framework for Teaching*. London: HMSO.

DfEE (1999) *English in the National Curriculum*. London: HMSO.

DfEE (2000) *Curriculum Guidance for the Foundation Stage*. London: QCA.

DfES (2003) *Excellence and Enjoyment*. London: DfES Publications.

Dombey, H. and Moustafa, M. (1998) *Whole to Part Phonics: How Children Learn to Read and Spell*. London: CLPE.

Drifte, C. (2003) *Learning through Phonics*. London: David Fulton Publishers.

Fisher, R. and Williams, M. (eds) (2004) *Unlocking Creativity*. London: David Fulton Publishers.

Funnell, E. and Stuart, M. (1995) *Learning to Read: Psychology in the Classroom*. Oxford: Blackwell.

Gentry, R. (1982) 'An analysis of developmental spelling in GNYS AT WRK'. *Reading Teacher,* **36** (2).

Goswami, U. (1994) 'Phonological skills, analogies and reading development'. *Reading,* **28** (2).

Graham, J. and Kelly, A. (2000) *Reading Under Control* (2nd edn). London: David Fulton Publishers.

Guppy, P. and Hughes, M. (1999) *The Development of Independent Reading*. Milton Keynes: Open University Press.

Harrison, C. and Coles, M. (1992) *The Reading for Real Handbook*. London: Routledge.

Lloyd, S. (1992) *The Phonics Handbook*. Chigwell: Jolly Learning.

McGuinness, D. (1998) *Why Children Can't Read*. London: Penguin.

McKay, D. (ed.) (1970) *Breakthrough to Literacy*. Harlow: Longman.

Moustafa, M. (1998) *Beyond Traditional Phonics*. London: Heinemann.

Mudd, N. (1994) *Effective Spelling*. London: Hodder & Stoughton.

O'Sullivan, O. and Thomas, A. (2005) *Understanding Spelling*. London: CLPE.

Palmer, S. (1995) *Playing with Language*. Truro: Language LIVE.

Peters, M. (1985) *Spelling Taught or Caught? A New Look*. London: Routledge.

QCA (1998) *Standards at Key Stage 2: English, Mathematics and Science: Report on the 1998 National Curriculum Assessments for 11 Year Olds*. Sudbury: QCA Publications.

QCA (1999) *Target Setting and Assessment in the National Literacy Strategy*. Sudbury: QCA Publications.

Riley, J. (1996) *The Teaching of Reading*. London: Paul Chapman Publishing.

Stanovich, K. (1980) 'Towards an interactive-compensatory model of individual differences in the development of reading'. *Reading Research Quarterly* 1, 32–71.

Taylor, M. (2005) *The Guardian*, 3 June.

Williams, M. (1998) *A Study which Explores the Impact of the English National Curriculum (1990) on the Work of Teachers at Key Stage 2*. PhD Thesis (unpublished). Brunel University.

Further reading

Drifte, C. (2003) *Learning through Phonics*, London: David Fulton Publishers.

Goodwin, P. (2005) *The Literate Classroom*, (2nd edn). London: David Fulton Publishers.

Williams, M. (ed.) (2002) *Unlocking Writing*. London: David Fulton Publishers.

Useful websites

BBC 'Spelling with the Spellits' website (www.bbc.co.uk/schools/spellits/).

BBC 'Words and Pictures' website (www.bbc.co.uk/schools/wordsandpictures).

Teaching grammar and knowledge about language

Françoise Allen and Gerry Gregory

There's an awful lot of 'grammar' in the Literacy Hour...

Introduction

Year 5, Term 3: 'Pupils should be taught...to investigate clauses through identifying the main clause in a long sentence.'

(DfEE 1998:48)

This is, arguably, the most 'difficult' item identified in the National Literacy Strategy Framework for Teaching (NLS) and one that, in our experience of 'delivering' INSET, many teachers find far from simple to grasp. It is potentially difficult for Year 5 pupils because in analysing a 'long sentence' it might be necessary to ask if it is a simple (single clause) sentence – and long only because it has many phrases – or a multiple sentence. If it turns out to be the latter, then a further question arises. Is it a compound sentence (two or more clauses of equal status joined by a connective like 'and' or 'but' or 'then') or a complex sentence (a main clause with one or more subordinate or dependent clauses)?

Before pupils meet main clauses they should, for example, have been taught, as part of 'Grammatical Awareness', to 'match verbs to nouns/pronouns' (Year 2, Term 3), 'use the term "verb" appropriately' (Year 3, Term 1), and 'identify adverbs and understand their functions in sentences' (Year 4, Term 1). Around the same time as they set about identifying main clauses they will be learning how to 'understand and use the term preposition' (Year 5, Term 3).

'...and there's a fair amount of 'grammar' in the National Curriculum (DfEE 1999), too'.

At this point some readers might be wanting to ask: So what? Those of us working with English in the National Curriculum are used to the idea of teaching explicit 'grammar' knowledge. 'Grammar' in the National Curriculum is sometimes used in relation to pupils learning how to apply the rules for making Standard English; sometimes it is used in relation to them learning about these rules and how to talk about them using standard terminology. However, it is noteworthy that, in contrast with NLS requirements mentioned above, it is only in the Programme of Study for Key Stages 3 and 4 that 'clause and sentence structure' are specifically targeted (DfEE 1999). For example:

A Year 6 class and their teacher have just started reading a novel. Following a shared reading session, the books are taken in. After school, the teacher word processes the next page and copies the text twice. Then she goes through one copy, deleting all the nouns and leaving in their place gaps of uniform length. She prints ten copies – on blue paper. Then she makes further versions deleting the verbs and adjectives respectively. She runs off sufficient copies for a third of the class to have a verb-less (pink) text, and another third an adjective-less (green) one.

Next day, she gives out the copies: two tables get blue, two more get pink, and the last two tables get green. The tasks are to fill the gaps plausibly and work out the *kinds* of words that are missing. On no account must blues confer with pinks, and so on. The class is familiar with 'Cloze Procedure'; they have used it to consolidate learning in technology, science and history. They have also used it with poetry, attempting to supply what is *not* there by making maximum use of what *is*, e.g. rhyme patterns, line lengths, patterns of alliteration, and – above all – meaning. Accustomed to Cloze work, they are quickly on-task. They find the second task harder: some of them can't find the term they need to refer to the missing words. 'Name', 'doing word' and 'describing thingy' are heard in groups' exchanges. On the wall are five faces: ranging from very grumpy (1) at one end to very smiley (5) at the other. In almost daily use in this classroom, 1 tends to get used to record negative verdicts and 5 positive verdicts. By using the faces, the teachers often gets pupils to vote, express opinions and hence collect *data* about their experiences and attitudes and preferences, rather than allowing the talkative and assertive and confident to appear to speak for all. She thinks of it as developing a sense of the importance of collecting *evidence* as against settling for a vague sense of how things stand – and as training for democratic citizenship. The question today is: 'How hard did you find it to understand your passage?' The children vote. As the votes come in, it quickly becomes apparent that the blue (noun-less) group have found far more difficulty than the others. On the computer a block graph is produced to record the average scores relating to the three word classes. It is printed, enlarged (twice), coloured (blue, pink and green) and displayed.

FIGURE 5.1 A Year 6 class

We return to this classroom later.

What 'grammar' refers to in this chapter

As we have already seen, the word 'grammar' means several different things, and this has been signalled by the single quotation marks surrounding the word up to this point. Sidney Greenbaum (1988) identifies half a dozen meanings in an expert discussion.[1] For present purposes just two points about meaning need to be made. First, this chapter is concerned with 'grammar' in a descriptive (rather than prescriptive) sense. That is to say, we focus on grammar as describing aspects of how language works rather than as prescribing how language should be used. Second, and amplifying 'aspects of how language works', the present focus is the study of how we make sentences. The emphasis is on taking sentences apart to see how they work, or, as one of our PGCE students memorably put it, on finding out what's going on 'under the bonnet' of language. (In passing, it is often said that you do not need to know what goes on under the bonnet to drive competently, and very often said, for example, by students and teachers whose education has not included work of the kind this chapter explores, that you can be a highly competent language user without having explicit knowledge of grammar. Both assertions are self-evidently true. However, a case for teaching explicit grammar knowledge – that is for helping pupils to make explicit a fraction of that vast amount of their implicit (grammar) knowledge which enables them, to paraphrase Chomsky, to generate and understand unique utterances – is made in the following section. Before we embark on that, it is perhaps worth noting that the analogy between effective driving on the one hand and using language on the other takes us only so far: the former entails a modest repertoire of skills plus the ability to 'read' and adapt to a range of road conditions and situations; the latter entails literally unlimited complexity and novelty of context.)

Is there a case for teaching explicit 'grammar' knowledge?

It should be made clear at the outset that we consider the primary business of the English curriculum to be the development of pupils as effective speakers, listeners, writers and readers. A plausible case for teaching grammar must show that knowledge of grammar, and skill in applying it, promotes that development.

The case against teaching 'grammar'

There have been many investigations into the usefulness and effectiveness of teaching grammar; and many studies have appeared to give it the 'thumbs down', for example:

> Wherever it has been seriously researched, the analytical study of grammar has failed to produce significant results in student writing across the board...It would be folly to ignore the avalanche of studies that point to minimal connection between the ability to parse, label, diagram, and correct exercises and a more generalized correctness, fluency and elegance in writing.
>
> (D'Eloia 1977: 1,20)

In view of the widespread agreement of research studies based upon many types of students and teachers, the conclusion can be stated in strong and unqualified terms: the teaching of formal grammar has a negligible or – because it usually displaces some instruction and practice in composition – even a harmful effect on improvement in writing (Hartwell 1985).[2]

Although Tomlinson (1994) has cast doubt on the methodology and findings of one such investigation – a study frequently quoted in Britain over recent decades to justify excluding grammar from the English curriculum – the trend is clear. However, what most of the studies referred to have in common is an appeal to direct improvement of pupils' writing as the yardstick for justifying grammar (e.g. Eppi-Centre 2004).[3] In relation to this, QCA (1998:55) has argued that it may be

> time to try to shift the criterion by which the usefulness of grammar is judged. Walmsley (1984) has questioned the premise that the only justification for teaching grammar is direct improvement of pupils' writing... It may be more profitable to promote the teaching of grammar on different grounds: as a strand in the teaching and learning of language, which like all other aspects, compositional and technical, does not have a straight transfer into writing.[4]

We can find a plausible case if we look to grammar study for other benefits.

A case for teaching 'grammar

There are two chief arguments for teaching grammar; both relate to the development of literacy.

First, it is useful to develop a grammar 'metalanguage' (a language tool for describing and discussing language). This can help pupils to describe, analyse, discuss and evaluate texts: their own and others. Arguably, describing a problem is a step on the road to solving it. Through shared grammar concepts, and vocabulary for labelling them, pupils and teachers are enabled to discuss, for example:

1. pupils' texts with precision and economy: for example 'too many adjectives' rather than 'too many describing words – you know, words like "red" – I mean, words that describe names, er, persons, places...I don't mean the ones that describe doing words...or state words...';

or

2. the language of sports commentary: for example the use of noun phrases (see below) such as 'the England midfielder', 'the unorthodox Costa Rican', which offer a change from using players' names only or 'buy time' while they are brought to mind;

   or

3. the use of 'nominalisation' (i.e. the turning of, for example, verbs into nouns/noun phrases, (see below)) in, say, letters from public utilities, as in 'Non-payment of bills may result in loss of supply' rather than 'If you do not pay up we shall cut off your supply';

   or

4. the use of active or passive voice in newspaper headlines – and the resultant effect, and likely intentions – as in: 'Police shoot rioters', 'Rioters shot by police', 'Rioters shot'.

Examples 3 and 4 above suggest the development of concepts and related vocabulary that potentially help pupils understand and articulate how, for example, advertising and political discourses work, and work upon them.

There is much of demonstrable value for pupils in...learning not simply to look through language, to the content of a message but rather to see through language and be empowered better to understand and explain the ways in which messages are mediated or shaped, very often in the interests of preserving a particular viewpoint or of reinforcing existing ideologies (Carter 1990:108).[5]

Pupils learning a modern foreign language or English as an additional language

Regarding pupils learning a modern foreign language, and the special case of pupils for whom English is an additional language (EAL), a shared understanding of 'grammar', accompanied by a joint possession of a shared terminology, can sometimes allow teacher and pupil to refer with precision to aspects of English and how its features either mirror or differ from other languages in pupils' repertoires. Examples include: considering English in relation to some Asian languages (the positioning of subjects, verbs, adverbs and objects, the use or non-use of articles and modes of transforming statements into negatives and questions); and considering English in relation to French/Spanish/German/Italian etc. (word order, e.g. positioning of nouns/adjectives and verbs/adverbs).

In the case of EAL pupils, our sense is that such explicit knowledge and reference are likely to help most those who are beyond the earliest stages of learning English, and when used in conjunction with deliberate exposure of the learner to an artificially large number of instances of some target structure in English on the assumption that the very high frequency of the structure...will attract the learner's attention to the relevant formal regularities.

(Terrell 1991:59)

Second, and related to the above, grammar study is valuable in helping to understand language itself; that is it is a dominant means of understanding the world, of much of our thinking, of making (and undermining) relationships and of developing and expressing our sense of ourselves. The importance of such understanding is as self-evident as that of experiencing and understanding literature, though in our experience this is less readily admitted by teachers (QCA 1998).

In addition to these fundamental justifications for teaching grammar, a number of others have been offered. The following are examples from Hudson (1992:181–8):

- building linguistic self-respect: dispelling the myth that non-standard languages have no grammar;
- help in learning foreign languages;

from the Cox Committee, DES 1989:

- some form of analysis (which may be more or less explicit) is necessarily a part of the interpretation of texts and of the production of accurate writing;

and, from QCA (1998):

- there is evidence that drawing explicit attention to the syntactic features of pupils' writing, in the context of an individual pupil's work and in relation to the type of task in hand, can increase pupils' awareness of how language works. This may in turn increase their sense of control over their writing.

Here the evidence is neither produced nor referenced: given that which is cited above, the 'may' speaks volumes. In a recent article, Gregory (2003), one of the present writers, has further explored the cases for and against grammar teaching, as well as issues of what grammar to teach and how.

For a succinct rationale for grammar we believe it would be difficult to improve on the case made by the Cox Committee (above) for teaching knowledge about language; namely: to the end that pupils 'achieve a working knowledge of its structure and of the variety of ways in which meaning is made, so that they have a vocabulary for discussing it, so that they can use it with greater awareness, and because it is interesting'.

Teachers' commitment to and preparedness for grammar teaching

Successful grammar teaching depends on teachers' (a) commitment to it, based on conviction of its importance; and (b) competence, based on their own secure grammar knowledge.

Teacher commitment

The British press reported considerable teacher opposition to grammar teaching around the time when the government of the day introduced the first version of the National Curriculum (English). It is our impression, supported by noting the views expressed in INSET programmes and a small-scale enquiry that is reported below, that this opposition has diminished, though by no means disappeared. Furthermore, the National Association for the Teaching of English (NATE 1997:2) has confirmed the importance of understanding grammar:

> The study of grammatical structures and systems allows pupils to explore for themselves an essential part of the rich complexity of language. It sheds additional light on the varieties and styles of spoken and written language, offering insights into how they work and how people choose to use them.

A small-scale enquiry

During 1998/99 a questionnaire was distributed to an 'opportunity sample' totalling 35 teachers of KS1/KS2 pupils across a range of schools in the Brunel University/local schools partnership. Overwhelmingly, these teachers recognised the importance of pupils developing explicit grammar knowledge, as follows: 86 per cent agreed that, 'if pupils are able to analyse/describe features of their writing using grammatical terminology, this is helpful towards their evaluating what they write and understanding how to improve it'. Of that 86 per cent, 43 per cent agreed strongly.

The identical percentage agreed that such analytical/descriptive ability is helpful towards pupils' understanding, response to and evaluation of the texts they read. Twenty-nine per cent agreed strongly. Ninety-one per cent considered developing such grammar knowledge important (given the other requirements of the National Curriculum), of whom 29 per cent considered it very important. Eighty-nine per cent indicated their belief that 'the teaching and learning of explicit grammar knowledge' can be enjoyable for pupils; 34 per cent thought it might be 'very enjoyable'.

Teachers' comments regarding the cases for and against, and the priorities in respect of teaching grammar included, on the 'for' side:

- We should focus on aspects of language children are having difficulty with at different stages...greater exposure (through reading) to more complex structures is partly the answer;
- Gives a shared vocabulary and helps with expression/fluency and pace;

and 'against':

- I would give this low priority. [Grammar] terminology is not child-friendly;
- More important things to teach – like writing process and developing lifelong readers and writers. Grammar not a priority for me. Was taught it very badly – in isolation, not related to anything 'real'. Was very turned off by it.

One teacher reported that 'Closer focus on grammar has led to improvement'. Tantalisingly, what sort of improvement is left unspecified. Another respondent reported: 'Year 6 top set cope well with grammar; average children in Year 6 find it hard'.

Teacher preparedness

Our routine 'audits' of the explicit grammar knowledge of both pre-qualified teachers and serving teachers joining our INSET programmes invariably suggest a gap to be bridged. Such findings confirm those of, for example, Williamson and Hardman (1995). This situation is hardly surprising, given the absence of grammar teaching from the English curriculum (and very often from the modern foreign language curriculum as well) experienced by most serving teachers. Helpfully, detailed guidance material has become available to support the teaching of grammar within the National Literacy Strategy. For instance, *Grammar for Writing* (DfEE 2000) contains explanations of grammatical points that are related to the sentence level objectives for Key Stage 2.

Grammar teaching: the 'how'

After they had begged me to reveal that afternoon's task, I reluctantly said: 'Grammar'. Groans slipped out ... and skipping turned into slouching. I overheard Ben make a two-pence bet with Ricky that it would be well boring.

(Pre-qualified teacher 1999)

Let's start by returning to our Year 6 classroom, at the point where it had been found 'experimentally' that nouns were missed most:

With the whole passage (with deletions restored and underlined in the original colours) now displayed on the interactive whiteboard, teacher and class are discussing the underlined words. The terms 'verb' and 'adjective' are recalled from earlier lessons – and the 'wordclass mobiles' that pupils made then, now turning slowly with the movement of air, are invoked. When they get to 'nouns', the word 'name' comes up and the teacher collects from pupils a list of the kinds of things that nouns name: people, places, things, animals, ideas. Someone wonders if, in a way, animals are 'things' – but is heavily, and in some cases indignantly, outvoted.

On slips of paper, the pupils now write their own sentences, with gaps where the nouns should be, and swap them with their friends. (One pupil says it reminds her of when they tried to write descriptions of seashells without using adjectives, so that others could make accurate sketches from the descriptions.) Then the teacher asks them to listen carefully and put their hands up when they think they know the story she is about to 'tell', as follows: mother, son, poverty, cow, market, pedlar, beans... The teacher now asks: 'Why is it so hard to understand a passage if you remove the nouns? And why was it possible to recognise a well-known story from a short list of nouns?' They think for a bit. Then someone says: 'Nouns are what it's all about...'.

FIGURE 5.2 Nouns are what it's all about

In her grammar (and related) work, this teacher exploits opportunities that crop up while working on other things. Her grammar work tends towards the experimental, the investigative, the statistical (Keith 1997), and she tends to work inductively (from language data to generalisation and naming concepts) rather than deductively (for example, from naming and defining a wordclass or phrase-type to consolidating such knowledge through working examples):

We should start with shared concepts and experience and develop a metalanguage out of these, rather than deciding upon the metalanguage and handing it down...as a set of rules.

(Francis 1994:223)

When undertaking explicit study of 'sentences', for example, our teacher is inclined to start by inviting pupils (working in pairs) to calculate the average length of their own sentences in the writing they have produced in the last few weeks (Jones *et al.* 1996). As pupils work on this activity, the teacher's attention may be taken by rising voices. She may note that some pairs are beginning to dispute figures:

'You reckon you've written six sentences on that page – but it's actually eight.'

'No it's not.'

'Yes it is. Number two isn't one sentence – it's two.'

'How come?'

'Well that [pointing] should be a full stop, not a comma.'

Via a practical, statistical activity, rather than by following a teacher definition (which is likely to be inadequate) (Harris and Rowan 1989), these pupils are beginning to consider what a sentence is (and there are few knottier problems in descriptive linguistics) (LINC 1992:352), to identify comma splices (Weaver 1996) (see below) and to focus on the need for appropriate sentence markers.

Contexts of grammar teaching

Arguably, grammar teaching is most effective when it occurs in the context of activities that are planned to develop pupils' competence in speaking/listening, writing/reading. This contextual approach to the teaching of grammar is exemplified in the teaching of modern foreign languages (MFL), where grammatical features are introduced within suitable topics and applied through communicative, oral or written activities, such as role-plays or letter-writing. Except in the case of bilingual pupils, there is, of course, a fundamental difference between the conscious process by which pupils develop competence in a foreign language and that by which they acquire their mother tongue – just as there is between the levels of competence attained in each. Nevertheless, it is interesting to note that the Key Stage 3 Strategy Framework for teaching MFL mirrors the NLS Framework in that the objectives are set at word, sentence and text levels and the terminology used is the same (DfES 2003a). Hence, whether dealing with the mother tongue or a foreign language, progress in literacy is charted partly through the conscious learning of grammatical features applied within different contexts of increasing complexity.

In English lessons grammar teaching works best when contingent opportunities are seized, and when, if the work of enough pupils raises the same issue so as to constitute a 'critical mass' (Peterson 1998:77), a 'minilesson' (Weaver 1998:26) is 'delivered'. In summary, grammar learning is likely to be most meaningful and secure when it is incidental to, and enhances other, learning.

'Delivery' of a coherent grammar curriculum cannot, however, be achieved contingently: that is, only by exploiting serendipity and as 'spin-off'. A succession of structured grammar teaching episodes, albeit expressly related to other language and literacy work in progress, is essential. This premise underpins the guidance provided in *Grammar for Writing* (DfEE 2000). A satisfactory grammar curriculum will feature activities of both sorts.

Grammar teaching in the context of other activities

'Knowledge acquired within the context of a meaningful writing activity...has a much better chance of being used and retained' (Peterson 1998:75). Some examples of exploiting opportunities that arise may serve to convey the nature of such grammar work.

In the context of pupils' writing

- Study examples in pupils' writing of 'comma splices' (commas used where full-stops/periods or semi-colons are required) (Weaver 1996), perhaps entailing use of such terms as 'clause', 'sentence' and 'sentence marker', and link this with study of published writers' practices.

- Find the incidence of sentence types in pupils' writing (simple, compound, complex; statement, question, command [imperative], exclamation). Study the effects of writers' choice of sentence types and draw on any insights achieved via improved redrafting.

- Consider, together, ways of improving dull, imprecise pupil writing. Here, we want to caution against the widespread advice to pupils to insert more and better adjectives and adverbs. Regarding adjectives, there is much to be said for the George Orwell/Mark Twain ('As to the adjective: when in doubt, strike it out') and the Sir Ernest Gowers tendency[6] to think twice before using them at all. Arguably, writing is more often sharpened by precise use of nouns and verbs than by the addition of adjectives and adverbs;[7] and if effective communication is the goal, then to counsel pupils deliberately to import 'grand' words into their writing is likely to be the opposite of sound advice. However, in some contexts adjectives can be indispensable, as we saw pupils recalling in the lesson reported above. Invite pupils to judge the effect of adding adjectives to, or removing them from, passages, or to repair sentences clogged with adjectives and to explain the improvement thereby achieved: such activities help bring these issues into focus by experiential means.

In the context of shared reading

- When reading an illustrated text, create Venn diagrams to record the nouns seen in the text, those seen in the illustrations and those seen in both.

- Identify the connectives (and, but, therefore, nevertheless, although etc.) used in a passage, especially of non-fiction, explaining the work they do and attempting to define them.

- Pupils place their copies of a text face down with the teacher reading on, stopping after the first word of a sentence (e.g. 'Although...' or 'Moreover...') and asking pupils to predict the structure of the sentence in question.

- Examine the verbs/adjectives used in telling a story.[8]
- Notice the use of verbs in the passive voice in fiction: for instance, in a passage from Chapter 5 of Jane Eyre:

> To this inferior class I was called, and placed at the bottom of it...the day's Collect was repeated, then certain texts of Scripture were said...By the time that exercise was terminated, day had fully dawned...the classes were marshalled and marched into another room for breakfast...'

then discuss the impression of lack of agency on the part of Jane and her classmates at Lowood School: the effect of suggesting that they were mostly having things done to them.

In the context of Media Education work (see also Chapter 12), pupils study:

- sentence/paragraph lengths/structures within broadsheets and tabloids;
- reasons for/effects of widespread use of phrases in newspaper reports ('Attractive brunette Maria, London-born animal rights campaigner and mother of three...');
- the nature of headlines (Are they 'sentences'? What word classes predominate/ disappear? ('COACH SEAT BELTS SAFETY VICTORY'; 'GERBIL GETS GENES'). What verbs/nouns are in especially common use (AXE/BID/ROW/SHOCK) and why? What verb tense is most used, and why? How are adjectivals formed to achieve compression? ('MASKED RAIDER BITTEN BY HAVE-A-GO GRANNY') (Sharples 1999:39);
- the incidence/effects of 'nominalisation'. This is the turning of verbs, especially, into nouns so that, among other things, human actions are turned into 'things', with often a loss of 'agency' and a hiding of responsibility. For example, the excuse note that refers to a 'family commitment' as opposed to saying 'We went to a party'; or the military briefing that refers to 'collateral damage' rather than saying 'We bombed a hospital by mistake'.[9] Nominalisation usually occurs more in written than in spoken language and tends to be valued by teachers where it occurs in pupil writing. For example, 'Many people are concerned that scientists are trying out new cosmetics on animals' may strike teachers (semi- or unconsciously) as linguistically less sophisticated than: 'There is widespread concern at animal testing of new cosmetics'. (This raises a number of issues about writing development and about the sorts of language teachers value, and why.)

Pupils might study the structural advantages of nominalisation, for instance that a writer is able to load meaning into a clause by piling up nouns or noun phrases, whereas there will normally be just the one verb; also that a 'technical' term can be substituted for a long-winded description of the same thing – for example 'enjambement', instead of something like 'overflowing the meaning from a line of poetry into the one that follows it (i.e. following punctuation and sentence-structure) so that the verse division is ignored in reading'.

In the context of work on advertising/commercial language uses

Pupils search through a pile of newspapers to find the adjectives most used in advertisements for domestic property or for holiday resorts and make graphs to represent the findings. They can then explore the possible purposes and evident effects of the choice of adjectives and create 'anti-ads', substituting unlikely adjectives and so forth. Through recourse to a journals collection in the local library it is possible to compare the adjectives pupils find with those used in advertisements some 50 or a 100 years before, hence raising the (non-grammar) issue of codes of law and practice governing advertising today. This will help establish that there are different kinds of adjectives, for example, 'spacious rooms' and 'dining-rooms'.[10] Perhaps teacher and class will get so interested in adjectives that they look up the origins of the word 'adjective': they will pass from puzzlement at, to fascination with, its relation to the word 'jet' (and the French 'jeter'); and from there note the significance, going far beyond grammar, of an early use recorded in the *Oxford English Dictionary*: 'The women were treated as adjective beings' (i.e. additional, appendages to the men) (Grote, 1794–1871).

'Set-piece' grammar lessons

> As far as my pupils are concerned, they shall not parse.
>
> (Teacher)[11]

Here we have in mind teaching lessons that are specified in schemes of work to ensure coherent coverage of appropriate grammar concepts: these are 'core' lessons to which the above activities are additional.

Many such lessons, for many teachers, will draw on published teaching materials. The latter are inevitably uneven; some may even contain information that is downright 'wrong'. A good deal of recently produced material consists of fairly standard grammar exercises published in a modern idiom: no change there, except in the modernist 'designer' packaging of traditional fare. Much material, perhaps inevitably, offers simplified, unproblematic language examples to which it is fairly straightforward to attach simple grammatical labels: 'the practice exercises in grammar books are carefully crafted to be relatively easy; they do not give students the opportunity to grasp the critical features of a concept like sentence' (Weaver 1998: 24).

The work of Sue Palmer (e.g. in her articles and Longman Book Project) and of Jim Crinson[12] are valuable, partly because they draw on an extensive study of linguistics and partly because they are a rich source of 'set-piece' grammar lessons.

Some material written for teachers or other adults includes activities that might arguably be adapted for use with pupils (Crystal 1996). The two language encyclopaedias edited by David Crystal[13] provide raw material for a range of language, including grammar, work.

In addition to using published grammar resources, you may find it useful to keep and draw on a file of other material that crops up, e.g. items such as the above from other language activities, environmental print, junk mail, journalism and transcribed spoken utterances (Bain and Bain 1996).[14] Examples from the latter categories that cropped up while this chapter was being drafted are:

1. 'Having worn the same dress to two consecutive balls, the Prince of Wales approached Lillie Langtry and exclaimed: "That damned dress again"' (*The Observer* 1999).[15]

2. 'Having served their sentences, their houses are firebombed.'

3. 'Like an awful lot of rich men, his finances are complex.'

Pupils might explore why, although meaning is arguably clear in each case, the actual construction of these sentences seems to suggest that 1. Prince wore the dress; 2. that houses served prison sentences; and 3. that finances are like men. From there it might be a matter of finding grammatical terms, like 'unattached' or 'misrelated' or 'dangling' participles ('having', in 1. and 2. for example), to use in crystallising such analyses.

It is a truism that having to explain a joke kills it stone dead. However, teachers may consider it worthwhile inviting pupils, after enjoying (DfES 2003b) such items as the following, to explain, using grammatical terms, the source of any humour that may strike them:

1. GENERAL FLIES BACK TO FRONT (World War II headline).

2. Girls like reading more than boys.

3. MPs discussed fox-hunting in the House of Commons.

4. We dispense with accuracy (sign in chemist's shop).

5. Please sign the form and return in the envelope provided.

6. This door is alarmed.

7. GIANT WAVES DOWN FUNNEL (much-quoted headline).

8. (a) My wife who is French has lived in England for ten years…
   (b) My wife, who is French, has lived in England for ten years…

9. Doctor: 'Did you drink your medicine after your bath, as I told you to?'
   Patient: 'No. By the time I'd drunk the bath I couldn't manage the medicine.'

Attempts at explanation of some of the above are given in an endnote.[16]

There is a good deal of grammar 'mileage' in studying:

- recipes (nouns and the occasional adjective among the ingredients – why? verbs and the occasional adverb within the 'method' – why?)
- menus (adjectivals like 'farm-fresh', 'drizzled', 'topped with coffee cream', 'smothered with gooey fudge frosty'...)
- product names (e.g. most of a clause used as an adjective noun in 'I Can't Believe It's not Butter'; the similar use of a subjunctive fragment – from Rudyard Kipling's poem 'Recessional' – in the name: 'The Richmond and Twickenham Lest-We-Forget Association').

These exemplify the remarkable flexibility of English, which allows words, phrases and clauses to do a variety of jobs in utterances. It is for this reason that care is needed in teaching pupils that, for example, a word is of a particular wordclass and, still more, that they may be associated it with a particular colour.[17]

Reference may be made to the pictures on the classroom wall. They may be full of nouns, to which adjectives can be attached, and verbs attracting appropriate adverbs, and whose description entails the use of prepositions: lady beside a spinet; cat beneath a table; table by the wall; seat near a cornfield.

Games have their place in grammar teaching, for example:

- Tie labels or stick 'Post-Its' on 'nouns' in the classroom.
- In drama, develop an adverbial dance (e.g. moving stealthily, confidently, cautiously, assertively, proudly...)
- Enact prepositions (under the desk, in the stock cupboard, behind the door) – or, more accurately, acting the prepositional phrases they introduce. (A pre-qualified teacher recently testified to the popularity of this: 'We played the preposition game. A few days later I noticed kids playing it during 'wet play'.)
- In reading a passage aloud, substitute 'sausages' for every noun (some authorities prefer 'coffee-pot', 'flump' etc.).
- Pupils are asked to bring in copies of poems cut into chunks for other pupils to reassemble. Were any chunks 'full sentences'? Why do you think so? (A 'back door' into sentence study.)
- Pupils produce lists, as follows: town, river, country, boy's name, girl's name, fruit, vegetable, animal, each starting with the same letter (Liverpool, Loire, Luxembourg). Why do some words have capitals? (This potentially consolidates understanding of proper nouns. For further work on proper nouns, *The Guinness Book of Names* is a rich, suggestive resource.)
- Make and use 'sentence-machines' (from kitchen-roll tubing, card and tape).

- Adapt a long-established playground activity (called 'fortune-tellers' in some playgrounds), making and using grammar 'quizzers'.[18]

Such gaming activity shades off into more familiar grammar exercises, for example:

- Reverse subject and object for humorous effect ('Mandy rode a horse').
- Identify that what wordclass a word belongs to depends on how it is used in a particular utterance (shop, bill, round, table, box).
- Finding (usually noun) phrases on the spines of books in the class library (*Charlotte's Web, The Iron Man, Harry Potter and the Philosopher's Stone, The Borrowers*) to consolidate understanding of the concept 'phrase'.
- Matching subjects and predicates:

  The League Champions   like to go shopping on Saturday morning

  Mandy and her Mum   did a lap of honour

  helps to reinforce these concepts. (Compare the teacher who started a lesson on the notion of the subject of a sentence by referring to our being the Queen's subjects. This established the expectation that a sentence subject will be human and led to confusion when the class reached 'An angry rhinoceros lumbered into view'.)

- Identify (as in the above lesson) the wordclasses of missing words and fill gaps appropriately. (A variation on the former part of this is using nonsense verse like 'Jabberwocky' by Lewis Carroll. 'Slithy' and 'toves' are likely to be identified as adjective and noun, respectively. However, given that we can't look them up, how do we know this? The answer is, of course, that we draw on our understanding of sentence structure. This, potentially, reinforces understanding that which wordclass a word should be allocated to depends on the work it does, the slot it occupies in an utterance. See again the caution, above, regarding pigeon-holing particular words within particular wordclasses, and especially associating them with particular colours further to strengthen the identification.)

- Compose theme poems following set wordclass patterns; for example each line to contain adjective, noun, verb and adverb, or lines to contain specified components:

  noun

  adjective adjective

  verb verb verb

  noun noun noun noun, etc.

- Write a few lines about a topic, each starting with one preposition and containing another.
- Write a scene from a play using all four sentence types.

A role for information and communication technology (ICT)

Use of ICT played a part in the lesson we visited earlier in this chapter and there is much 'grammar mileage' bound up with use of ICT generally (see also Chapter 11). For example, altering sequences of clauses/phrases within utterances so as to understand the changes of emphasis this can achieve; similarly, transforming sentences from active to passive (see above); combining clauses to form multiple sentences; highlighting all adverbs, say, and inviting pupils to identify what the highlighted words have in common and then attaching the agreed label ('adverb'); inviting pupils to make the changes to a well-known poem suggested by a grammar checker and to discuss the effects of such changes; in a passage of 'teen fiction' finding/replacing female with male names, and vice versa, and noting the effects, e.g. do the linked verbs, adverbs, adjectives etc. still feel appropriate, or are some strongly linked with males/females?

Conclusion

> A child does not need any special cognitive abilities or teaching to be able to think and talk about language.
>
> (Sharples 1999:20)

This chapter has suggested a modest role for grammar in the English curriculum, and has offered suggestions as to how grammar might be taught effectively and enjoyably. The challenge we have posed is that, discarding the unproductive aspects of the grammar curriculum of the 1950s and earlier, we can help pupils develop their understanding of language in use, both their own and that of others, and of the options from which we all choose in our daily attempts to make meaning.

Time for a final visit to our Year 6 classroom...

There is still plenty more 'mileage' in the interactive whiteboard passage. The teacher now asks for two lists: of nouns starting with lower-case and capital letters, respectively. This leads to discussion and labelling of 'proper nouns'. The teacher makes a mental note that next time they work on the history of English, she will bring in her copy of Gulliver's Travels to show them how all English nouns were once capitalised, as in German they still are. Still pondering proper nouns, someone sings, sotto voce, 'There's only one Steven Gerrard'; the teacher hears it and remarks that there are grammar lessons to be had everywhere, even at the footy!

Now two more lists: nouns referring to just one thing, and nouns where there are two or more. (The second list includes 'craftsmen' and 'gentlemen', but the majority end in 's', including 'experts' and 'ladies'.) The books are given out and the incidence of '-s' plurals and other types is researched. Another block graph results. One of the words found is 'donkeys', and someone asks why it becomes 'donkeys' while lady becomes 'ladies'. There is talk of when there is and when there isn't a vowel before the '-y'. The teacher considers mentioning where the different plural forms have come from, but decides, again, to save it for the aforementioned forthcoming lesson in her language change series.

Notes

1. S. Greenbaum (1988) *Good English and the Grammarian* (Ch.2). Harlow: Longman.
2. R. Braddock *et al.* (1963) 'Research in written composition'. Urbana, Ill.: National Council of Teachers of English, cited in P. Hartwell, 'Grammar, grammars, and the teaching of grammar', *College English*, **47** (2), 105, February 1985. In this country, Connie and Harold Rosen wrote (in *The Language of Primary School Children*, (London: Penguin, 1973: 253): 'We have assumed that the teaching of grammar in the primary school is as discredited as teaching capes and bays and copperplate... What teachers have discovered for themselves is that... the return for trying to teach children about language was very low in terms of its effect on how they used language... Clearly, "the more you know about the language the better you use it" does not stand up to examination'
3. Eppi-Centre (2004) 'The effect of grammar teaching (syntax) in English on 5–16 year olds' accuracy and quality in written composition'. http:// eppi.ioe.ac.uk/EPPIWeb Content/reel/review_groups/english/eng_rv6/eng_rv6.doc; see also the press release http://www.york.ac.uk/admin/presspr/pressreleases/grammar.htm
4. Quality and Curriculum Authority (QCA) (1998) *The Grammar Papers*. London: QCA, p. 55. Details of the article alluded to are: J. Walmsley, 'The uselessness of formal grammar?'. Committee for Linguistics in Education Working Paper No.2. Birmingham: Language Studies Unit, Aston University (1984, reprinted 1993).
5. R. Carter (1990) *Knowledge about Language and the Curriculum*. London: Hodder & Stoughton, p. 108. Note also the 'cultural analysis' role of the subject English: DES (1989) *English for Ages 5 to 16*. London: HMSO, para. 2.24.
6. E. Gowers (1951) *ABC of Plain Words*. London: HMSO, pp. 2–3.
7. See, for example, C. Weaver (ed.) (1998) *Lessons to Share on Teaching Grammar in Context*. Portsmouth, NH: Boynton/Cook, pp. 28–30.
8. See, for example, E. Bearne (1998) *Making Progress in English*. London: Routledge, p. 206.
9. Nominalisation is discussed for example in K. Perera (1984) *Children's Writing and Reading* (Oxford: Blackwell, pp. 188–9 and 293–4), R. Bunting (1997) *Teaching about Language in the Primary Years* (London: David Fulton Publishers, p. 41), and G. Cook (1992) *Discourse of Advertising* (London: Routledge, p. 97).
10. See D. Crystal (1991) *Language A–Z for KS 3/4* (Harlow: Longman, pp. 6–7); and D. Shiach (1998) *Grammar to 14* (Oxford: Oxford University Press, p. 22).
11. We are grateful to Sue Palmer for passing this on.
12. See the series of articles in *Primary English*, starting from No. 2, 1997. Other useful material is to be found in *The Cheshire Cat* (Jones and Selby 1996) and in G. Keith (1994) *Get the Grammar*. London: BBC.
13. *The Cambridge Encyclopaedia of the English Language*. Cambridge: Cambridge University Press (Crystal 1995) and *The Cambridge Encyclopaedia of Language* (Crystal 1997). Cambridge: Cambridge University Press. Gill Francis (1994) refers to another source of language data: Cobuild – the 'Bank of English – a large collection of natural language, indexed and stored on computer and accessible for interrogation'.

14. E. Bain, and R. Bain (1996) *The Grammar Book* (Sheffield: NATE, pp. 6, 114) makes useful suggestions about developing a 'language variety box' and using 'junk mail'.
15. *The Observer* (Review) 21 March 1999, p. 11.
16. (1) GENERAL (noun, grammatical subject) FLIES (verb) then <u>EITHER</u> BACK (adverb) TO (preposition) FRONT (noun meaning 'foremost line of an army, nearest the enemy') OR BACK TO FRONT (adverb phrase meaning 'in reverse, in disorder'). (2) An example of 'ellipsis' (omission of a word or words necessary to complete a sentence, something which is common in headlines to keep them short and snappy). Could mean...<u>EITHER</u> boys do (noun/verb) OR they like boys (pronoun/verb/noun-object etc). (8) (a) No commas around the subordinate or dependent clause 'who is French' makes it a 'restrictive' (sometimes called a 'defining') clause, so that the speaker seems to be making it clear that he is talking about his French wife rather than his Norwegian wife, his Russian wife, and so on! Providing the commas in (b) signals that it is a 'non-restrictive' (sometimes called a 'non-defining') clause: an additional but inessential piece of information.
17. Department for Education and Employment (DfEE) (1998) *The National Literacy Strategy: Framework for Teaching*. London: HMSO. (Teaching Grammar through Shared and Guided Reading and Writing). DfEE (1998) advises: 'Colour-code different parts of speech to create sets of words on coloured cards, e.g. nouns on blue card, adjectives on red, adverbs on green...'. Which colour for 'fast', for example?
18. In, respectively, S. Brownjohn and G. Gwyn-Jones (1996) *Spotlight on the English Language*. London: Hodder & Stoughton, pp. 30–1; and S. Hackman and C. Humphreys (1997) *Grammar and Punctuation 9–13*. London: Hodder & Stoughton, p. 74.

References and further reading

Bain, E. and Bain, R. (1996) *The Grammar Book*. Sheffield: NATE.

Bearne, E. (1998) *Making Progress in English*. London: Routledge.

Barton, G. (2005) *Grammar Survival – A Teacher's Toolkit*. London: David Fulton Publishers.

Brownjohn, S. and Gwyn-Jones, G. (1996) *Spotlight on the English Language*. London: Hodder & Stoughton.

Bunting, R. (1997) *Teaching about Language in the Primary Years*. London: David Fulton Publishers.

Carter, R. (1990) *Knowledge about Language and the Curriculum*. London: Hodder & Stoughton.

Chomsky, N. (1957) *Syntactic Structures*. The Hague: Mouton & Co.

Cook, G. (1992) *Discourse of Advertising*. London: Routledge.

Crinson, J. (1997) 'Step-by-step grammar.' *Primary English Magazine*, 2.4–5.2. Sheffield: NATE.

Crystal, D. (1991) *Language A–Z for KS 3/4*. Harlow: Longman.

Crystal, D. (1995) *The Cambridge Encyclopaedia of the English Language*. Cambridge: Cambridge University Press.

Crystal, D. (1996) *Discover Grammar*. Harlow: Longman.

Crystal, D. (1997) *The Cambridge Encyclopaedia of Language*. Cambridge: Cambridge University Press.

D'Eloia, S. (1977) 'The uses – and limits – of grammar'. *Journal of Basic Writing* 1, Spring/Summer, 1–20.

DES (1989) *English for Ages 5 to 16*. London: HMSO.

DfEE (1998) *The National Literacy Strategy: Framework for Teaching*. London: HMSO.

DfEE (1999) *English in The National Curriculum*. London: HMSO.

DfEE (2000) *Grammar for Writing*. London: HMSO.

DfES (2003a) *Framework for Teaching Modern Foreign Languages: Years 7, 8 and 9*. London: DfES.

DfES (2003b) *Excellence and Enjoyment: A Strategy for Primary Schools*. London: DfES.

English, E. and Williamson, J. (2004) *Meeting the Standards in Primary English*. London: Routledge Falmer.

Eppi-Centre (2004) 'The effect of grammar teaching (syntax) in English on 5–16 year olds' accuracy and quality in written composition'. http//eppi.ioe.ac.uk/ EPPIwebcontent/reel/review_groups/english/eng_rv6/eng_rvb.doc.

Francis, G. (1994) 'Grammar teaching in schools: what should teachers be aware of?'. *Language Awareness* **3**(3) and **3**(4).

Gowers, E. (1951) *ABC of Plain Words*. London: HMSO.

Greenbaum, S. (1988) *Good English and the Grammarian*. Harlow: Longman.

Gregory, G. (2003) 'They shall not parse! Or shall they?' *Changing English* **10**(1), 13–33.

Hackman, S. and Humphreys, C. (1997) *Grammar and Punctuation 9–13*. London: Hodder & Stoughton.

Harris,M. and Rowan, K. (1989) 'Explaining grammatical concepts'. *Journal of Basic Writing* **8**(2), pp. 21–41.

Hartwell, P. (1985) 'Grammar, grammars, and the teaching of grammar'. *College English* **47** (2), February.

Hudson, R. (1992) *Teaching Grammar: A Guide for the National Curriculum*. Oxford: Blackwell.

Hurford, J. (1994) *Grammar: A Student's Guide*. Cambridge: Cambridge University Press.

Jones, M. and Selby, J. (1996) *The Cheshire Cat*. Chester: Cheshire Education Authority.

Keith, G. (1994) *Get the Grammar*. London: BBC.

Keith,G. (1997) 'Teaching yourself English grammar'. *The English and Media Magazine* **36**, pp. 8–12, (Summer).

LINC (1992) *LINC Materials for Professional Development*. Nottingham: Department of English Studies, University of Nottingham.

National Association for the Teaching of English (1997) *Position Paper: Grammar*. Sheffield: NATE.

The Observer (Review), 21 March, 1999.

Perera, K. (1984) *Children's Writing and Reading*. Oxford: Blackwell.

Peterson, S. (1998) 'Teaching writing and grammar in context', in Weaver, C. (ed.) *Lessons to Share on Teaching Grammar in Context*. Portsmouth, NH: Boynton/Cook.

QCA (1998) *The Grammar Papers*. London: QCA.

Rosen, C. and Rosen, H. (1973) *The Language of Primary School Children*. London: Penguin.

Sharples, M. (1999) *How We Write: Writing as Creative Design*. London: Routledge.

Shiach, D. (1998) *Grammar to 14*. Oxford: Oxford University Press.

Terrell, T.D. (1991) 'The role of grammar instruction in a communicative approach'. *The Modern Language Journal*, **75**(i), 59.

Tomlinson, D. (1994) 'Errors in the research into the effectiveness of grammar teaching'. *English in Education*, **28**(1), 20–6, Spring.

Walmsley, J. (1984 – reprinted 1993) 'The uselessness of formal grammar?'. Committee for Linguistics in Education Working Paper No. 2. Birmingham: Language Studies Unit, Aston University.

Weaver, C. (1996) *Teaching Grammar in Context*. Portsmouth, NH: Boynton/Cook.

Weaver, C. (ed.) (1998) *Lessons to Share on Teaching Grammar in Context.* Portsmouth, NH: Boynton/Cook.

Williamson, J. and Hardman, F. (1995) 'Time for refilling the bath? A study of primary student-teachers' grammatical knowledge'. *Language and Education* 9(2) 117–34.

Further reading

Bain, R. and Bridgewood, M. (1998) *The Primary Grammar Book.* Sheffield: NATE.

Barton, G. (1997) *Grammar Essentials.* Harlow: Longman.

DfES (2003) *KS3 National Strategy: Grammar for Reading: Course Handbook.* London: DfES.

Mallett, M. (2005) *The Primary English Encyclopaedia* (2nd edn). London: David Fulton Publishers.

Mason, M. (1999) *Knowledge about Language for Primary School Teachers: A Self-Access Course.* Wigan: Wigan and Leigh College.

Medwell, J., Moore, G., Wray, D. and Griffiths, V. (2002) *Primary English – Knowledge and Understanding.* Exeter: Learning Matters.

Smee, M. (1997) *Grammar Matters.* Oxford: Heinemann.

Wilson, A. (2004) *Language Knowledge for Primary Teachers* (3rd edn). London: David Fulton Publishers.

'Is this write?': learning to write and writing to learn

Mary Williams and Robert Fisher

Dear JPM WW HYP the L f Hannah (Hannah, aged 5)
(Dear Jolly Postman we will help you post the letters from Hannah.)

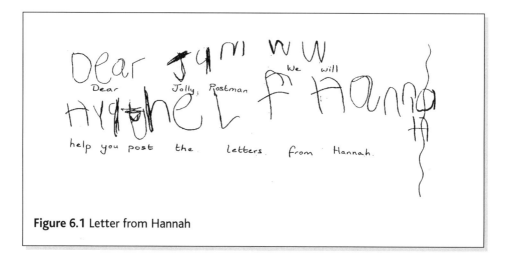

Figure 6.1 Letter from Hannah

Writing helps me think what I say.
(Sophie, aged 8)

Introduction

At one time very little emphasis in learning to write was placed on what young children wanted to 'say'. Writing in the early years of school was often little more than handwriting practice copied from the blackboard. However, researchers have found that children's earliest marks, as observed in preschool settings and the home, are both systematic and logical, as in Hannah's example in Figure 6.1, where a letter stands, for the most part, for a whole word. It seems that children develop hypotheses about the process that gradually emerge as they encounter written words in the world around them, most predominantly from books that are read to them. Among the assumptions they tend to make about the writing process are: that there is a minimum word length, i.e. that a word should have at least three letters (not one to which Hannah conforms); that there is a relationship between the size of the object they are writing about and the letters they use, e.g. an elephant would be written in large letter-like forms whereas a mouse would be written much smaller; or that length of word relates to the ages of the people involved, as with Mariana who decided that she has four letters in her name because she was four years old, whereas her father, who she thought to be very old, had a thousand![1] As children develop as writers they are able to cope with a wide range of written styles, learning to use these to get across their thinking compellingly and with ever-increasing precision in terms of style and form. How they can be helped to achieve this will be discussed in this chapter.

Developing writing in the Early Years

The process of writing begins with the story. It can be the story of what happened on the way to school or of an imagined world full of fantastic creatures. Like all stories it begins with the telling, so it can be shared with one's friends and classmates and thereby writing has a purpose. How can the story survive for longer than the moment it takes to tell if it is not recorded in some way?

Children should have the opportunity to put their thoughts into writing from as young an age as possible, so that they begin to understand the process, but before they do this they need to be encouraged to tell stories as this gives them a growing sense of authorship. To further develop confidence as writers, and when the time comes, for more focused composition, children need to compose their stories orally before writing them down (DfEE 2000a) because this allows them to structure what they are going to write. It encourages them to think of a beginning, middle and end, preventing endings like 'then they went to bed' or, more prosaically, 'the end', when they run out of ideas or energy! Oral composition helps them to sequence a story to ensure that it is cohesive and meaningful; although 'speech' cannot be replicated exactly in writing (see below). When they begin to write short stories they should be given the chance to 'say' what they like about their writing (or the writing of others) as well to make suggestions about what should be altered, possibly during a writer's workshop or conference with the teacher or during the plenary of the Literacy Hour, as this helps them develop a critical response to the written word.

When children start to write they experiment with a number of principles about the process that are integral to understanding its symbolic nature (as above). These relate to the arrangement of letters and words on the page.[2] For example, Lisa, aged 3 years 9 months, demonstrated a *recurring* principle in her writing, knowing that letters are made up of circles and lines which she replicated with great care in her pattern-making by covering a strip of centimetre-squared paper with a series of circles and downward strokes. Edward, aged 4, showed *flexibility* in his first attempt at writing his name 'Ed2wrd', thinking, at this stage, that letters and numbers are interchangeable. (To fully appreciate the logic of his response you would need to hear him say his name aloud.)

Harshita, at 5, knows that writing is made up of shapes that are generated over and over again and uses the letters she is familiar with in both English and Urdu, i.e. those in her own name, as well as word-length squiggles to produce her writing. In addition, she is aware that print is *permanent* and was able to tell her teacher what her story, modelled on Alan Ahlberg's *Funny Bones*, was all about:

> Funny Bones went to the park and the dog skeleton bashed into a tree and it tipped over a park bench. Funny Bones never ever went there again.

In the following example, Ben, 6, shows that he has not fully come to terms with the arrangement of letters and words on the page:

> I went to a spooky yard and a witch came out nad she cot me and
>
> dna tuo dpmuj I dna top nicoc a ni em tup ehs
>
> I went bak home

These examples show how children's understanding of writing conventions grows with time and experience of print in the environment around them.

Developmental, emergent process approaches such as these were endorsed in the first English National Curriculum (DES 1990) in which a 'growing mastery' of the process was recognised as important. This was derived from the recommendations in the earlier Cox Report[3] in which 'a measure of tolerance of errors' was advocated and seen to be useful for assessment purposes (see Chapter 10) as a means of establishing a child's current state of knowledge and understanding.

Of equal importance is the fact that developmental approaches to learning to write do not conflict with the following widely accepted principles of education in the Early Years that underline how:

- learning can be achieved through discovery and play; and
- assessment of progress should be based on what children can do, rather than what they cannot do.

As with other aspects of learning, experimentation through play[4] will increase young children's knowledge, skills and understanding of the writing process. So it is important that teaching approaches adopted for four-year-olds in reception classes are not too formal. Preschool children should be encouraged to use pictures, symbols, familiar words and letters to communicate meaning, showing some awareness of the different purposes of writing as in the *Curriculum for the Foundation Stage* (DfEE 2000b)[5] and as advocated for the reception year of the National Literacy Strategy (DfEE 1998a) in which it is stated that they should 'use writing to communicate in a variety of ways, incorporating it into play and everyday classroom life'.[6]

Table 6.1 shows how approaches to teaching writing in the reception year (4/5 years) mirror the stages the young child goes through as an 'emergent writer'.

Table 6.1 Emergent writing and the National Literacy Strategy

Emergent skills of the young writer	Learning objectives in the reception year (DfEE 1998a)
Knows which is their drawing and which is their writing.	Distinguishes between writing and drawing.
Understands the permanent nature of written language.	Knows that words can be written down to be read again for a wide range of purposes. Understands that writing remains constant, i.e. will always 'say' the same thing.
Invents spellings starting with a '3 letter' hypothesis.	Invents spellings derived from phonic analogy making.
Develops increased phonetic regularity and accuracy in orthographic spelling.	Experiments with writing and recognises how their own version matches and differs from the form.
Uses own name as the base for experimentation with the writing process.	Writes own name and explores other words related to the spelling of own name.
Understands concepts of directionality in writing.	Knows that words are ordered from left to right and that they need to be read in this way to make sense. Tracks the text in the right order – left to right. Understands how writing is formed directionally.

Early writing and the Literacy Hour

Fortunately there is now an emphasis on creativity in literacy teaching in the early years (especially in the Foundation Stage and Reception classes). Teachers need to resist any pressure to return to over-formalisation of the early years curriculum. They must continue to stand firm in what is known to be right for young children. Equally, because of all the competing demands on time they need to be creative and flexible as they teach writing through the Literacy Hour with young children (Fisher and Williams 2004).

However, children need to be offered more than just time to play as play can so easily become unchallenging if they are left to their own devices.[7] In successful Early Years settings, an adult – either a teacher, a nursery nurse or a learning support assistant plays alongside them in order to model aspects of the writing process, for example, in the context of a theme such as Postman Pat's post office or the 'Three Bears' cottage (see below for an example of a writing task on the theme of this). If the role-play area is set up to reflect the theme of the book being used for shared reading within the Literacy Hour in some way, this will help to provide an interesting and motivating context for learning. It is essential that shared sessions in reading and writing retain children's interest so they need to vary in format as young children can become restless, and long sessions 'on the carpet' are not productive. This view was confirmed by a higher ability child, already capable of writing her own poetry, who responded with a sigh when asked what she thought about the Literacy Hour when it was first introduced: 'On Monday you have a Big Book and you read it again and again, and on the next Monday you have another Big Book and you read it again and again!' (Katie, aged 5).

Young children need to hear stories read from the beginning to the end in order to experience 'being taken into other worlds' (Meek 1991). Without time being given to this, they are unlikely to find their own 'voice' in writing. Equally, teachers need to model writing across a range of genres such as daily plans, shopping lists or written instructions, to increase and broaden children's understanding of the writing process (Williams 2002). To avoid a sense of frustration, like Katie's, it is essential that a flexible approach to the Literacy Hour be adopted.

This is most easily achieved if several texts relating to a single theme are included each week from which it is possible to develop understanding and skills at word, sentence and text level as advocated in the termly objectives for the particular age group.

Example of a Key Stage 1 stimulus for writing

As part of a series of Literacy Hour lessons based on the 'Three Bears' story, select a range of books which relate to this theme including relevant extracts from fiction and information books about bears.

In one lesson, as part of 'shared reading' read the children the letter from the *The Jolly Postman or Other People's Letters*[8] which Goldilocks sends by way of apology for the havoc she has wreaked in the three bears' household. Then ask a guided writing group of children of similar ability to compose the letter that initiated this response, i.e. a letter of complaint from Father Bear and Mother Bear. This activity involves children in 'higher order thinking' as they have to analyse and synthesise what they know about the story from the various sources on offer in order to assess how the aggrieved parents of baby bear would feel.

Figure 6.2 is the first draft of a response from a gifted and talented six-year-old in which he shows considerable awareness of his audience.

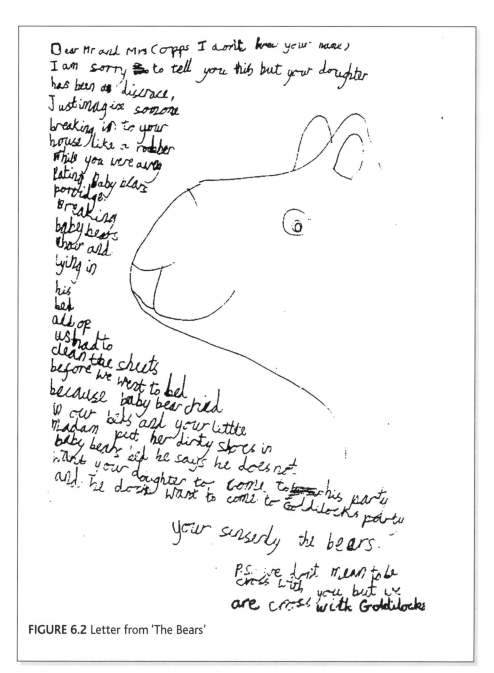

FIGURE 6.2 Letter from 'The Bears'

This lesson could also be used to develop and assess spelling ability – word level work (see Chapter 4) – as the children could be asked to act as Goldilocks's teacher who is going to correct the spelling mistakes she has made in her letter to the three bears; or to work as response partners to help each other edit the first drafts of their own letters (see above). Another very useful strategy to develop standard spelling is to ask children to underline words that are spelled incorrectly even if they do not know what the correct form is yet.

By these means, in National Literacy Strategy terms, work at text, sentence and word levels will have been undertaken:

- text level: developing composition styles appropriate to audience and purpose
- sentence level: developing an understanding of sentence construction and punctuation
- word level: developing spelling, vocabulary and handwriting.

Developing a range of writing

What kind of writing are we doing today?
(Sean, aged 7)

In the past the form of writing that dominated teaching in schools was that of story, but as children's writing ability develops they need to have their repertoire broadened. During Key Stage 1 they should be introduced to other forms of writing such as signs, labels, captions, lists, instructions, recounts, non-chronological reports and, building on this in Key Stage 2, they should learn how to proceed, report, argue, persuade, explain and discuss in their writing (DfEE 2000c). The advantage of beginning with story writing is that it mirrors more closely the habits of spoken speech than does non-fiction writing. We dream, gossip and make sense of the world through stories. However, written stories are not the same as spoken ones. With speech, it is possible to convey subtle meanings through intonation, facial expression or gesture, whereas in writing this is much more difficult. With speech, immediate feedback is given so the message can be altered accordingly by explaining points further, repeating certain words or phrases and so on. With writing, feedback may be offered some time later or not at all. With speech, others have to prompt us into further utterance or explanation. There is no prompting between a writer and a sheet of paper, so teachers or response partners (Williams 2002) have a key role in bridging this gap by challenging children to put their meaning across effectively.

Writing a text – whether story or non-fiction – provides the child with the most complex of intellectual and physical challenges. If the writing is by hand, not only must the child manipulate pen or pencil in skilful, regular, abstract patterns, but they must also get spelling, grammar (syntax) and style right in order to give meaning to others (semantics). To maintain sense in a passage, children need to master complex cohesive devices to help keep 'the thread' of meaning alive, for example in the use of pronouns for nouns.

With non-fiction writing, children have to develop their skills still further, which can be even more challenging, as technical vocabulary and more formal and impersonal registers are used. Non-fiction is organised in a variety of ways, and these need to be learnt. Recent research has shown how both reading and writing can be enhanced through familiarity with non-fiction genres, in particular, by introducing children to different forms of factual and non-narrative writing.[9] The term 'genre' is used to identify the different forms that texts take according to the social purposes they serve. As children emerge as writers they need to learn how to apply their skills across a range of writing genres.

Children also need to be introduced to the ways writing can be processed on the computer. Young children can, for example, learn to type their names into a Word document, as was recently seen in a Reception class where children were taking turns to 'book their holidays' in role-play as a travel agent. The skills of using the computer should be developed alongside the physical skills involved in writing by hand. They need to be introduced to different aspects of the writing process whatever form their writing might take. The range of features they need to learn and think about include:

Features	Questions to consider
Purpose	Why are we writing this? What other reasons are there for writing?
Audience	Who are we writing this for? Who else might we be writing for?
Style and form	What kind of writing is this? What other kinds of writing are there?

FIGURE 6.3 Questions to consider

Purpose

Through reading, and being read to, from a wide range of different genres children will become aware of the way style differs according to the purpose of the text. However, they will not just pick this up for themselves. Teachers need to help them to develop understanding of the purposes of writing. Three broad purposes for writing might be identified as:

- personal – writing for yourself, e.g. personal notes, diary, letters;

- imaginative – writing for others, e.g. stories, poems, plays; and
- functional – writing for practical purposes e.g. recipes, instructions, information.

One way of developing this understanding is to ask children to explain the qualities they would expect to see in different kinds of writing. For example, what do they think the differences are between personal, imaginative and functional writing?

The following are qualities in different forms of writing as identified by a Year 4 class (8–9-year-olds):

Personal writing

- 'You use it when you know someone well.'
- 'It is about your personal life.'
- 'The word 'I' is used.'
- 'The word 'we' is used.'
- 'It is about you not anyone else.'
- 'It tells about your thoughts and feelings.'
- 'You are speaking to yourself.'

Imaginative writing

- 'It's not real.'
- 'It is an untrue story, for example, about dinosaurs.'
- 'It uses interesting words.'
- 'It's made up in your head.'
- 'You can see pictures in your head.'
- 'It is made up, not true.'
- 'It can be funny or scary.'

Functional writing

- 'It tells you how to do things.'
- 'It is not real or made up.'
- 'It gives information about things.'
- 'It can tell you things you don't know.'
- 'It is serious.'
- 'It gives you advice about what to do.'

Children also need to know that the same piece of writing can fulfil different functions. For example, an e-mail can be personal, imaginative and functional at the same time. They should be given different pieces of writing to sort and discuss what kind or type of writing they think each piece is. 'Why are we writing this?' or 'Why has this been written?' are questions that can be asked about any piece of writing. Another question to ask is 'Who is it written for?'. Recently, text-messaging has created a whole new written genre that children can be very adept at using (see Chapter 12).

Audience

In the early stages, children's audience for writing is likely to be either themselves or known recipients such as parents/carers, and, possibly at a later date, their teachers. They need to know that writing for unknown audiences places certain demands on a writer in terms of establishing the context, explaining terms and spelling out relationships. Children need to be aware of the needs of their audience and to anticipate problems in understanding that might occur as they write. Audiences are not, of course, limited to time and place. They might be writing for distant and unknown audiences, as on the internet.

Our research shows that many children do not know, or find it difficult to say, who it is they are writing for.[10] As Sonal, aged 6, said, 'I don't know who it's for, you just write what your teacher says,' whereas Claire, whose writing was going to be included on her school's website, certainly knew who she was writing for: 'I am sending this to everyone in the world'.

It is important, therefore, to discuss with children the possible audiences they might be writing for, and to give them experience of writing for those which are both known or unknown to them:

Type of audience	Known/unknown
Self	known
Parent	known
Teacher / other pupils / friends	known
Other teachers / classes	partially known
Family members	partially known
Children in other schools / pen pals / internet connections	unknown
The media / councillors / local businesses / community	unknown

FIGURE 6.4 Type of audience

Style and form

Recent research has shown how both reading and writing non-fiction genres can be enhanced through introducing children to different forms of factual and non-narrative writing.[11] 'Genre' can be further defined as types of text whose form varies according to the purpose it serves. For example, early genres that children experience could include labels, stories and nursery rhymes. Fictional genres include fiction, poetry and plays. Non-fiction genres identified in the National Literacy Strategy are recount (past tense), report (present tense), explanation, procedural (such as a recipe), persuasion (argument) and discussion (arguments from different viewpoints, as in the persuasion writing frame in Figure 6.5).

Non-narrative factual forms have been neglected in the past and were identified as causing problems in terms of children's learning through writing (QCA 1998). The range of writing children experience in school needs to include both story forms and non-narrative types of writing such as: letters; reports; descriptions; instructions; reviews; explanations; arguments.

The following are some writing activities planned by a teacher to link to a story about mice that she was studying with her class:

- Write a letter from a mouse to a person who is scared of mice, telling them why they should not be afraid. (persuasion)
- Write a description of a mouse to match an illustration. (description)
- Write a review of two books about mice saying which you prefer and why. (review)
- Make a scrapbook of information about mice using material from books and the internet. (report)
- Write instructions on how to care for a mouse. (instruction)
- Design a mouse trap and explain how it should be made and used. (explanation)
- Write arguments to persuade someone why you would rather be a country (or town) mouse. (argument)

One way to generate non-narrative writing is to pose a problem. When a challenging problem is set (Fisher and Williams 2004), for example 'What is air?', children can be asked to think about it for themselves initially, then discuss it in pairs and share ideas with the group or class. This process of 'think–pair–share' provides an important means of accessing prior knowledge and for sharing ideas that will later form the basis for writing. Information can then be gathered from a range of relevant books and recorded in a manner suitable to the subject, including the use of computer resources and ICT.

Matching 'style to audience and purpose' can be taught not only through shared reading and writing of the Literacy Hour but also through other encounters with print. These take place across the whole curriculum as children use information books to extend their knowledge and understanding, e.g. in history and science. Every opportunity should be taken to discuss the key features of a broad range of texts with children and it is important to evaluate the quality of writing in all curriculum areas and not just what is produced in the Literacy Hour.

Extending writing within the Literacy Hour

The 'shared' aspect of the Literacy Hour provides an ideal opportunity for teachers to model aspects of the writing process (DfEE 2000a). They should be questioned about the effectiveness of a particular author's style during shared and guided reading. In shared writing, there are several ways that this can be achieved.

The first is modelling, where teachers should model, through 'thinking aloud', what needs to be considered when using a particular style for writing, bearing in mind the needs of an intended audience. During such sessions the teacher can act as a scribe for children's (or their own) ideas in order to demonstrate what real writers do during the act of creating words on paper or on a computer screen. As one teacher commented, 'I should not expect my children to write if I have not shown them again and again what to do and how to do it'. The second is the joint creation of a written text with the children, based on the genre or a theme from a text being used during shared or guided writing (as in the three bears example above). Here the teacher shares information about the features of the genre and models the sorts of questions that skilled writers ask themselves (as listed above) as they write. During group or independent time the children can go on to construct new texts in the same genre, both drafting and editing the text in consultation with peers, prior to final publication and evaluation in a debriefing or plenary session. The cycle should be repeated to cover increasingly more challenging aspects of genre. Research shows that this model has been found to be most helpful in supporting children's development as writers and is a characteristic of 'effective teachers of literacy'.[12]

A Literacy Hour might be turned into a 'writer's workshop' focusing on either fiction or non-fiction writing. During the hour this might include:

- sharing and discussing with pupils examples of how one or more writers have dealt with a theme or issue in writing;
- asking pupils to compose orally for themselves during shared writing time, while you write down the children's ideas;

- giving pupils 20 minutes to write for themselves, while you concentrate on helping one focus group of writers; and

- reassembling the class in the plenary ten minutes to share and review, identifying what is good about each piece of writing and how it might be improved.

In writing fiction, focus on one or more aspects of the writer's art, for example the plot (theme or genre), narrative structure (especially good beginnings and endings), interesting characters, evocative settings, and use of dialogue.

The following are ten tips from teachers to help children write stories in a short time:

Writing short stories

1. Use only one or two main characters.

2. Plan a good beginning to capture the reader's interest, but keep it short.

3. The main part is the 'middle', then move the problem quickly on to a resolution.

4. Describe the setting, and any changes within it as the story goes along.

5. Tell your reader how characters think and feel.

6. Make characters talk about what is happening (but don't always use the word 'said').

7. Use a variety of sentence lengths, and avoid repetition of words, e.g. at start of sentences.

8. Finish the story with a good last line or sentence.

9. As you write, read the story through to yourself to see if it makes sense.

10. Finish with five minutes to spare, to check your draft for punctuation and spelling.

An effective strategy to help children to write either fiction or non-fiction is through the use of 'writing frames' (Hodson and Jones 2001). This is another scaffolding approach that can help support young writers by giving starters and key questions to help prompt and structure the writing and to bridge any gaps in understanding.[13] Figure 6.5 is an example of a writing frame that helped Year 4 children to structure their arguments into a discussion for and against whether children should wear school uniform. Speaking and listening can provide the oral groundwork for writing, helping children to argue through ideas in their own minds, as well as expressing them in dialogue before planning their writing.

Name: Jane Brewster	
Title: Should children wear school uniform?	

Make notes in the boxes below listing arguments for and against...

Arguments for...	Arguments against...
1. There is not the problem of parents not knowing what to buy their children for school.	1. Children cannot choose what to wear for school, everyone has to have the same.
2. School uniform makes you feel proud of going to your school.	2. School uniform is expensive. Some parents can't afford it and have to get it from second-hand shops.
3. You know who goes to your school if they are wearing the uniform.	3. School uniforms can be boring and muddy colours.
4. Some children get way out ideas about fashon [sic] and everyone copies them.	4. If your school uniform is in the wash in the morning you've [sic] got trouble!
5. School uniform makes you look smart.	5. You can choose comfortable clothes for yourself.

My conclusion based on these arguments is:
I think children should be allowed to choose whether they wear school uniform or not

because
there are arguments for both sides.

FIGURE 6.5 Writing frame for an argument or discussion completed by a nine-year-old

Composition and transcription: finding a balance

One of the possible weaknesses of the Literacy Hour, initially, was that the time allowed for independent or group work (20 minutes) was insufficient for children to engage in extended pieces of writing, although this has now largely been overcome.[14] This relates to the problem of deciding how much attention should be given to the composition and transcription aspects of the process, respectively. The best solution is to take a balanced approach, viewing both these elements as mutually dependent and, therefore, needing equal attention. When there is a balance between composing and transcription, children are encouraged to express their thoughts and feelings on a wide variety of subjects that are meaningful to them in appropriate styles for their intended purpose. To achieve this, children need to be:

- motivated by the use of good books and stories;
- taught to write legibly and use spelling, grammar and punctuation accurately;
- shown how to plan, draft, revise and edit their writing;
- understand the learning objectives and success criteria for the writing;
- supported in the writing process by a 'response partner' (see below), writing group, or teacher, to help improve their writing;
- given sufficient time to complete extended pieces of writing; and
- encouraged to share, judge and evaluate their writing and the writing of others.

Children need to be motivated by good models of writing and of the process of planning, drafting and revising writing. When children come to write for themselves it is important that they have a clear objective. They also need to discuss and understand the criteria by which a piece of writing is judged to be a success. They should also be made aware of the purposes or long-term goals of learning to write.[15] Some teachers help younger learners focus on learning objectives, success criteria and long term-goals by cartoon drawings of animals or people such as OLI, WALT, WILF and TIB:

- OLI = Our Learning Intention ('In this lesson our learning intention is to...')
- WALT = We Are Looking To (learning objective)
- WILF = What I'm Looking For (success criteria)
- TIB = This Is Because (long-term goal)

Some teachers have found it helpful to post advice on the process of writing and responding to writing, such as the reminders to a class of ten-year-olds in Figure 6.6.

Acting as a 'response partner' will help children to gain awareness or metacognitive understanding of writing in progress. It helps children to engage with the question that is a challenge for every teacher: 'How do you help someone to improve their writing?'.

Shared reading and textual analysis of samples of writing with children can enhance their understanding of the process of writing and what it means to be a good writer. Discussion of writing through conferencing between the child, or group of children, and a teacher will help to develop a shared vocabulary for discussing writing. Such discussions should help older children become familiar with the technical language of English including the use of grammatical terms (see Chapter 5), as well as understanding the importance of textual features such as cohesion, voice, style and the use of imagery.

When you have drafted your writing:

1. Read it aloud to yourself.

2. Ask yourself, 'Is there anything I want to add or change?'

3. Read your writing to a 'response friend'.

4. Ask if he / she has any good ideas to improve your writing.

5. Give your revised draft to an adult to read.

How to be a good 'response' friend:

1. Listen carefully to your friend read his / her work.

2. Tell your friend what you liked about the writing.

3. Think how it might be improved:

   - Will the audience understand it?
   - Will they find it interesting?
   - Is there anything missing?
   - Can you suggest any words or changes?
   - Is it the right length?

4. Suggest how the writing might be improved.

FIGURE 6.6 When you have drafted your writing

Another approach is to involve children in assessing writing, and in particular to discuss the criteria used for judging a good piece of writing. Figure 6.7 gives some criteria brainstormed by Year 4 children and their teacher.

Other questions that can challenge children (as well as teachers) to think about and articulate their understanding of the writing process include:

- Why is it good for children to learn to write?;
- What five hints would you give a younger child to help them become a good writer?; and
- What must you do to improve your writing?

Children	Teacher
'Be a good story'	Understanding of story (or genre) structure, e.g. a story should have a good: beginning (setting the scene, interesting the reader) development (interesting events/characters/problems) resolution (ending where the problem/s are resolved)
'Have good words'	Use of vocabulary: Writing should be expressed in 'best words'. e.g. use of imaginative expressions for detail and description: range of adjectives, verbs, adverbs expanded noun phrases, e.g. 'One cold, frosty morning...'
'Explain things well'	Use of stylistic features: Writing should have a good style. e.g. through use of: varied sentences, short and expanded metaphor and simile repetition and alliteration
'Make sense'	Use of Standard English. e.g. use correct written forms of expression, including: range of appropriate connecting words to extend sentences correct use of punctuation and spelling consistent use of tenses
'Be interesting to read'	Awareness of the needs of the reader; e.g. written with audience and purpose in mind, including interesting content that is well paced/sequenced.

FIGURE 6.7 What makes a good piece of writing? (success criteria)

Conclusion

Part of the value of writing is that it enables us to record our thinking both as a product and a process of learning. Writing can help develop meta-cognitive awareness at three levels:

- knowledge of task: what is the writing task – its form, audience, and purpose?
- knowledge of process: what do you do – draft, revise, edit, share?
- knowledge of self: what kind of writer are you – what helps you to write well?

But to give the last word to a child. Here, Tom, aged 10, explains what the writing process means to him:

When I write I find it easier at first to discuss my ideas with others, then have a go. I like to think what to write about without rushing into it. I prefer to write in rough first, because I can change things like boring words to unboring words or my lines if they are too long. I don't like too much noise when I write so I can hear myself think. I like to write a lot of ideas and only keep the ones [sic] that are good, so it makes sense and sounds right. I then read it through and check for spelling mistakes. Sometimes it helps to discuss what you are writing with a friend. When I give it in I hope the teacher will say 'good work'.

Notes

1. E. Ferreiro and A. Teberosky (1979), researching in Argentina, showed that children's emergent mark-making was not merely haphazard scribbling as had once been thought.
2. Marie Clay (1972) showed through research that children did not automatically acquire 'concepts about print', such as directionality, letter and word concepts, book orientation and punctuation, but needed them taught explicitly. Nigel Hall (1987) and A. Browne (1995) have investigated further the principles children adhere to as they emerge as writers.
3. These approaches in the English National Curriculum (DES 1990) were derived from recommendations in the earlier Cox Report (DES 1989, 10.8).
4. T. Bruce (1991), T. David (1998) and C. Nutbrown (1999) have identified from research key principles in effective teaching of young children, in particular the importance of structured play in the early years.
5. *Curriculum for the Foundation Stage* (DfEE 2000b) lays out what children under 5 in nursery and reception classes in schools in England and Wales should be taught.
6. *The National Literacy Strategy* (DfEE 1998a: 19). Similarly, in the English curriculum there is endorsement of developmental principles, for example, in the statement that '*during* the key stage they [pupils] should become independent writers of texts which are correctly spelled, with sentences punctuated correctly' (DfEE 1999b:5).
7. C. Meadows and A. Cashdan (1988) were influential in showing that adults need to engage in meaningful dialogue with children if the learning opportunities afforded by play are to be

maximised.

8. Based on Janet and Allan Ahlberg (1986) *The Jolly Postman or Other People's Letters*. London: Heinemann.

9. R. Beard (1999) offers a useful review of research related to writing in the National Literacy Strategy. J. R. Martin (1989) outlines and discusses the important role of factual writing.

10. M.Williams and R.Fisher (1998) *Brunel Research Into Literacy* (unpublished).

11. See D. Wray and M. Lewis (1997) *Extending Literacy: Children Reading and Writing Non-fiction* (Routledge), which draws extensively on the Exeter Extending Literacy (EXEL) project. Wray and Lewis's work, in turn, strongly influenced the emphasis on using non-fiction in the National Literacy Strategy (DfEE 1998a).

12. J. Medwell *et al.* (1998) in a report for the Teacher Training Agency aimed at identifying the characteristics of effective teachers of literacy.

13. D. Wray and M. Lewis (1997) offer approaches to 'scaffolding' writing based on the earlier theories of L. Vygotsky (1962) and J. Bruner (1983).

14. M. Williams (2001) researched the dissemination of the National Literacy Strategy and its effect on practice in primary classrooms from the perspective of student teachers, and this was a critical feature relating to writing at Key Stage 2. The problem has been overcome by removing 'guided group work' from the Literacy Hour on some occasions or by giving children the opportunity to develop a longer piece of writing over several sessions. Sometimes children can engage in parts of the drafting process as part of homework. Then discuss work in progress during the hour itself.

15. For more on feedback and formative assessment strategies in the classroom see the work of Shirley Clarke, including her book *Feedback Matters in the Primary Classroom* (Hodder Arnold, 2003)

References

Beard, R. (1999) *National Literacy Strategy: Review of Research and Related Evidence*. London: DfEE.

Browne, A. (1995) *Developing Language and Literacy*. London: Paul Chapman.

Bruce, T. (1991) *Time to Play*. London: Hodder & Stoughton.

Clarke S. (2003) *Feedback Matters in the Primary Classroom*. London: Hodder Arnold.

Clay, M. (1972) *Reading: The Patterning of Complex Behaviour* (2nd edn.) London: Heinemann.

David, T. (1998) 'Learning properly! Young children and desirable outcomes'. *Journal of the Professional Association of Early Childhood Educators*, 18(2), Spring.

DES (1989) *English for Ages 5 to 16*. London: HMSO.

DES (1990) *English in the National Curriculum (No.2)*. London: HMSO.

DfEE (1998a) *The National Literacy Strategy: Framework for Teaching*. London: HMSO.

DfEE (1998b) *Teachers Meeting the Challenge of Change*. Green Paper.

DfEE (1999a) *English in the National Curriculum*. London: HMSO.

DfEE (1999b) *The Review of the National Curriculum in England*. London: HMSO.

DfEE (2000a) *Developing Early Literacy*. London: NLS.

DfEE (2000b) *Curriculum for the Foundation Stage*. London: QCA.

DfEE (2000c) *Grammar for Writing*. London: NLS.

Ferreiro, E. and Teberosky, A. (1979) *Literacy Before Schooling*. London: Heinemann.

Fisher, R. and Williams, M. (eds) (2004) *Unlocking Creativity*. London: David Fulton Publishers.

Hall, N. (1987) *The Emergence of Literacy*. London: Hodder & Stoughton.

Hodson, P. and Jones, D. (2001) *Teaching Children to Write*. London: David Fulton Publishers.

Martin, J.R. (1989) *Factual Writing: Exploring and Challenging Social Reality*. Oxford: Oxford University Press.

Meek, M. (1991) *On Being Literate*. London: Bodley Head.

Meadows, C. and Cashdan, A. (1988) *Helping Children Learn*. London: David Fulton Publishers.

Medwell, J., Wray, D., Poulson, L. and Fox, R. (1998) *Effective Teachers of Literacy: A Report of a Research Project Commissioned by the Teacher Training Agency*. Exeter: University of Exeter School of Education.

Nutbrown, C. (1999) *Threads of Thinking* (2nd edn). London: Paul Chapman.

QCA (1998) *Standards at Key Stage 2: English, Mathematics and Science: Report on the 1998 National Curriculum Assessments for 11-Year-Olds*. London: QCA Publications.

Williams, M. (2001) 'Trainee teachers' perceptions of the effectiveness of the Literacy Hour in primary schools in England'. *Early Child Development and Care, 166,* 53–61.

Williams, M. (ed.) (2002) *Unlocking Writing*. London: David Fulton Publishers.

Wray, D. and Lewis, M. (1997) *Extending Literacy: Children Reading and Writing Non-fiction*. London: Routledge.

Children's literature

Ahlberg, A. (1980) *Funny Bones*. London: Heinemann.

Ahlberg, J. and A. (1986) *The Jolly Postman or Other People's Letters*. London: Heinemann.

Further Reading

Graham, J. and Kelly, A. (2003) *Writing Under Control*, 2nd edn. London: David Fulton Publishers.

CHAPTER 7

It's good to talk: reinstating the place of speaking and listening in the primary classroom

Pam Hodson

'I like talking in the classroom when I'm doing tricky work – it's how I learn best – when I can share ideas with my friends.'

Introduction

Safiya, aged 8, had been engaged in a maths investigation with four of her peers. She highlighted the fact that through talk, discussion and interaction with other children this 'tricky work' had become a meaningful and manageable task; observation of the processes they engaged in also demonstrated that significant learning had taken place.

This chapter will aim to put into context the recent guidance on speaking and listening – *Speaking, Listening, Learning: Working with Children in Key Stages 1 and 2* (DfES 2003a) – and consider ways to implement its recommendations in the classroom. The teaching of speaking and listening has always been a richly controversial and much debated field and its re-emergence as being central to children's learning and literacy development also brings to the fore complex and challenging issues, not least in reappraising the way in which literacy is taught in the classroom. Robin Alexander (2005) pulls no punches when he states that the 'literacy and numeracy strategies have promoted classroom interaction which all too often is low-level and cognitively unchallenging'.[1]

The value of talk as a means of learning is widely accepted. However, it is true to say that for the last ten years, while there has been a firm emphasis on raising standards in reading and writing in primary schools, the explicit teaching of speaking and listening has been neglected. This, despite the fact that the English National Curriculum (DfEE 1999) firmly retains speaking and listening in its prominent position as its first Programme of Study. Similarly, the National Literacy Strategy (DfEE 1998), which has had a significant impact on how English is taught in the primary classroom, acknowledges the role that oral work plays in children's literacy development, yet its many objectives address mainly reading and writing. Aspects of speaking and listening are implicit: 'Literacy…also involves speaking and listening which, although they are not separately identified in the Framework, are an essential part of it' (p. 3). The words 'discuss' and 'summarise orally' do appear, but the Strategy's drive has focused predominantly on the teaching of reading and writing and classroom practice has reflected this.

In 2003, as a result of a partnership between the QCA and the National Literacy Strategy, new guidelines, in response to a perceived need for support from teachers, were developed to raise the profile of speaking and listening in the primary classroom (DfES 2003a). As the guidance highlights, its aim is to complement the Strategy's objectives for reading and writing and reflect the National Curriculum programmes of study for speaking and listening both in English and across the curriculum.

History and context

National initiatives for the development of speaking and listening are not new. In 1987, the National Oracy Project was established to enhance the role of speaking and listening in the learning process by improving children's performance across the curriculum and encouraging active learning.[2] The late 80s and early 90s proved to be an extremely rich era in teaching where the profile of speaking and listening was high and debate was fierce. In addition to the National Oracy Project, the LINC Project (Language in the National Curriculum 1989–1992) was designed to support teachers' effective knowledge and understanding of language as they implemented the introduction of the National Curriculum. The project proved to be highly controversial, although in many areas highly successful with teachers for whom this was their first taste of professional development and enhancement of subject knowledge or INSET, as it is now known. Influences from both of these projects can be seen in the new guidance on speaking and listening.

Speaking, listening, learning: working with children in Key Stages 1 and 2

The guidance is related to the four interdependent aspects of speaking and listening in the National Curriculum programmes of study for English:

Table 7.1 The four aspects of speaking and listening in the English National Curriculum

Speaking	Listening	Group discussion and interaction	Drama
Being able to speak clearly and to develop and sustain ideas in talk	Developing active listening strategies and critical skills of analysis	Taking different roles in groups, making a range of contributions and working collaboratively	Improvising and working in role, scripting and performing and responding to performances

As its title suggests, the central role of oral language in children's learning is a fundamental aspect of the new guidance, in parallel with the desire to 'raise standards further'. It identifies 67 distinct objectives for speaking and listening which are organised in two ways: chronologically, and then divided into the separate key strands of speaking; listening; group discussion and interaction; and drama. The difficulty of presenting any linear model of language is that language development is not linear; it is recursive. To a certain extent, the objectives do reflect this, identifying language skills which are revisited and developed in different years, for example increasing development of the ability to tell a story and developing confidence and sophistication in operating as an effective member of a group. However, children's progress in speaking and listening will vary tremendously according to each individual, so teachers also face the challenge of setting goals that are achievable and appropriate to each child's language development.

The guidance is also linked to key objectives from the Literacy Strategy Framework, for example Year 3, Term 3, objective 35:

> To use the language of possibility to investigate and reflect on feelings, behaviour or relationships

is linked to the NLS text level objective 5 of the same term:

> To discuss characters' feelings, behaviour, relationships, referring to the text and making judgements.

Literary texts such as narrative, poetry and drama texts also provide the stimulus for exploration, analysis and discussion in the objectives. In addition, investigating language use and variety in a range of contexts is also embedded in the guidance as well as critical engagement with media texts such as advertisements or TV broadcasts (see Chapter 12).

The ways in which speaking and listening can be taught and used as a means of learning in other subject areas is also emphasised. Moral issues discussed in PSHE can be used as a way of engaging actively in group work through the resolution of differences by exploring alternative viewpoints, making decisions and justifying choices. PE presents opportunities to describe performance; science and maths to use appropriate technical language, ask questions, decide how these can be investigated and explain reasoning.

Metalanguage and a grammar for talk

The guidance highlights the need for children to be taught to use technical languages that are relevant for each subject area. The same is true for reflecting on and discussing language. Children need to be taught a metalanguage, a specialised form of language used when discussing or describing the structure of language, in order to engage critically and explicitly with language. In this way, grammar, word classes and figures of speech can be used in a rich and stimulating context where children will feel free to hypothesise and speculate, not merely be required to label parts of speech (see Chapter 5). Carter (2003)[3] takes this debate further and argues for a grammar for spoken language that identifies the differences between spoken and written English.

The guidance also highlights the requirement that children should use, where appropriate, standard English; a complex issue which is addressed next in some detail.

Standard English

The view adopted by the Working Group for National Curriculum English (1989) that standard English is a social dialect associated with particular uses, especially in areas of power, proved to be highly unpopular among people who wanted it to be viewed as the 'correct' way to talk. The Group stated that standard English was not inherently superior to all other forms of English and highlighted research which demonstrated that all other dialects were rule-governed and systematic, not deviant forms of standard English. Undoubtedly, it is vital for teachers to respect the child's home dialect, but it is equally true to say that not having the ability to use standard English will exclude adults from areas of power, such as government, law, education, commerce and the media. The National Curriculum, English (DfEE 1999:17) states that at Key Stage 1 'Pupils should be introduced to some of the main features of spoken standard English and be taught how to use them', progressing through to Key Stage 2 where they 'should be taught the grammatical constructions that are characteristic of spoken standard English and to apply this knowledge in a range of contexts'.

English as an additional language

The need to respect and value children's home language is equally important for children whose first language is not English. Teachers need to demonstrate an awareness of and foster an interest in the languages that children speak at home, as well as extending children's development in English. It is also evident that providing opportunities for children to use their own language repertoires in school enhances the child's self-image and increases confidence in their learning.

Children need to be made aware that standard English can be spoken with any accent (regional newsreaders provide ready-made evidence of this) and that its use is not confined to speakers who may use an accent such as 'Received pronunciation', or BBC English as it is sometimes known. Both media and internet resources offer the opportunity to extend children's encounters with different speakers beyond the classroom. If children's reading of literature was confined to texts written by the class teacher or their peers, 'their knowledge of language would be unnecessarily limited' (Hewitt 2003);[4] the same must also be true of providing a limited number of role models for speaking and listening. Therefore, in providing both audiences and appropriate role models for spoken language, teachers need to exploit opportunities beyond the classroom.

The explicit study of standard English provides all children, irrespective of their language(s) background, with a rich resource for language study in the classroom and is most effective when explored in context. Many children, from an early age, demonstrate the ability to change their language according to whom they are with and why they are speaking. Observations of children's self-corrections in whole-class teaching demonstrate this. For example, children in a Year 4 class were discussing the actions of the characters in the story they were reading. Anna responded to her teacher's question by stating emphatically, 'He didn't do nothing wrong'. After a moment's pause, she restated, carefully, 'He didn't do *anything* wrong', with a deliberate emphasis on the 'anything' to underscore her knowledge. In this context, the teacher had allowed time for Anna's self-correction before intervening or remodelling her response, providing the opportunity for the child to demonstrate her growing proficiency in using language appropriately. This knowledge can be exploited and developed further through role-play, formal debates and presentations in the classroom where the appropriate use of standard English can provide both the focus for use and reflection on language usage.

As standard English is the form of language most commonly used in writing, the need to develop children's competence in this area is unquestionable. However, within standard English, there are differences of style, particularly in the continuum between formal and informal language and between standard English spoken in different parts of the wider English speaking world. Most children, used to exposure to films and TV series from America and Australia, can readily identify different word usages; the BBC website (www.bbc/ voice.co.uk) provides an excellent resource of regional accents and dialects.

Excellence and enjoyment

In the same year as the guidance on speaking and listening was produced *Excellence and Enjoyment. A Strategy for Primary Schools* (DfES 2003b) was published, advocating a more flexible approach to teaching the Literacy Hour. It suggested that schools should be adapting the strategy to meet their own particular needs, highlighting the non-statutory nature of both the Literacy and Numeracy Strategies.[5]

So, has there been a considerable shift in primary classroom practice towards a more balanced approach to teaching speaking and listening, reading and writing? Initial research (Hodson 2005)[6] would seem to indicate that the new guidance has not been universally adopted. At best, schools' and teachers' responses to implementing the guidance have been tentative, and practice patchy. Some schools have identified that it is not a priority and there is often an assumption that speaking and listening occurs 'naturally' and happens implicitly as part of the normal school day. In many instances, teachers demonstrate a suspicion of speaking and listening, fearing that they will 'lose control' and while 'Good listening' is often rewarded in the classroom, 'Good speaking' is rarely celebrated. Children, too, often seem to perceive talk as something furtive which goes on when the teacher isn't looking or behind a strategically placed hand when they can 'get away with it' in assembly. For many children, talk is something that they do in the playground, before lessons begin and something 'you don't do when you need to concentrate when you're learning'. Children's perceptions are not all negative, however, as is evidenced in Safiya's opening quotation. In contrast, when children had been given opportunities to work in groups, they were able to articulate how talking had helped them to learn. Several children discussed the pleasure they gained from reading and sharing books with their peers and collaborating over a writing task. When engaged in explicit discussion about the nature of talk, children demonstrated insightful perceptions of what makes a good speaker and a good listener and considerable enthusiasm for the topic of speaking and listening as a whole.

For teachers, the guidance presents considerable challenges, not least in generating a change in a classroom ethos which, since the inception of the Literacy Strategy, has focused largely on teacher-led and -controlled discussion to promoting a whole-school ethos where speaking and listening is valued. In addition, speaking and listening is an extremely complex and controversial topic.

Many teachers face pressure from parents and the media to promote a more traditional view of learning, where a quiet classroom is perceived as the most effective for successful teaching and learning.

The teacher's role

An understanding of how children acquire language is fundamental to informing how speaking and listening is taught in the classroom and this has been recognised for a long time.[7] Joshua, aged 6, when asked 'How did you feel when you spoke in assembly?' replied, 'I feeled nervous'. Joshua will not have heard the verb 'feeled' from an adult but he is, in fact, applying known rules of grammatical construction – that is, adding 'ed' to the present tense of a verb to make the past tense - to a new situation. In this context, Joshua's use of language is recognised as a sign of growth, a child's understanding that language is a system, and rule-governed, but he has not yet acquired mastery of that system.

There are clear implications for the crucial role that a teacher plays in building a bridge between the child's current knowledge – what they already know about language – and helping them towards progressively more advanced levels of competence (Vygotsky 1978). This makes significant demands on the teacher's knowledge and understanding of each individual child's competence in speaking and listening and highlights the need for effective assessment and rigorous planning in order to provide the child with appropriate scaffolding. As the expert role model for spoken language, teachers also need to present an appropriate model for spoken standard English in the classroom and to present opportunities for children to use and explore appropriate contexts for using standard English. This is an integral part of the National Curriculum programmes of study for speaking and listening and the objectives for speaking and listening.

Teachers also need to reflect on the kind of speaking and listening that they promote in the classroom. It is evident that there is a significant difference between spoken discourse in the classroom and that in the community outside. In essence, a lot of classroom practice is typified by the IRF (Initiation, Response, Feedback) or IRE (Initiation, Response, Evaluation) sequence, where the teacher initiates talk with a question, children respond, and through the teacher's feedback the teacher controls the language and meaning, signalling what is to be viewed as relevant knowledge within the classroom. This kind of sequence is characteristic of many of the teacher–pupil interchanges that take place during whole-class teaching in the Literacy Hour, both in shared reading or writing and the plenary. Research into classroom interactions by Alexander (2003)[8] highlights the fact that interactions between teachers and children tend to be brief rather than sustained; closed questions predominate and children are very much focused on giving the 'right' answer. He recommends a move towards 'dialogic teaching' and identifies four conditions for teaching this effectively. These are:

- Collective: pupils and teachers address learning tasks together, whether as a group or as a class, rather than in isolation;
- Reciprocal: pupils and teachers listen to each other, share ideas and consider alternative viewpoints;
- Cumulative: pupils and teachers build on their own and each others' ideas and chain them into coherent lines of thinking and enquiry;
- Supportive: pupils articulate their ideas freely, without fear of embarrassment over 'wrong' answers, and they help each other to reach common understandings.

(Alexander 2003:36)

In contrast, the community outside the classroom presents a rich and varied picture of language use, changing language styles and of different communication practices. Many children whose mother tongue is not English are extremely adept at switching between two or more languages, depending on who they are with. Although it is not always possible to replicate these practices in the classroom, teachers also need to take account of the children's linguistic repertoires outside of the school and find ways to celebrate it in the classroom.

Planning for speaking and listening

When planning for talk, it is important to consider the nature of talk and it is helpful to identify four discrete, but interdependent, aspects of speaking and listening:

- social – for developing relationships;
- communicative – for transferring meaning;
- cultural – different meanings are adopted by different speech communities; among children these might be associated with popular culture; and
- cognitive – using talk as a means of learning.

Therefore, in planning effective speaking and listening opportunities, we are also planning for effective learning.

> Learning is the product of the interaction between the old and the new, the known and the not known...Through talk it is possible to explore and clarify new meanings, review and revise old meanings, until there can be an accommodation between the two.

(Baddeley 1992:41)

117

Research by Mercer (2000)[9] highlights the value of this kind of exploratory talk but observational research indicates that very little of it occurs naturally in the classroom. However, research from Australia (Cormack *et al.* 1998)[10] shows that, despite fears from teachers that children would not be focused, when they were provided with structured opportunities to work with their peers, they were able to use speaking and listening to:

- interrogate their own understanding
- aid recall
- instruct others
- work on ideas and propositions
- problematise
- argue a personal point of view
- rehearse subject specific language
- progressively shape knowledge
- generate ideas
- 'sponsor' learning.

(Cormack *et al.* 1998)

The research also highlights that the effective use of speaking and listening for cognitive purposes was dependent on the clarity of the task (children knew what kind of talk was required) and the appropriate selection of a topic that allowed children to build on their previous knowledge and understanding.

Several schools that are implementing the new guidance have started by focusing on current practice in relation to the development of children's spoken language. In doing so they have adopted the functional approach to language which is evident in the Professional Development materials for the guidance (DfES 2003a:39). This approach is based on functional linguistics (Halliday 1978) where the structure of the language we use and the structure of the social action are mutually determining. Put simply, we vary what we say and how we say it according to who we are with (the audience) and why we are speaking (the purpose). For children, development and progression in their speaking and listening skills are marked by an increasing confidence and competence in achieving these aims.

A preliminary analysis of the kinds of speaking and listening children engage in at the beginning of the school day could look like Figure 7.2:

Again, observational evidence would seem to indicate that although children may implicitly be able to vary how they speak according to whom they are with, the opportunities for extending their speaking and listening repertoire need careful planning.

Table 7.2 Analysing children's speaking and listening

Activity	Audience	Purpose	Setting
Arriving at school with parents/carers	Parents/carers	To say goodbye. To reaffirm arrangements for after school. Social and communicative.	Playground
Meeting friends	Peers	To share information. To re-establish relationships Social, communicative, cultural.	Playground
Teacher greeting pupils	Teacher	To greet communicative.	Classroom
Circle time	Teacher/teaching assistant	To listen to other children. To give a sustained, individual account/anecdote/story. Communicative.	Classroom

The National Oracy Project (1992) identified four key questions that teachers need to consider in order to plan successfully for speaking and listening:

1. What should the children be learning?
2. Where can talk contribute effectively to the children's learning?
3. Where are the children now in their learning?
4. What period of time is the planning due to cover?

Fundamentally, speaking and listening should be embedded in the curriculum and not a 'bolt on', decontextualised activity. Teachers need to identify areas of the curriculum where the activities and the children's learning would be aided by speaking and listening. As has already been discussed, it is vital that teachers have observed and assessed children's speaking and listening development in order to plan for progression (see Chapter 10). Time is also a key factor: some speaking and listening activities may need to be planned for over an extended period of time; some may constitute just a part of one lesson. For example, a Year 2 class were focusing on the literacy strategy objective for term 1 on 'instructions'. The class teacher planned, over four weeks, an extended activity where the use of a digital video provided the children with an initial context for exploring this area in a medium other than writing. The children were engaged in group work where they each had different roles in filming and giving instructions to visitors on how to navigate around the school. Reflection and analysis of the video created by the children formed an integral aspect of the work they completed, as did explicit discussion of what constituted appropriate language in different contexts. This carefully planned extended unit of work provided the children with a real context both for exploring the language of instruction, and also engaging in meaningful group work where negotiation, co-operation and teamwork were essential. The children then had the opportunity to edit their films and add written text to the visual images they created, demonstrating how speaking and listening can successfully underpin more traditional writing activities.

Classroom organisation and resources

The physical organisation of the classroom is also vital. Children, particularly at Key Stage 1, are used to moving in order to accommodate different contexts for learning: the movement from whole-class teaching on the carpet, group work around tables and back to the carpet for the plenary is an integral aspect of the children's daily lives in the classroom. Teachers need to consider whether their classroom layout supports the particular kind of speaking and listening activity they are planning for and adjust it accordingly. Some children may feel more comfortable in presenting their ideas on tape, where they have the opportunity to stop, re-frame ideas and work on a polished presentation. Increasingly, as described earlier, children are being given opportunities to work with digital video cameras, both in front of and behind the camera. Again, this resource allows them to edit and adapt their talk before presenting it to a wider audience. Both audio and video technologies present opportunities for children to analyse and reflect on speaking and listening.

A climate for talk

A classroom ethos needs to be created where positive achievements in speaking and listening are valued and celebrated. The transitory and ephemeral nature of speech makes this difficult, but teachers can raise the profile of speaking and listening by making it the end product of an extended scheme of work (a debate which identifies arguments for and against a key question), or a role-play (see Chapter 8) which demonstrates children's understanding of a text they are reading. Talk can form the basis for discussion and analysis:

- Who do you feel most comfortable speaking and listening with?
- When do you feel most comfortable speaking and listening?
- Where do you feel most comfortable speaking and listening?
- What do you like discussing?
- Why?

Talk Diaries can raise the profile of speaking and listening for children. The first two hours of football-mad James's (aged 11) diary, looked like this:

Table 7.3 A Child's Talk Diary

Who	When	Where	Types of language
Brother	Before school	At home	Questions – asking where he'd put my football
Friend/Mum/brother	On the way to school	Mobile phone in the car	Asking friend to bring football to school. Listening to mum. Arguing with brother.
Friends	Before school	Playground	Discussing England's match the night before. Arguing/negotiating – who was the best player? Organising – to meet at break time.
Teacher	Beginning of school	Classroom	Answering my name.

A talk diary such as this also recognises children's speaking and listening outside of the classroom/school context and presents opportunities to discuss contextualised language in its social context. Children, with the support of the teacher, can then begin to identify and discuss the kind of language they are using.

Children as young as 6 can provide thoughtful responses, demonstrating that they do in fact have a great deal of implicit understanding of the nature of talk and the role of the critical friend. Again, the focus for discussion was based around sport – rugby.

'So what do you think makes a good speaker?'

Joshua thought for a moment and then replied, 'I think my friend Liam is a good speaker…because he watches me play rugby and then talks to me about it afterwards. He tells me what I do right…passing the ball…but then he tells me what I could do better…like, running faster.'

Providing different audiences is also a valuable way of raising the profile of speaking and listening – inviting other classes, teachers and parents to observe children engaged in a purposeful activity can fulfil a variety of functions, not least demonstrating that talk is a valued part of classroom practice. Children should also be part of the process for valuing speaking and listening in the classroom: discussions of what makes a good speaker and a good listener can provide the basis for establishing shared and agreed ground rules for effective speaking and listening that can then be displayed on the classroom wall. This is a key objective from the new guidance:

> Objective 37: To use and reflect on some ground rules for dialogue.

Table 7.4 Objective 37

Ground rules for dialogue
Listen to the views of others
Respond to the views of others
Reinforce the views of others
Initiate ideas
Ask questions of others
Encourage others to join in
Take turns
Participate in discussion

Speaking and listening in the Literacy Hour

The National Curriculum for English (DfEE 1999) stresses the interrelatedness of the four modes of language: speaking, listening reading and writing. Research into effective practice in writing (Frater 2001) also demonstrates that children make successful progress in their writing development when opportunities for speaking and listening are an integral part of work on reading and writing. Although teachers may feel there is immense pressure on time to fulfil the objectives from the Literacy Strategy in reading and writing alone, Goodwin (2001:xi) states that: 'If anything, fulfilling the guidance of the framework requires more talk in the classroom rather than less'.

Whole-class teaching

Whole-class teaching provides the teacher with opportunities to model standard English in appropriate contexts and also to demonstrate the tentative and speculative nature of talk. Teachers' questions also play a key role in scaffolding children's learning, particularly in making progressively greater cognitive demands of the children through the use of higher order questions (Fisher 2002).

When time is given for thought, reflection and support from talk partners, this context also provides a ready audience for children to give structured and extended contributions and to listen to and respond to the contributions made by other children in the classroom. Children's oral responses, moreover, provide opportunities for a teacher to assess a child's understanding and learning in a medium other than writing.

Group work

Children are used to sitting in groups as part of the organisational structure of the Literacy Hour. However, observational evidence shows that, in general, children are working as individuals within those groups and not engaged in genuine collaboration on tasks that require exploratory talk. Teachers also need to consider carefully how they organise children for speaking and listening activities. Placing children in mixed-ability groups can provide them with opportunities to interact with children who may be more linguistically competent. Gender is also another significant consideration and, depending on the nature of the task, it may be appropriate to organise children in single-sex groups. Children should also be given the opportunity for some autonomy on how groups are organised; this, in itself, can provide an interesting area for debate.

Drama activities can create the context for exploratory talk by encouraging the expression of hypothesis and opinion (Johnson 2000). In addition, children can be actively involved in making meaning from literary texts through the appropriate and selective use of DARTs (Directed Activities Related to Texts) activities (Lunzer and Gardner 1979). These activities are not new; they were developed in the 1970s in response to research into reading which showed that children did a great deal of copying from texts, rather than actually gleaning information from their reading.

DARTS (Directed Activities Related to Text)

- Cloze
- Sequencing
- Prediction

Teachers frequently make use of the latter strategy by stopping reading at a critical point in a narrative and asking children to predict or hypothesise what could happen next. Sequencing activities can work equally well with both fiction and non-fiction texts, requiring children to read and re-read parts of text in order to make meaning from the whole. Cloze activities provide interactive learning experiences where children can discuss, negotiate speculate and justify word choices. In all DARTs activities, it is important to reassure children that they are not seeking the 'right' answer – but are searching for an appropriate answer.

The poem below provides an example of a text that is cognitively challenging but accessible to children of a range of abilities when presented in the right context. This was presented to Year 5 children as part of an extended scheme of work when other related issues were being explored such as the plight of evacuees in World War II as depicted in *Goodnight Mister Tom.* Children worked together in pairs to negotiate and speculate about which words could fit into the spaces. This work was extended further by asking the children to reflect explicitly on the knowledge they used in order to make their choices. This included knowledge of poetry and poetic forms (rhyme scheme) and knowledge about grammar (for example, the first word had to be a noun) which is underpinned by an increasing understanding of the meaning of the poem and the poet's intentions:

Evacuee

The slum had been his _____ since he was born;

And then war came and he was rudely _____

From all he'd ever known; and with his case

Of mean _____, brought to a place

Of _____ and space; just boom of sea

And sough of wind; small wonder then that he

Crept out one night to seek his _____ slum,

And thought to find his way. By dawn he'd come

A few short _____; and cattle in their herds

Gazed _____ as he trudged by, and birds

Just stirring in _____ light, awoke to hear

His lonely _____, born of abject fear

Of sea and hills and _____; of silent night

Unbroken by the sound of shout and _____.

(Edith Pickthall)

The plenary

The plenary offers time for children to engage in extended speaking and reflective listening. It also provides the teacher with the opportunity to assess children's understanding of texts through talk, as an alternative mode of assessment to writing.

Children are often able to make positive, supportive comments about each other's work, but find it more difficult to be critical. Scaffolding their critical responses with language that articulates a speculative, considered approach, should empower them to offer supportive criticism without being unduly undermining of their peers. In addition, speaking frames (example below) can provide useful scaffolds to support the language development of all children, particularly those for whom English is a second language.

Table 7.5 Speaking Frame

Speaking frame: review of writing (composition)
I really enjoyed the description of
I found it really interesting when
I thought the character was really
My favourite part is where
The most exciting part was where
I liked it because
Perhaps you could
Do you think it would be better if?
Could you add
Maybe if
I'd like to know more about
Tell me what would happen if

Conclusion

While it has to be acknowledged that speaking and listening have been undervalued in the past, the new guidance presents opportunities for schools to evaluate their own practice and place speaking and listening at the heart of the primary curriculum, not just in literacy teaching, but in all subjects. It is apparent that not all schools embraced it as wholeheartedly as they did the National Literacy Strategy, but its re-emergence cannot fail to have a positive effect on children's learning. Through it teachers have been given a mandate to loosen the grip of the Literacy Hour and to reaffirm the fundamental role that speaking and listening play in children's literacy development and learning as a whole.

Notes

1. Robin Alexander, writing in the *Education Weekly* section of *The Guardian* 19 April 2005. The full text is available on:
   www.education.guardian.co.uk/egweekly/story/0,,1462428,00.html
   See also Alexander, R. (2005) *Talking to Learn; Oracy Revisited* (National College for School Leadership *Teaching Text*). Nottingham: NCSL.
2. The National Oracy Project (1998) was highly influential in informing the recommendations for the Speaking and Listening requirements of the English National curriculum.
3. Carter, R. (2003) 'Teaching about talk – what do pupils need to know about spoken language and the important ways in which talk differs from writing?' *New Perspectives on Spoken English in the classroom*. Suffolk: QCA Publications.
4. Hewitt R. (2003) 'Is there a case for considering talk as part of the oral heritage and as a performance skill?' *New Perspectives on Spoken English in the Classroom*. Suffolk: QCA Publications.
5. *Excellence and Enjoyment* (DfES 2003b) was intended to give more autonomy back to schools so that schools themselves decide which aspects of a subject pupils will study in depth, how long to spend on each subject and how to arrange learning in the school day. It also identifies that one of the key ways to support literacy and numeracy is by reaffirming the place of speaking and listening both as a key foundation for literacy and also an essential aspect of all effective learning.
6. Unpublished research by Hodson based on data collected from 60 primary schools in west London. However, some LEAs, notably Barking and Dagenham, and North Yorkshire have launched major programmes focusing on classroom talk.
7. In the 1970s and 1980s, work done by Britton, J. (1972) *Language and Learning* (London: Penguin); Halliday, M.A.K. (1978), and Tizard, B. and Hughes, M. (1984) *Young Children Learning: Talking and Thinking at Home and at School* (London: Fontana), demonstrated that children play an active role in their language learning and are not merely imitating the language of adults. They build up a linguistic system (Halliday 1978) that is based on their current knowledge of language structures.
8. Research by Alexander explored in *New Perspectives on Spoken English in the Classroom*. QCA, 2003.
9. Mercer, N. (2000) *Words and Minds: How We Use Language to Think Together*. London: Routledge.
10. This research by Cormack, Y.P., Wignell, P. and Nichols, S. is part of the *Classroom Discourse Project* undertaken in Australia in 1998. It is available on:
    www.griffith.edu.au/schools/cls/clearinghouse/1998_classroom/cal.pdf

References

Alexander, R. (2003) *New Perspectives on Spoken English in the Classroom*. London: QCA.

Baddeley, G. (ed.) (1992) *Learning Together through Talk*. London: Hodder & Stoughton.

Britton, J. (1972) *Language and Learning*. London: Penguin.

Cormack, Y.P., Wignell, P. and Nichols, S. (1998) Classroom Discourse Project. Canberra: Commonwealth Department of Employment.

DfEE (1998) *The National Literacy Strategy*. London: HMSO.

DfEE (1999) *The National Curriculum: Handbook for Primary Teachers in England*. London: DfEE.

DfES (2003a) *The Primary Strategy. Speaking, Listening, Learning: Working with Children in Key Stages 1 and 2*. Norwich: HMSO.

DfES (2003b) *Excellence and Enjoyment: A Strategy for Primary Schools*. Nottingham: DfES Publications.

Fisher (2002) 'Boys into writing: raising boys' achievement in writing', in Williams, M. (ed.) *Unlocking Writing*. London: David Fulton Publishers.

Frater, G. (2001) *Effective Practice in Writing at KS2*. London: The Basic Skills Agency.

Goodwin, P. (ed.) (2001) *The Articulate Classroom* (2nd edn). London: David Fulton Publishers.

Halliday M.A.K. (1978) *Language and Social Semiotic: The Social Interpretation of Language and Meaning*. London: Edward Arnold.

Hewitt, R. (2003) 'Speaking and listening', in *New Perspectives on Spoken English in the Classroom*. London: QCA Publications.

Johnson C. (2000) in Williams, M. and Fisher, R. (eds) *Unlocking Literacy*. London: David Fulton Publishers.

Lunzer, E. and Gardner, K. (1979) *The Effective Use of Reading*. London: Heinemann Educational.

Mercer, N. (2000) *Words and Minds: How We Use Language to Think Together*. London: Routledge.

Norman, K. (ed.) (1992) *Thinking Voices: The Work of the National Oracy Project*. London: Hodder & Stoughton.

QCA (2003) *New Perspectives on Spoken English in the Classroom*. London: QCA.

Tizard, B. and Hughes, M. (1984) *Young Children Learning: Talking and Thinking at Home and at School*. London: Fontana.

Vygotsky, L.S. (1978) *Mind in Society*. Cambridge, MA: Harvard University Press.

Children's literature

Magorian, M. (2004) *Goodnight Mister Tom*. London: Puffin Modern Classics.

Pickthall, E. (1998) ' Evacuee', in *The Quest for Peace*. London: Longman Publishing Pelican.

Further reading

Alexander, R.J. (2005) *Towards Dialogic Teaching: Rethinking Classroom Talk*. York: Dialogos.

Dawes, L., Mercer, N. and Wegerif, R. (2000) *Thinking Together: A Programme of Activities for Developing Speaking, Listening and Thinking Skills for Children 8–11*. Birmingham: Imaginative Minds.

Dawes, L. and Sams, C. (2003) *Talk Box: Speaking and Listening Activities for Learning at Key Stage 1*. London: David Fulton Publishers.

Education Department of South Australia (2004) *Oral Language Developmental Continuum*. Rigby-Heinemann.

Education Department of South Australia (2004) *Oral Language Resource Book*. Melbourne: Rigby-Heinemann.

Grugeon, E., Dawes, L., Smith, C. and Hubbard, L. (eds) (2005) *Teaching Speaking and Listening in the Primary School* (3rd edn). London: David Fulton Publishers.

Hodson, P. and Jones, D. (eds) (2006) *Unlocking Speaking and Listening*. London: David Fulton Publishers.

Useful websites

Classroom Discourse Project
www.griffith.edu.au/school/cls/clearinghouse /content_1998_classroom.html.

BBC Voices website (www.bbc.co.uk/voices/).

Appendix 1

Complete text of 'Evacuee', in *The Quest for Peace*, by Edith Pickthall:

Evacuee

The slum had been his home since he was born;
And then war came and he was rudely torn
From all he'd ever known; and with his case
Of mean necessities, brought to a place
Of silences and space; just boom of sea
And sough of wind; small wonder then that he
Crept out one night to seek his sordid slum,
And thought to find his way. By dawn he'd come
A few short miles; and cattle in their herds
Gazed limpidly as he trudged by, and birds
Just stirring in first light, awoke to hear
His lonely sobbing, born of abject fear
Of sea and hills and sky; of silent night
Unbroken by the sound of shout and fight.

(Edith Pickthall)

'Sparks which make learning vivid': speaking, listening and drama

Colleen Johnson

Aiden:	*'Miss, are we doing drama after play?'*
Teacher:	*'We certainly are.'*
Class 4J:	*'Yesss!'*

Introduction

It was the start of playtime and already the children were looking forward to coming back into the classroom to get on with their work. As teachers we know the importance of motivation in learning. Children are often highly inspired by their involvement in both creating and reflecting upon drama. Fleming (1994:3) suggests that 'drama's motivational force...harnesses the inclination to play...'. If this inclination can be used to promote learning, then a powerful argument for the place of drama in the primary curriculum is offered. Could moments of drama in the classroom provide those 'sparks which make learning vivid' (DfES 2003b)'?[1]

There are many references to drama throughout the National Literacy Strategy (DfEE 1998). Indeed, the helpful 'Opportunities for drama in the framework of objectives' (DfES 1999a) offers a comprehensive list, citing a range of strategies applicable to promote all aspects of language learning. More recently, the subject's heightened status is there for all to see as a core strand in Speaking, Listening and Learning (DfES 2003a).[2] Major acceptability at last! This chapter considers some of the ways in which the subject can enhance children's learning, specifically in relation to language learning and literacy. The drama strategies used do not require specialist knowledge and the activities described illustrate ways in which drama can help teachers realise the objectives of these initiatives.

Why drama?

Drama is an art form in itself. All primary school children participate in dramatic performance, for example by taking part in and watching 'assemblies' and plays and by visiting the theatre and taking part in theatre-in-education visits to the school. Most see drama daily on television – soaps such as *Hollyoaks*, written specifically for a young audience. Children enjoy talking about what they have seen on television the night before.

Drama is a learning medium through which children can explore concepts and acquire knowledge and understanding. For example, to recreate historical events by working in role as archaeologists, identifying artefacts to discover more about how certain people lived, or as scientists conducting experiments on 'samples from the moon' as a means of learning more about minerals.

Drama is unique in that it enables teachers and children to create an unlimited variety of contexts: from the inside of the giant's castle at the top of the beanstalk to the Frank family's secret attic in Amsterdam; from the village post office to a space station on Mars. Children can explore these imagined worlds from within by engaging actively with specific aspects of a story or situation. They do this by empathising with the characters involved and exploring human behaviour in dilemmas that may well be beyond their own experiences, while being able to make connections with their own lives. Making these connections demands perception, imagination and interpretation (Johnson 1998).[3] By engaging in a dramatic situation, and then, out of role, reflecting upon that situation, the teacher and children are involved in a metacognitive process of imaginative thinking both individually and collectively (Johnson 2004).[4] Such experiences enhance learning across all areas of the primary curriculum. However, the focus of this chapter will be the role of drama in the teaching of language and literacy. Through drama we can create different contexts in which children experience diversity in language and through these experiences develop confidence in their own use of, and knowledge about, language. Such experiences enhance all language learning, including standard English and language study.

Drama, language and literacy

Good oral work enhances pupils' understanding of language in both oral and written forms and of the way language can be used to communicate (DfEE 1998:3).

The relationship between oracy (speaking and listening) and literacy (reading and writing) is central to language and literacy teaching. Talk is at the core of learning. The National Curriculum for Speaking and Listening (DfEE 1999b) and the Primary National Strategy (DfES 2003a) refer to developing talk for different purposes and audiences. When a teacher uses drama to create contexts for talk, the range of contexts, purposes and situations is without limit and the wide range of types of talk required will challenge children's creative use of language. Such approaches are characteristic of 'excellent teaching of speaking and listening' which 'enhances children's learning and raises standards further' (ibid).

Drama can give a purpose to reading and writing, requiring the children to interrogate, respond to and generate text. Having been engaged in dramatic activity to explore an aspect of a story aimed at predicting 'what comes next', children are encouraged to 'read on' in order to find out how their predictions match up with those of the writer. In addition, to develop understanding of a text written to be performed, children should have the opportunity to experience the text through performance, both their own and that of others.

The Primary National Strategy advocates whole-class, group and individual teaching that engage pupils in active learning. Drama can stimulate the best in whole-class teaching through discursive and interactive talk, fostered and modelled by the teacher, for example during shared text work and the plenary session of the Literacy Hour. Good quality independent group work can be maintained when such talk continues while the children are working without teacher support. Through drama, the teacher can create a context for exploratory talk, developing children's confidence in the expression of hypothesis and opinion.

Teaching strategies

All of the approaches to drama work described in this chapter took place in the *classroom*. This is particularly advantageous in schools where space is at a premium and it is difficult to have access to larger spaces such as the gym or hall for lessons other than PE. In addition, a drama activity that may not demand more than a few minutes can be highly beneficial in stimulating further reading or written work.[5] In this case, it is useful for the children to have near at hand the resources they will need, such as pens and books, and to be able to get to work immediately at their tables.

Still image

This strategy requires children to organise themselves into creating a three-dimensional image to represent a dramatic moment or a visual 'summing up' of a situation. Children are already familiar with the convention of the still image under many guises: for example, a pause on a video is a 'freeze-frame', or they may have played 'musical statues', or sequenced a story using cartoon strips and added captions to 'snapshots'. (See also the use of 'still image' in Chapter 3.)

For the teacher with little or no experience of drama, this is one of the most accessible approaches. It is useful as a control device, as a point of focus at the start of a lesson when recapping what has gone on before and as a safe way of presenting a moment of aggression or violence in a story; for example the moment in Shakespeare's *Macbeth* when the hero is slain by Macduff. It enables the teacher to 'slow down' the pace of a narrative and examine a key incident in detail. It does not require a lot of space, nor is it usually a 'noisy' activity. It is immediate and, because of a limitation of time, the children must work quickly and with concentration.

A Year 3 class had been reading a story about Krishna and the Hydra, where a young boy saved a village from the sea monster by dancing on its many heads. The teacher stopped reading the story at the moment when Krishna walked to the water's edge, watched by the villagers.

Teacher: *'If we could put a picture in the book to illustrate this scene, what would it look like?'*

One child volunteered to be Krishna and came to stand at the front, in the middle, facing towards the class. One by one, children put up their hands to join the image. After each had taken her or his place, the teacher asked the children to look at the image to see how it was changing and to think about where they might put themselves within it. She 'froze' the image once seven or eight children were in place. Then she introduced a second drama strategy.

Thought tracking

The teacher invited those in the still image to contribute the thoughts of the characters they were representing, one at a time:

Teacher: *'At that moment I thought to myself...'*

She moved around the image, touching each child on the shoulder, inviting them to speak:

First villager: *'He must be mad!'*

Second villager: *'He'll be eaten up!'*

Krishna: *'It's now or never.'*

Another way of combining these strategies would be to have those in the audience volunteer the thoughts of individuals already in the image. This makes an already active learning situation even more interactive. Additionally, the audience could be asked to invent a caption to go with the image; those watching are in the best place to do this as they see the complete picture.

The teacher went one step further with this strategy. She asked all the children, those *in* role and those *out of* role, in turn, to predict what might happen next. The predictions of those in the still image – most said that Krishna would perish – were considerably gloomier than those of the children watching. The teacher invited the children, out of role, to consider why this might be so. Discussion focused upon the children knowing that stories about Krishna as a child always ended happily because 'we know he grew up to be a god, so he must have been OK'. Out of role, the children knew that all would end happily. In role, however, as the villagers, the children experienced the immediacy of the moment when lives were held in the balance. As the thought tracking exercise had shown, most of the 'villagers' had no confidence in the ability of a young boy to defeat a powerful monster.

The still image approach, once modelled by the teacher with the whole class, is useful for children to use for themselves independently of the teacher. For example, children in groups can be asked to choose the most significant part of a chapter in a story and then to create a still image to represent this, to present to the rest of the class. This involves highly focused discussion as the children negotiate meaning and how to convey their interpretation to an audience. It is more fruitful, and less time-consuming, to have an image to interpret than a short improvisation as children have been required to 'crystallise to the essence' (Baldwin 1991)[6] the significant moments of the narrative. The image created by a group will represent two things: a key moment or event and the quality of learning achievable through exploratory talk. The approach demands group discussion and interaction – a core objective of 'Speaking, Listening and Learning' (DfES 2003a) that has direct links with the Literacy Strategy.[7]

The teacher could use the still image to stimulate collaborative written work, for example by asking children to write a short piece of dialogue suggested by the image produced. In this case it would be helpful to have the children's chairs set up in a 'double horseshoe' arrangement. Two rows of chairs are placed in the shape of a horseshoe, with desks between them, leaving a space in the middle for 'performance'. When the children are required to work in pairs, the children on the front row turn around and work with those behind.

Teacher and children in role

The range of questioning which a teacher is able to use is significantly expanded if the teacher uses the strategy of working *in role,* an approach which enhances the power of teacher talk in the scaffolding of children's understanding. In a Year 1 classroom, to support a theme of shops, services and dealing with money, the role-play area was set up as a post office with stationery, stamps, receipts, TV licences and a till with money. The children were involved in the sorts of activities that they may have observed in high street post offices and other shops.

They were highly motivated by having 'real' objects with which to work. A context for the role-play itself was established where the children were already happily playing spontaneously. The teacher was watching a small group at work and after a while entered the post office as a customer:

> Teacher: *'Can you help me? I need to send a letter to India.'*

The 'counter assistants' gave her an airmail letter.

> Teacher: *'This envelope is different to those. [pointing to ordinary weight stationery] Why is that?'*

Some assistants talked about the need for air mail stationery to be lighter than that for surface mail, and identified the colour (usually blue) and the stripes. They discussed the cost in relation to weight.

> Teacher: *'Why is it more expensive to send a letter abroad?'*

The assistants may already have the answer, or, with careful questioning, the teacher can develop their reasoning and help them to make the connection between transporting something by plane, which would suggest long-distance travel, the number of people involved in the process and so on.

> Teacher: *'Can you help me read my list? I've left my glasses at home.'*

An assistant reads the list out loud. Other activities which are taking place in the post office, exploiting opportunities for literacy and numeracy, include letter writing, stocktaking, having to write an order for more stock and sorting and redirecting mail.

By intervening in role the teacher gained the opportunity both to assess and extend the pupils' learning by:

- questioning the children to assess their current state of understanding;
- giving them opportunities to use subject-specific language, such as lighter/heavier, cheaper/dearer, even subtotal/total;
- scaffolding their understanding (as in the questioning about the cost of sending mail abroad);
- differentiating, supporting and extending the children's understanding where appropriate; and
- giving a purpose to reading and writing in the role-play area and even adding a sense of urgency with her 'time limit'.

Teachers do not need to spend much time playing in role but brief interventions such as these can serve to increase the quality of the play and the learning that is derived from it.

Hot seating

This activity usually takes place with the children seated on the floor with one or two chairs placed in front of them, as in the Literacy Hour.

A Year 2 class had been reading a version of the story of Goldilocks and the Three Bears. The teacher asked the children if they would like to interrogate Goldilocks about her visit to the bears' home. She could have played the part herself as *teacher in role* but instead asked for a volunteer to play Goldilocks who would sit on a chair placed centrally, or the *hot seat*. The children questioned Goldilocks about her actions, what her intentions had been and what she felt about the distress she had caused.

There are several variations to this technique that can be chosen to fit the levels of confidence of particular groups of children. The teacher can begin, as Goldilocks, to help establish the role and then can ask for a child to take over the role. After a short while, the teacher can swap another child into the role and onto the *hot seat*. This adds to the level of interaction, and can help keep the drama from flagging while relieving any one child of the pressure of having to maintain the role for too long. There may be two or more *hot seats* with more characters, for example, in this case, Goldilocks and her mother, as responses from one character may elicit a question from the children for the other. The *hot seat* can be left empty and children can offer randomly the character's responses to questions. Further discussion is possible when conflicting answers are offered, with the teacher asking individuals to say why they believe that the character would answer in that way.

This approach encourages children to listen carefully as they need to build their questions onto what has already been said. Also, they hear the teacher and other children framing effective questions and this helps them to develop their own. Teaching children to listen permeates the National Curriculum for English, with children's ability to pay attention being a central feature of the shared and group elements of the Literacy Hour. Listening is another of the four core objectives which permeate 'Speaking, Listening and Learning'[8] (see also Chapter 7).

Mantle of the expert

In the simplest form of this technique, pioneered by Dorothy Heathcote,[9] the children take on the role of experts whose knowledge and experience are greater than those of the *teacher in role*. When children wear the mantle of the expert, the roles of teacher and child are temporarily reversed. The child is the 'one in the know', who has the expertise, understanding and experience, with the teacher being the 'one who needs to know', seeking clarification, advice and help. While all in this process are aware that they are simply acting, this reversal of status adds a fruitful new teaching and learning strategy to the repertoire.

When tied into a topic that the children have been studying, an opportunity is provided for the use of subject-specific knowledge and language and for the teacher to assess the levels of understanding achieved. For example, a Year 4 class had been studying the Vikings. When the children entered the classroom for their drama lesson the desks had been pushed back, chairs had been placed in a circle, and on a table in the middle was a small collection of dusty looking objects. The children sat down in the circle. The *teacher in role* introduced herself as a local historian, who addressed the children as:

> the world's leading experts on Viking settlements. It is a great honour to welcome you to this important meeting. During a preliminary investigation of a site being cleared for building work by a developer, these artefacts have been discovered and we believe that they may suggest the presence of a Viking settlement.

Here the teacher is using language with which the children might not be familiar. They are being addressed as adults and 'experts'. She is modelling formal language by using standard English appropriate to the situation, which helps to underline the serious nature of the enquiry. Children in role as experts respond with the language that they believe to be appropriate to the situation. As each offers suggestions and advice, there is confidence and authority in their speech.

The items were passed around carefully and the 'experts' conferred with each other:

Teacher: *'Could you advise us on how to conduct an investigation of the site and what we should be looking for?'*

A sense of urgency was added:

Teacher: *'We only have a week. Builders will begin work on the site after that.'*

The children began to talk to each other, still in role:

Maria: *'The builders will have to stop work.'*

Jamil: *'They will damage the ruins.'*

Teacher: *'How can we stop them?'*

Paris: *'We will get the police.'*

Jamil: *'I'll phone the government.'*

Out of role, the teacher and children reflected on the learning which had taken place. She drew attention to the language they had used in order to play the parts convincingly. Encouraging constructive criticism, she asked leading questions such as:

'In our drama, what worked well and why?'

Children commented on each others' roles, how what had been spoken and the way it had been said made the drama believable: a metacognitve process implicit in the cycle of making, performing and responding which demonstrates the importance of reflection in drama.

Generating text

Drama can provide children with a variety of contexts in which to write for a range of purposes and audiences. It is a vehicle both for demonstrating and extending understanding.

Writing in role

Taking the Viking stimulus further, an emphasis was placed on the investigation running out of time, so a campaign was launched to halt the building work for a while. The children looked at a variety of newspaper articles and then produced their own about the archaeological investigation in styles appropriate to a particular type of media. There were 'sensational' reports for the tabloids, exploiting the children's knowledge and use of alliteration. Thirty-second scripts were written for radio and television coverage, the range and style of writing needing to match with the type of programme. For example, some 'reporters' attempted to write serious, factual accounts of the campaign for the *BBC Nine O'Clock News* and Weather, others for Channel 4's *The Big Breakfast* news slot, whose coverage features sensational language similar to that typifying tabloid front page journalism, rich in alliteration and 'catchy' phrases:

Newsreader: *Good morning. Hot sounds from under the ground. There's a to-do at Sutton Hoo. The archaeologists are up in arms and down in the dumps about the crafty contractors creeping onto their dig to build homes on some old bones. (Michaela, aged 8)*

A group of children wrote a script for a short item on the campaign for *Blue Peter*, tailoring their writing to suit a 'younger' age group with a more limited understanding of archaeological issues. As a result, the children were learning about genre and writing for a variety of audiences.

Scribing

To extend the potential for writing that can be obtained through drama, the whole class, *in role*, could write with the teacher acting as scribe. This activity has a number of benefits:

- the teacher models the writing and thereby shows the correct style;
- the teacher and children compose collaboratively;
- as they refine and edit, the children are having to pay close attention to both the composition and transcription elements of the text;
- the teacher can provide differentiation in a number of ways: for example, by targeting specific children with different questions, reading the text aloud with those who lack confidence, and so on;
- children who might only manage one or two tortured lines unaided are able to contribute to the whole text; and
- most children will feel a sense of achievement from having contributed to the composition of a piece of writing which is of a higher standard of work than would have been possible if they had been working on their own or with a group of peers.

The children of a Year 3 class, as citizens of Hamelin, had sent letters to the local council to complain about the growing rat problem. A 'letter' had come back to them all saying that 'as only a small number of you are affected' the council did not think it to be a serious problem. Children as individuals, groups or the whole class respond very positively to letters written to them within the context of drama. That they should have been sent a reply reflects the 'seriousness' of their endeavour and, assuming they know that it is the teacher who has produced the letter, shows them that their work is respected and taken seriously by her or him.

The 'citizens', with the teacher as scribe, decided to send a communal letter, with a forceful message:

Dear Mayor,

We are ALL very serious about this rat problem, not just a few of us. We're fed up with it. Please will you do something about it? We have to keep our children in the house. They can't go out to play in case the rats get them. How would you like it?

Rats spread diseases. If we are ill, we don't go to work. Then who will work for you? No-one!

Take a trip to other cities. See how they keep rats out and ask them to tell you how to do it.

Don't forget, we voted for you. It's your job to look after us. If you don't ,we won't vote for you again.

Clear up our city before it's too late.

Yours sincerely,

The citizens of Hamelin

Once the children had gone through the process, aided by the teacher, of composing, refining and editing the letter, the teacher wrote it out and brought it back into the classroom for the children to sign, which they did with pride. Drama had given a sense of purpose to their work and enhanced their understanding of how to write effectively in a persuasive style.

The quality of learning within independent group work is enhanced when children have experienced whole-class teaching such as this, based on teacher modelling, discussion and interaction, maximising their potential for exploratory talk. The guidelines for English in the National Curriculum identify that for group discussion and interaction to be successful, children should:

(a) take turns in speaking and listening;

(b) relate their contributions to what has gone on before;

(c) take different views into account;

(d) extend their ideas in the light of the discussion;

(e) give reasons for opinions and actions.

(DfEE 1999b)

Children of a Year 5 class, in the role of detectives, were investigating the disappearance of a teenage boy. The classroom was set out as normal, with children seated in their groups around tables. This suited the layout of an 'incident room', with groups of detectives working together on the case. After an initial briefing by the co-ordinator of the investigation (*teacher in role*) the detectives (assuming the *mantle of the expert*) were shown possible clues surrounding the case to date, which included a note purportedly written by the boy, a letter he had received the day prior to his disappearance, a train ticket and a brief statement from his mother. Through group discussion, the teams were to come up with a possible scenario and suggestions for ways forward with the investigation, including a plan of action. The activity involved them in both reading and writing in role. Each group had to prepare their findings in the format of a brief report to be fed back to the whole group in the plenary (Wray and Lewis 1997:10).

Groups of children working in role demonstrated a sense of purpose and clear awareness of each other's function. They listened and argued with the respect appropriate to the 'expert' part they were playing, assessing evidence, responding to the thoughts and opinions of others and taking into account different views, while having to justify their own.

Eavesdropping

The teacher interrupted the groups as they worked:

Teacher: *'Remember the point in the discussion you have just reached. Let's listen to each group of experts as they discuss the case.'*

She allowed time for groups to recap and then asked for silence. She moved around, pausing for a minute or so by each group, which was the signal for that group to resume their discussion, loud enough for everyone else to hear. When all groups had presented their 'snapshots', she asked questions of everyone, based on what they had just heard:

Teacher: *'Which groups were thinking along the same lines in their theories of what had happened? What were the main areas for disagreement for this group?'*

The strategy of eavesdropping, accompanied by teacher questioning, is highly focused and constitutes a brief interruption that allows time to observe everyone's work. It brings together work in which the whole class is engaged, in this case, heightening the dramatic tension and purpose of an incident room. It also reinforces the need to listen to each other and gives children the opportunity to hear others engaging in exploratory talk, sometimes working with unfamiliar language. The teacher did not need to monitor the groups closely. This was high quality and largely independent oral work, but they would not have been able to achieve this had they not learned to work in this way with the teacher in previous lessons.

Drama and text

All the strategies described so far can be used to help children interrogate text, such as the use of still image to represent key moments in a chapter, slowing down the narrative, especially with texts that are plot-driven; hot seating characters and role-playing events which contribute to the sub-plot of a story and writing in role.

The empathy/understanding dimension of drama work is inevitably stimulated through texts of one sort or another. Therefore, drama can be used to aid understanding at text level as envisaged in the Literacy Hour. For example, the children in a Year 6 class were reading *The Diary of Anne Frank* as part of a topic on the 1930s. In using drama strategies to explore the text, the intended learning outcomes were that the children would:

- interrogate a text 'with challenging subject matter that broadens perspectives and extends thinking' (DfEE 1999b);
- gain a perspective about a historical issue; and
- reflect upon their own responses to change.

Like Anne at the start of her diary, the children were approaching puberty. Some were anxious about the transition to secondary school. One girl was a Bosnian refugee who had recently joined the school. The safe context of the story helped the children explore and reflect upon the anxieties they were experiencing about changes taking place in their own lives.

An initial improvisation coincided with the time when the class had reached the part of the diary where Anne describes the family's preparations for going into hiding. The children, working in role and in groups which represented families or flatmates, were asked to make decisions about which of their possessions they would take with them if they were asked to go into hiding. Part way through the improvisations, the teacher interrupted to ask them to imagine that each group had been given a large cardboard box which, due to lack of space, was all they would be allowed to take with them. By these means extra pressure was put on the children to argue, discuss, prioritise and ultimately compromise on their original list.

Some 'families' agreed to scale down what they would take in terms of size and quantity of objects. Some members had chosen to take a lock of hair, pictures of loved ones, letters, and gifts given to them by friends they might never see again. They listened attentively to each other. The atmosphere was one of sustained concentration, mutual respect and a communal sadness at leaving their homes.

This activity, conducted in groups, with little or no intervention from the teacher, demonstrates ways in which drama contributes to creating and sustaining purpose for independent group discussion and interaction. In this lesson, group talk featured through taking turns in speaking and listening, taking different views into account with sympathy and understanding, extending ideas in the light of discussion and giving reasons for opinions and actions. Such activities promote oral work that is discursive and interactive, a significant aim of the National Literacy Strategy. The teacher asked the children if this moment had reminded them of any time in their own lives which they were invited to share with the rest of the class. Their responses included moving house, leaving an area, saying goodbye to a grandparent going home to India, coming home from holidays, hiding in a bomb shelter in Kuwait and leaving friends made while away.

While it is possible to plan a drama activity and identify clear learning outcomes, the teacher cannot know what personal response the drama may generate. In this instance, the experience had provided a vehicle for the children to put into words their own emotional response to events that they may never have discussed before. The children were learning to empathise both with characters as well as with each other. At the end of the lesson, the teacher invited the children to reflect upon the quality of the exploratory talk that they had achieved in their groups and the way in which such talk enhanced their learning and understanding; a metacognitive process stimulated by engagement in, and reflection upon, drama.

Some of the drama work on the Anne Frank story had stimulated writing *in role*: diary entries of different characters, letters from hiding, letters sent from outside to those *in* hiding, giving news of events, some even written in elaborate codes. They all displayed and extended understanding of the issues the children explored through the drama. Of equal importance is reflective writing *out of role*, articulating thoughts and emotions that arise through dramatic engagement with a text, demonstrating empathy and conveying this to an audience. As Naomi, aged 11, commented, 'I think that people who are witnessing a war, losing friends and family and homes can never recover. For this must be like a knife cutting through their lives.' The children were finally engaged in the process of moving from improvisation to performance in that they prepared a piece of drama to present during a whole-school assembly.

Reading text aloud

When working with text, children should be encouraged to read aloud, with expression, characterisation and pace, as modelled by the teacher. This approach is of particular significance in the shared reading aspect of the Literacy Hour. In this way most teachers, when reading or telling stories to their classes, incorporate drama to some degree in their delivery, changing their voices with volume, tone and pitch, adopting accents, using facial expression, establishing eye contact with the 'audience', all of which enhance enjoyment and understanding. Children will then develop awareness of how meaning can be both illuminated and altered by the ways in which text is spoken, and their listening skills, as well as their understanding, can be developed in this way. Text which was written to be performed should be lifted from the page and heard, encouraging 'attentive listening and response'.[10] But how is a teacher to manage reading aloud a play text written for a small number of speakers, with a class of 30 or more?

With a script written for two characters, the class can be divided into two lines facing each other. Everyone is given a copy of the text. All those in one line play part A and all those in the other, part B. Begin with the first pair and move down the lines as the script progresses. Come back to the first pair and continue until the script is finished. The teacher, or a child, reads stage directions. In this way, everyone will need to concentrate on following the text, to look ahead for their turn, and all of the children will speak. There will be a variety of delivery. When the text has been read through once, with difficult or unusual words being identified and discussed, teachers can ask a range of questions, all of which will require the children to re-examine the text or to reflect on what they have heard.

They can ask children to consider directions, pauses and actions that will add or enhance meaning: how, for example, speaking the text with an angry, sad, happy or frightened vocal expression can create a different context and meaning. Again, working in groups, using just a part of the whole text, children could plan and rehearse their own version of it to be performed to the rest of the class.

Understanding a challenging, dramatical text

Classical texts can be used, even with very young children. Shakespeare, for example, is challenging to all, adults and children alike, and of those people going to see a performance of one of Shakespeare's plays very few will have a thorough understanding of the language used. However, carefully selected short scenes and speeches can provide highly enjoyable dramatic experiences in the classroom. Drama objectives within Speaking, Listening and Learning frequently require children to perform, and to 'engage the interest of the audience' (DfES 2003a).[11] To this end, here are some examples of the ways in which teachers could work with excerpts in the primary school.

> Be not afear'd: the isle is full of noises. Sounds,
> and sweet airs, that give delight and hurt not.
> Sometimes a thousand twangling instruments will
> hum about mine ears, and sometimes voices,
> that, if I then had waked after long sleep,
> Will make me sleep again: and then, in dreaming,
> The clouds methought would open and show riches
> Ready to drop on me, that, when I waked,
> I cried to dream again.
>
> The Tempest, Act III, Scene 2: Caliban's speech

Activities: Suitable for Key Stages 1 and 2

Whole class
- Read through together, aloud.
- Identify difficult words.
- Question children about possible meanings of unusual words and phrases.
- Read through, singing the word which precedes punctuation.
- Read through, kicking up a balloon or scarf at the end of each phrase.
- Allot each child a phrase (each will be spoken by at least two children).

- Place chairs all around the room to represent trees in a forest; each child stands behind a chair and when it is that child's turn to speak their phrase s/he must do so while running from one 'tree' to another.

- Discuss ways in which children may, additionally, animate their phrase. For example: hopping/skipping/singing/doing a cartwheel and so on. As two speak the phrase at the same time, co-ordinate how it is to be done.

- Heighten the sense of drama by suggesting that in the trees are monkeys with custard pies. As the speakers leave the shelter of their 'tree' they may have to dodge the custard pies being hurled at them!

> When shall we three meet again?
> In thunder, lightning, or in rain?
> When the hurly burly's done.
> When the battle's lost and won.
> That will be ere the set of sun.
> Where the place?
> Upon the heath.
> There to meet with Macbeth.
> Fair is foul, and foul is fair:
> Hover through the fog and filthy air.
>
> Macbeth, Act I, Scene 1: The Three Witches (adapted)

This is one of the shortest scenes written and it is highly charged because it is the dramatic opening scene and involves the supernatural.

Activities suitable for Key Stages 1 and 2

Whole class

- Seat the children in a circle.
- Set the scene for the 'blasted heath' by discussing what the place would look like. Possibly there will be trees, bushes, ditches, fog and marsh. What would we hear in this place? Build up the atmosphere by asking the children, one at a time, around the circle, to add their sounds to create a *soundscape*. 'Conduct' the soundscape, bringing volume up and down and cueing parts of the circle. Hand over the job of conductor to one of the children.
- Read through the scene together.

Group work

- Divide the class into small groups. Each group will be given a phrase. Brainstorm different ways the words may be delivered, e.g. whispering, echoing each other, varying pitch and volume, singing and so forth.
- Groups should be given time to rehearse.

Whole class

- Go through the scene, each group performing their phrase in turn.
- Discuss 'what worked well and why' and possible refinements.
- Repeat performance.
- Recap on the soundscape.
- Rehearse, performing the text over the soundscape.
- Add refinements, such as deciding when the volume of the soundscape should be raised/lowered.
- Give the final 'performance'.

Lady Macbeth:

Yet here's a spot

Out, damned spot! Out, I say!
One, two; why then 'tis time to do it.
Hell is murky.
Fie, my lord, fie! A soldier and afear'd?
What need we fear who knows it, when none can call our power to account?
Yet who would have thought the old man to have so much blood in him?
The Thane of Fife had a wife; where is she now?
What, will these hands ne'er be clean?
No more o' that, my lord, no more o' that; you mar all with this starting.
Here's the smell of the blood still.
All the perfumes of Arabia will not sweeten this little hand.
Oh, oh, oh!
Wash your hands, put on your nightgown, look not so pale.
I tell you again, Banquo's buried; he cannot come out on's grave.
To bed, to bed; there's knocking at the gate.
Come, come, come, come, give me your hand.
What's done cannot be undone.
To bed, to bed, to bed.

Macbeth, Act V, Scene 1: Sleepwalking (adapted)

145

Activities suitable for Key Stage 2

Whole class

- Cut the text into strips – one line per strip.
- Seat the children in a circle.
- Allot lines, randomly around the circle so that each child has one.
- Set the context by reading a description of the sleepwalking scene.
- Choose a child to represent Lady Macbeth.
- Lady Macbeth walks around and across the inside of the circle. Each child she passes speaks her/his line (sometimes the lines will overlap).
- Discuss 'what worked well and why' in relation to individual delivery, combination of lines, and so on. Refine: 'How can we improve upon the performance of the scene?' Possibly add a *soundscape*.
- Read through again, with added effects.
- Tape record the scene, as if making a radio drama.
- Ask, 'Where have we come across these lines before – to which parts of the plot do they refer?'

Extension: (some children may search text of play using a Macbeth CD-ROM)

Group work

- Give each group an envelope containing a complete set of lines, cut into strips.
- Ask the groups to attempt to put their lines in the order in which they think they were written.
- Plenary: compare and contrast versions. Look at copies of scene as written, including other characters.
- Compare with an earlier speech of Lady Macbeth, in verse. Why did Shakespeare choose to write this final speech of Lady Macbeth in prose?

Conclusion

In the examples of classroom practice which have been discussed in this chapter, it is evident that drama:

- has a unique contribution to make in the teaching of speaking and listening;
- has potential for literacy learning;
- offers a range of strategies applicable to text level work;
- is a vehicle for imaginative response to, and generation of, text;
- helps children gain an understanding of the deeper meanings in books;
- stimulates enquiry;
- builds confidence; and
- promotes discursive, exploratory talk, which is a significant aim of the National Primary Strategies for Literacy, Speaking, Listening and Learning, particularly in fostering independent group work, group discussion and interaction.

In adopting drama approaches, not only is the teacher enhancing her/his repertoire of teaching strategies, but the children are learning many skills which will contribute to their development as independent learners, not just in literacy and language learning, but also across the curriculum. Teachers must embrace the subject's welcome heightened status. We should all be saying 'Yesss!' to drama.

Notes

1. The DfES (2003b) encourages teachers to be creative and innovative in their teaching in order to foster *Excellence and Enjoyment* in children's learning processes.
2. *The Primary National Strategy: Speaking, Listening, Learning* (DfES 2003a) identifies best classroom practice in fostering talk in the classroom. Drama can provide a range of strategies for this purpose.
3. The author, cited in J. Bowden and F. Marton (1998), explores children's thinking when generating and shaping drama to convey meaning to an audience.
4. The author (2004) explores this process further in relation to strategies that help promote children's creative and critical thinking.
5. The author (2002) explores further drama's potential to stimulate, and enhance the quality of, children's written work, in Williams, M. (ed.) (2002) *Unlocking Writing: A Guide for Teachers,* (London: David Fulton Publishers).
6. An expression coined by P. Baldwin (1991) to represent the process of negotiating meaning children undergo when creating a 'still image'.
7. *The Primary National Strategy: Speaking, Listening, Learning* (DfES 2003a), Year 4 Term 1, Objective 40, Drama: to comment constructively on performance, discussing effects and how they are achieved. This links with NLS text objectives 5, 6 and 13.

8. *The Primary National Strategy:* Speaking, Listening and Learning (DfES 2003a), Year 2 Term 1, objective 14, Listening: to listen to others in class, ask relevant questions views and follow instructions.
9. D. Heathcote and G. Bolton (1995) explore the 'mantle of the expert' approach.
10. D. Wray and M. Lewis (1997) advocate giving children the opportunity to explore formal and abstract writing through preparing reports.
11. *The Primary National Strategy: Speaking Listening and Learning* (DfES 2003a), Year 6 Term 3, objective 67, Drama: to devise a performance considering how to adapt the performance for a specific audience.

References

Baldwin, P. (1991) *Stimulating Drama – Cross-curricular Approaches to Drama in the Primary School.* Norwich: Norfolk County Council.

Bowden, J. and Marton, F. (1998) *The University of Learning.* London: Kogan Page.

DfEE (1998) *The National Literacy Strategy: Framework for Teaching.* London: HMSO.

DfES (1999a) *Opportunities for Drama in the Framework of Objectives.* London: HMSO.

DfEE (1999b) *English in the National Curriculum.* London: HMSO.

DfES (2003a) *Primary National Strategy: Speaking, Listening and Learning: Working with Children in Key Stages 1 and 2.* London: QCA.

DfES (2003b) *Excellence and Enjoyment: A Strategy for Primary Schools.* London: QCA.

Fleming, M. (1994) *Starting Drama Teaching.* London: David Fulton Publishers.

Heathcote, D. and Bolton, G. (1995) *Drama for Learning: An Account of Dorothy Heathcote's 'Mantle of the Expert' Approach to Education.* Portsmouth, NH: Heinemann.

Johnson, C. (2002) 'Writing aloud: drama and writing', in Williams, M. (2002) *Unlocking Writing: A Guide for Teachers.* London: David Fulton Publishers.

Johnson, C. (2004) 'Creative drama: thinking from within', in Fisher, R. and Williams, M. (eds) *Unlocking Creativity: Teaching across the Curriculum.* London: David Fulton Publishers.

Wray, D. and Lewis, M. (1997) *Extending Literacy: Children Reading and Writing Non-fiction.* London: Routledge.

Children's literature

Frank, O. and Pressler, M. (eds) *Anne Frank's Diary.* Harmondsworth: Penguin.

Garfield, L. (1988) *Shakespeare Stories.* London: Heinemann.

Garfield, L. and Foreman, M. (1985) *Shakespeare Stories.* London: Victor Gollancz.

Further reading

Clipson-Boyles, S. (1998) *Drama in Primary English Teaching.* London: David Fulton Publishers.

Gibson, R. (2001) *Stepping into Shakespeare.* Cambridge: Cambridge University Press.

Hendy, L. and Toon, L. (2001) *Supporting Drama and Imaginative Play in the Early Years.* Buckingham: Open University Press.

O'Neill, C. (1995) *Drama Worlds.* Portsmouth, NH: Heinemann.

Pollard, A. (1997) *Reflective Teaching in the Primary School.* London: Cassell.

Winston, J. (2000) *Drama, Literacy and Moral Education.* London: David Fulton Publishers.

Winston, J. and Tasndy, M. (2001) *Beginning Drama 4–11* (2nd edn). London: David Fulton Publishers.

Woolland, B. (1993) *The Teaching of Drama in the Primary School*. Harlow: Longman.

Useful websites/CD-Roms

BBC (1996) Shakespeare's *Macbeth*. London: BBC Education/HarperCollins.

The National Journal of Drama (www.nationaldrama.co.uk)

QCA Creativity: Find it, Promote it, (www.ncaction.org.uk/creativity)

Sparks that make learning vivid

CHAPTER 9

'Where am I going?': planning and assessing progress in literacy

Deborah Jones

Assessment helps me know where I'm going.

(Robena, aged 10)

Introduction

Assessment and planning are inextricably linked. As Robena has noticed, knowing what we have achieved and how well we have achieved it enables us to plan for the future and to map out the way ahead. This process is at the heart of effective teaching and learning. Planning, teaching, learning and assessing form a cycle with each aspect being bound up with the other, so that they are, in a sense, interdependent. Planning must be based on what children can actually do, as awareness of their knowledge, skills and understanding is integral to effective further teaching. Language pervades the curriculum; therefore the assessment of literacy is of fundamental importance. Accurate assessment can be a powerful motivator for both teachers and children as they see what has been achieved and are enabled to plan the next learning steps. What is good practice in the assessment of literacy applies to assessment in any aspect of the curriculum. The aim of this chapter is to consider the role of assessment in planning and teaching literacy and to show how the use of a variety of strategies can catapult children forward in their thinking and learning.

National Curriculum assessment has undergone many changes since its introduction. Each year, handbooks of guidance (DfES 2005) are published by the Qualifications and Currirculum Authority (QCA), laying down the statutory assessment requirements for each Key Stage.[1] Currently, in literacy, children are required to undergo both standardised assessments and teacher assessments for the Programmes of Study 'Reading' and 'Writing', but teacher assessment only for 'Speaking and Listening'. Recent documentation (DfES 2003) provides brief guidelines for the assessment of Speaking and Listening at Key Sta

There have been several important influences on the way a approached. As a result of extensive research, Black and Wiliam (19 five key factors that improve learning through assessment:

- the provision of effective feedback to pupils;
- the active involvement of pupils in their own learning;
- adjusting teaching according to assessment results;
- recognising the huge influence assessment has on pupil self-esteem and motivation; and
- the need for pupils to be able to assess themselves and understand how to improve.[3]

In 2002, the Assessment Reform Group produced 'Assessment for Learning: 10 Principles'.[4] In addition, QCA 'Assessment for Learning' materials have been provided for teacher support. An important distinction has been made... 'assessment *for* Learning' being defined as 'the process of using classroom assessment to improve learning, whereas assessment *of* learning is the measurement of what children can do'.[5] All these initiatives have impacted on how assessment in schools is perceived and carried out.

Assessment – power and mystique

Assessment is a powerful force as its results are used to categorise individuals. The process starts at a very young age and culminates with the award of various qualifications that can ultimately decide the course of adult lives. For some, assessment is viewed positively; for others it is something to be endured or, at worst, something to be feared. Individual teachers and whole schools are held accountable for the standards they achieve, as is evidenced in published league tables in which assessment has a crucial part to play. Results have been used by both government and media and are often at the centre of disputes about falling standards. The equally hot topic of *poor standards in literacy* has been in the press for a long time. Therefore, mixing literacy and assessment together makes an explosive cocktail! There seems to be little in common between teachers' views and those of the wider public. Why is this? Could it be that as a profession we have perpetuated a mystique surrounding our knowledge of teaching literacy and our knowledge of assessment? There are many doors to be unlocked concerning the assessment of literacy and the main aim of this chapter is to examine ways of sharing this knowledge with parents and children, so dispelling this mystique in order to create effective partnerships with all concerned in the education of the child.

The purposes of assessment

> I did it because I had to. My records were complete and levels assigned –
> but I never quite got to grips with using them to help me plan really
> specifically.
>
> (Year 2 teacher)

Here, one teacher describes her experience of assessment. This is where we should start, as examining what we believe will influence our actions. Asking certain questions will be helpful in this – for instance, why are we assessing children? What are the real reasons for this? Clearly the purposes of assessment are many and varied. They include:

- to record progress;
- to diagnose particular difficulties;
- to provide feedback for parents;
- to inform planning and teaching;
- to comply with legal requirements;
- to be accountable to outside bodies;
- to help children learn; and
- to gauge how effective teaching has been.

It is a useful exercise to consider the reasons why we, as teachers, assess children and what the most important motivators are likely to be.

The principles of assessment

In order to guide our thinking and practice in assessing pupil progress the following principles can be identified. Assessment should be continuous, curricular, consultative and communicative. The importance of each of these will be considered in turn.

Assessment should be curricular

Traditional approaches to assessment have been one-shot procedures often bolted on to the curriculum but not integral to it. End-of-term examinations and isolated tests characterise this approach. The Task Group for Assessment and Testing (TGAT) (1987) stated that assessment should be an integral part of the curriculum and that it needs to take place within a strong context of meaning, as it is crucial that children make connections between what they are doing now and what they need to learn next.[6] The emphasis within the assessment for learning process underscores this: children should reflect on and review their performance with teachers. This is a joint venture.

Assessment should be continuous

If assessment is central to teaching and learning then it must be built into the daily routines of the classroom. It needs to provide both 'feedback' and 'feedforward', showing what children have achieved and how this will enable them to move on. If learning is a continuous process then assessment must be, too. Some traditional approaches have viewed assessment as occasional rather than continuous but this does not fit in with what we know about how children learn. It is essential that they are given several opportunities to show what they can do, as catching them on an off-day will do very little to help them move forward or to inform future teaching.

Assessment should be consultative

Teachers do not have exclusive knowledge of the child. Parents and carers have a wealth of information that can be drawn upon to support teaching and learning. We have all worked with children who exhibit completely different behaviours at home from those at school, and, discovering why this is can trigger a whole new range of approaches to teaching.

Assessment is not solely the domain of teachers, as other adults, for example volunteer reading helpers (when informed appropriately), can be used to note achievement and gather information. Central to this process, however, are the children themselves. Why should assessment be seen as the exclusive domain of the teacher? Conferencing with children to discover what they know and to elicit reflections on their learning can be a most powerful aspect of assessment.[7] Enabling parents, carers and children to contribute to this process is at the very heart of effective assessment. Cultivating such partnerships needs to be integral to both our practice and our thinking.

Assessment should be communicative

Similarly, if assessment is not the exclusive domain of the teacher, then methods of recording and the ways in which progress is discussed should be accessible to all. Therefore, letting parents and children in on the processes of assessment is vital, including setting up strategies in which all the parties concerned know what is being assessed and why. Results of assessments also need to be transparent – for example through avoiding jargon for non-professional audiences and by taking care to communicate in ways that are meaningful to all. (This will be discussed in more detail later.)

Think back to your own experiences of assessment:

- What are your earliest memories?
- What do you remember about assessment in school?
- What other types of assessment have you experienced outside of a school context?
- What feelings characterise your different experiences?
- Apply these four principles of assessment to your own reflections about yourself and to your classroom practice. How do they match up?

Methods of assessing literacy

The four principles above should underpin any form of assessment undertaken in schools and underlie the various methods of assessing literacy discussed below. Several different methods need to be used so that a range of evidence is collected relating to each child's achievements. These could include:

Methods of assessing writing

- National Curriculum criteria, as in the level descriptions
- Alternative criteria from other published sources
- Standardised Assessment Tests (SATs) materials
- Samples of children's writing
- Annotated samples of writing across a range of genres
- Developmental checklists
- Conferencing and self-assessment.

(See also Jones, D. 'Keeping track: assessment in writing', in Williams, M. (ed.) (2002) *Unlocking Writing*. London: David Fulton Publishers.)

Methods of assessing reading

- National Curriculum criteria as in the level descriptions
- Using the 'Framework of Objectives' of the National Literacy Strategy
- Alternative criteria from other published sources
- SATs materials

- Reading scheme levels
- Miscue analysis/running records
- Standardised reading tests
- Observation samples
- Book reviews
- Developmental checklists
- Conferencing and self-assessment.

Methods of assessing speaking and listening

- National Curriculum criteria as in the level descriptions
- Alternative criteria from other published sources
- Observation grids
- Developmental checklists
- Conferencing and self-assessment.

Examples of these methods are given below.

Using specific criteria is a common way of assessing children. Such criteria may be selected from the *English in the National Curriculum* (DfEE 1999) documentation.[8] The Primary Strategy Handbook, *Speaking, Listening and Learning* (DfES 2003), for example, provides formats for recording comments on the four aspects of Speaking and Listening.[9] Alternatively, the teacher may also identify her/his own criteria for a particular learning activity that the child can be assessed against. Developmental checklists may be used to record progress across each of the Programmes of Study for English.[10]

Observation grids or formats are a means of recording what a child is doing during a specific activity and provide evidence of the child's achievements at that time. The example in Figure 9.1 may also be used as a checklist/planner for individuals or groups.

Activities	Participants	Types of talk
	(e.g. pair, individual to group, individual to class)	

FIGURE 9.1 Speaking and listening checklist/planner

Speaking and listening may be assessed within any curriculum area and the observation grid in Figure 9.2 has been devised for this purpose.[11] While focusing on the chosen child, tick off those words around the edge which best describe this speaking and listening behaviour. This may then be written up in prose form in the 'record of observation' section and becomes evidence for the assessment of speaking and listening.

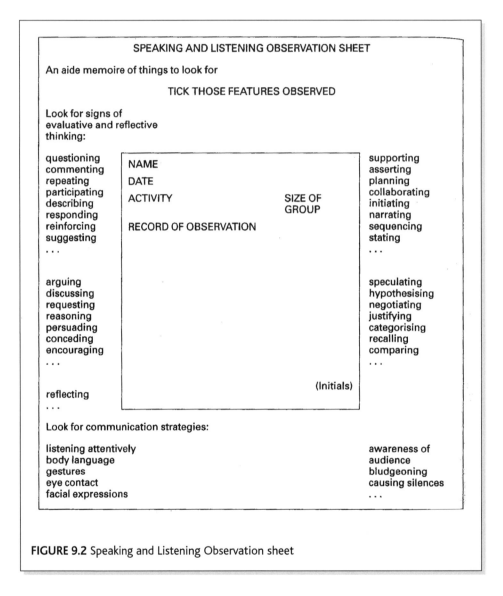

FIGURE 9.2 Speaking and Listening Observation sheet

Collecting a range of samples of children's work to be kept as evidence of achievement is most helpful, particularly when annotated so that their significance can be recalled at a later date (see Figure 9.3).

Name _____

Year group _____

Subject/Activity _____

Date _____

Activity: Individual   Pair
Group (Please circle)
Degree of Peer group support:
None 1 2 3 4 5 Much
Teacher support: None 1 2 3 4 5 Much

Description of writing
(audience, purpose, type, draft number etc.)

Child's own response to writing

FIGURE 9.3 Writing context sheet

In addition, book reviews may provide useful records of the child's reflective thinking about the content of a book (Figure 9.4).

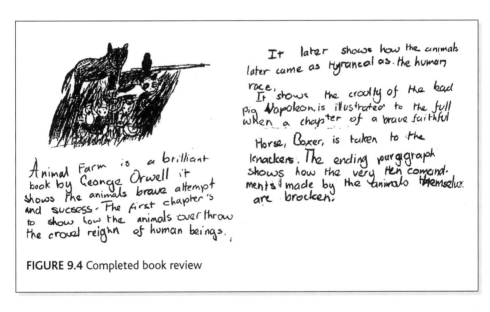

It later shows how the animals later came as tyranical as. the human race,
It shows the croolty of the bad pig Napoleon. is illustrated to the full when a chapter of a brave faithful Horse, Boxer, is taken to the knackers. The ending paragraph shows how the very teh comond. ments made by the animals themselve. are brocken.

Animal Farm is a brilliant book by George Orwell it shows the animals brave attempt and sucsess. The first chapter's to show how the animals over throw the croud reighn of human beings.

FIGURE 9.4 Completed book review

Literacy conferences (i.e. conversations about children's perceptions and abilities) with both parents and children may also be used to gather evidence for all aspects of language development.

Miscue analysis is a method by which the teacher analyses the child's miscues when reading a text aloud. This procedure, devised by Goodman[12] in 1973, has been simplified into the form of a running record. These approaches may be used with young children learning to read or with children experiencing reading difficulties. Useful insights may be gained into how a child decodes print that can inform future teaching in a specific and effective way.

At the end of each key stage, teachers are required by law to administer SATs for reading and writing that are used to determine levels of attainment for each child and these are communicated to their parents. For speaking and listening, the level is assessed by the teacher alone, so it is important that a range of assessment tools are used to ascertain children's achievement for this particular attainment target.

Teachers need to decide what is to be assessed, how they should do it and when it should be done. At selected points throughout the year, all, or some, of these methods may be slotted in as part of a systematic process. How such a systematic approach can be achieved will be discussed next to show ways in which assessment can be built in to the teaching and learning cycle.

The process

I've been a teacher for years and I suppose it all comes naturally, but when I take time out to really think about what I'm doing, that's when I realise changes are needed for myself and the children to grow.

(Year 6 teacher)

How can teachers teach and children learn in an effective way and what part does assessment play in this? After some time in the profession this may become an almost intuitive process, but nevertheless reflection on practice can give continuing fresh insights.[13]

● Reflect on the process of teaching, learning and assessing in your classroom.

● What actually happens? Identify the different stages.

● Note down who takes responsibility for these.

● How are the children involved in the various stages identified?

● Compare your list with the one below.

● What are the differences and similarities?

This process may be represented diagrammatically, as in Figure 9.5, to indicate possible stages that may occur in any process of teaching and learning. It can be viewed as a cycle in that setting targets is an integral part of planning itself.[14]

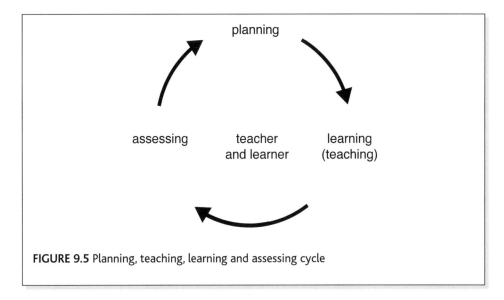

FIGURE 9.5 Planning, teaching, learning and assessing cycle

The following need to be considered when using the cycle:

Planning

- Selecting/choosing the curriculum content
- Planning specific learning intentions for particular lessons, sessions or activities
- Planning activities which support the learning of these
- Planning assessment of selected learning intentions.

Teaching, learning and assessing

- Sharing learning objectives
- Fixing learning objectives
- Sharing assessment objectives
- Fixing assessment objectives
- Undertaking activities
- Sharing learning
- Sharing assessments
- Sharing targets
- Fixing targets
- Recording assessments.

These stages are not rigid within the actual teaching situation and they may not always occur in the same order. For example, assessments may be recorded while the children are undertaking the activity as well as at its end. Equally, targets may be identified and shared in the middle of an activity, as significant learning moments are not restricted to the end-point. However, there is a sense in which isolating stages and devising formats enables us to deepen our understanding of the teaching situation. Nevertheless, the child must be allowed the freedom to follow individual learning leads within any planned session, difficult though this may be within the constraints of the Literacy Hour.

I will now examine some of these in more detail.

Planning

One of the most important features of planning is the linking of assessment objectives to the learning intentions by devising them at the same time. It is at the planning stage that assessment needs to be considered, not afterwards. When it becomes an afterthought or is viewed as a totally separate entity, its power as an integral and dynamic part of the teaching/learning process is weakened. A chart on planning formats will help make these issues clear (see Figure 9.6).

Activity focus	Date
Learning intentions	Assessment focus ● Who? ● How? ● When?
Activity stages ● Introduction _____ _____ _____	Differentiation
Plenary focus	
Assessment results	

FIGURE 9.6 Planning format

Fixing learning

> When I'm starting my work, I need to get it fixed in my head what I'm
> doing, so then I'll remember it.
>
> (Sarah, aged 8)

The notion of 'fixing' is important. Ensuring that children understand what is required of them and fixing it in their memory is crucial. In other words, children, having been told the learning intentions, need to be given a framework or structure to help them remember what they are doing. A written target is a way of fixing in the memory a goal to be achieved - although, it is often left out of the process - and is critical in securing progress in learning. This process of 'fixing' is one in which children should be given concrete support (see below) to help them make certain aspects of the learning process more explicit. 'Fixing' involves providing aids that enable them to be aware of *how* they are learning in the course of developing new knowledge and to help them to make their implicit knowledge explicit through becoming more metacognitively aware. If written targets are locked away in the teacher's mind and not shared with the pupil this 'fixing' will not occur.

What follows are suggestions for developing the different stages of the teaching, learning and assessment process within the classroom context.

Sharing learning intentions

> I always work out exactly what I want them to learn, but I don't always
> share the detail with them. Perhaps I need to be more specific.
>
> (Year 3 teacher)

Learning objectives need to be specific and based on both knowledge of the curriculum and awareness of the children's abilities. Lack of clarity on exactly what children are being expected to learn can result in little learning taking place. Nevertheless, despite clearly formulated plans and sharply focused learning intentions, these aims may be of little use if they are not shared with the children, for their aims may be very different from ours. As a consequence, they may only understand a portion of what we want them to achieve and so may only partially succeed in their learning. It is important, therefore, for teachers to make learning intentions comprehensible to children by converting them into a language they can understand. The term 'childspeak' has been coined to describe this process.[15] The teacher may have a distinct focus for learning but this needs to be conveyed clearly to children.

In sharing learning objectives, children need to know about the following:

- The **what**: the activity needs to be clearly explained – for instance: what it is, who it is to be done with, and how long children should spend doing it.

- The **why**: children should understand what they have to do and why they have to do it. David, aged 7, said, 'I do my work because my teacher says', and this response is typical of what many children think. Helping children to understand real reasons for activities will increase their motivation. They need to be let in on the secret that there is more to a day's work than satisfying their teacher.

- The **audience**: children should know who will read their writing or listen to them reading or talking. Equally, they need to know what will happen to their work once it is completed. Discussing the options and making decisions with children builds up a climate of trust in which they are free to focus on their work without worry.

- The **genre**: children need to know whether they are focusing on reading, writing, speaking or listening. If writing, for example, what type, or genre, are they using, e.g. newspaper report, narrative etc.? Making these aspects explicit is part of the teaching and learning process.[16]

- The **teacher's role**: you, as their teacher, should be clear about what you want from the activity and what you will be doing to help pupils as they take part in it. Clearly, depending on the task or type of assessment you wish to undertake, your role will vary. Sharing this with children will help eliminate confusion on their part and make it clear what they can expect of you.

In summary, children need to be clear about what work they need to do, its purpose, its audience, and what will happen to it. They need to know both what they should be doing and why, and what the teacher is doing and why. When these issues are clarified through planning formats, such as the one given under 'Planning' (above), the working environment will be appropriately supportive, so that effective learning can take place.

Sharing assessment objectives

> I always tell the children what I'm doing and why. It's important that they know we're all in this together.
>
> (Year 2 teacher)

Children need to know *who* will be assessing them: will it be the teacher, another adult or themselves? They should be learning a way of working whereby they constantly evaluate their own performance. Ways of achieving this should be built into daily classroom routines (see below). It is important that children understand what the teacher's role is to be during any session. If you are undertaking specific assessments then they should share this knowledge – what you will be focusing on, why you will be doing it and exactly how. There is no reason why children should not see your observation grids or other means of recording. Findings should be shared with them, however briefly, either individually, in groups, or at whole-class level within a plenary session. If they understand the process and feel a sense of partnership, then fear, suspicion and awkwardness are removed. They will view positively the fact that teachers are assessing them because they will recognise it as a normal part of a teacher's role. When teachers create secure contexts, children will be unafraid to take risks.

Providing visual aids and using specific strategies to fix intentions and objectives in children's minds are important. The following list gives examples:

- using a wall chart with stick-on symbols;
- asking children to write down one specific intention before they start;
- cards with learning intentions on them in the middle of the table;
- reminding groups of their learning intentions once they've begun; and
- setting up a quick memory game/quiz before starting the activity.

Remember that learning intentions and assessment objectives can be used for individuals, groups or for the whole class. Figure 9.7 provides a format for this.

The following openers might be helpful to start sessions in order to sharpen the focus on both teaching and learning:

- 'In this session we are going to...' (describe the activity itself, who it is to be undertaken with, and how long it will last)
- 'The type of work we are doing is...' (describe the type/genre of text)
- 'We are going to do this because...' (describe the general aim of the activity)
- 'What I want you to learn is...' (identify your specific learning intention)
- 'During the session I will be...' (describe your role as teacher)
- 'We will see if we achieve this by...' (describe any assessment activity)
- 'What will happen to your work is...' (discuss the options for the end result)
- 'At the end of the session we will...' (describe the focus of the plenary review)

Sharing Learning

This may take place with individuals, groups or with the whole class. A useful way of sharing learning is within a plenary session, for example in the last ten

GROUP 1 ACTIVITY We're going to:	We need to learn:
GROUP 2 ACTIVITY We're going to:	We need to learn:
GROUP 3 ACTIVITY We're going to:	We need to learn:
GROUP 4 ACTIVITY We're going to:	We need to learn:

FIGURE 9.7 Class wall chart (learning objectives)

minutes of every lesson, as in the Literacy Hour. Much of a plenary's effectiveness will be lost if it is used as a rushed 'show and tell' session or a part which is bolted on to the end of other seemingly more important activities. Careful planning can transform it into a strong motivator and a time when work can be shared and targets developed.

A plenary session can be used to:

- teach children to be reflective;
- teach children to be analytical;
- develop speaking and listening skills;
- develop confidence in themselves as thinkers and learners;
- develop a community of enquiry;
- develop a secure learning environment;
- consider whether or not learning intentions have been met; and
- enable children to share assessments of themselves and others.

Crafting the plenary is of enormous importance. The following is a suggested format for leading a plenary session:

1. Remind the class of the learning intentions of the lesson.

2. Ask groups or individuals to feed back and share what they have done and learnt.

3. Invite the class to question or comment on the work of the group or individual.

4. Question or provide teacher feedback to individuals, groups and the whole class, asking, for example, 'Have we met our learning intentions?'. Teachers and children can decide upon this together, in an informed way.

Ways of feeding back

Having one group feed back thoroughly will be more effective than trying to get half the class to merely say what they have achieved. It is important to be explicit about the nature of the feedback and what language mode(s) the child is being asked to use. We should model the questions and types of talk, such as interviewing, that we want children to become more confident in and use themselves.

There are several ways in which this can be achieved as outlined below.

Reporting

Structuring the end of an activity using plenary focus cards enables children to see where they are going and provides a framework and focus for their work. Questions may be written on a card and discussed with children at the start of the activity. They need to know at this stage what is expected of them so that they can structure their work accordingly. Questions they might ask include:

- What have I/we done?
- What have we learnt?
- What do we need to learn next?

This provides a baseline format but may, of course, be extended according to the age and ability of the children or, indeed, the nature of the activity itself. The following questions illustrate how reflection may be further developed.

- What did we enjoy most?
- What were we good at?
- What did we have trouble with?
- Who did what?

- Did we work well together?
- If we were doing it again what would we change?
- Did we meet our targets and how do we know this?

Interviewing
One child should be given a selected question(s) to ask another individual, pair or group.

Persuading
The plenary may be set up so that the child or children must persuade the rest of the class that this was a useful and interesting activity.

Instructing
Children may give others in the class instructions, based on their own experience of the activity, in order to let them know how to go about it when it is their turn.

Debating
Two children may debate certain aspects of the task taking opposing points of view.

Describing still images/objects
Children may be asked to present a still image representing a significant moment in the activity and then one or two of them describe it to the rest of the class. (For more on still images see Chapter 8.)

Setting post-activity targets

Purposes

Targets spring from reviewing and reflecting upon work achieved and this is one of the most critical points in the process. Discussing possible targets is at the centre of the learning process. Setting targets consolidates and moves understanding forward, with the target conference providing an essential link between what has been learnt and what the child still needs to know. As part of this process children realise what they have learnt and are enabled to become explicit about it. By these means they become more metacognitively aware as they come to understand their strengths and appreciate which areas need further development.[17]

Teachers have traditionally been the target setters but children also need to learn how to review their own performance and to set themselves meaningful targets. They are more likely to pursue them if they have been involved in their selection. Within the process of target setting a balance should be maintained between recognising achievement and focusing on points for further development. The teacher's input will be crucial in enabling pupils to do this. As children become more familiar with the process, they will be able to take on more responsibility and will learn to set their own targets with increasing relevance.

In setting targets there are a variety of issues to consider, for example whether:

- targets should be set by the teacher, the teacher and child, or by the child alone;
- targets should be set with the whole class, groups or individuals;
- targets should be set for each of the Programmes of Study for reading, writing, speaking and listening;
- targets should be set for literacy in general.

Children need to become used to working in this way and a variety of mechanisms can be used to support them. Some of the targets will be facilitated through talk, whereas others may be written down.

Fixing targets

Targets may be fixed in the child's memory in a variety of ways, for example by using cards, sheets, folders or wall charts. Reflective journals may also be used as a means of clarifying what the targets should be and could be in the form of a blank diary to be filled in by pupils. When learning how to use them children could keep a series of key questions in the front of the journal to help them structure their writing. These could be similar to those suggested for the plenary focus cards (see 'Reporting' above).

Target books are another much sharper and more focused form of target setting. The two formats shown in Figures 9.8 and 9.9 have been found to be accessible to children and may be adapted according to age and ability. The first (Figure 9.8) is one that may be used by young children and requires only a simple form of evaluation and review.

The second Figure (9.9) is more advanced with the children being required to ask themselves three basic questions, which are:

- 'What have I done well?' (in order to encourage and focus on achievement);
- 'How do I know this?' (in order to show the importance of specific evidence);
- 'What do I need to work on?' (in order to focus on an area for development, thereby setting the new target).

I am good at:	I am going to work on:

FIGURE 9.8 Literacy targets: Key Stages 1 and 2

READING DATE	DATE
What do I need to work on?	How well have I done? What have I done well? How do I know?
WRITING DATE	DATE
What do I need to work on?	How well have I done? What have I done well? How do I know?
SPEAKING / LISTENING DATE	DATE
What do I need to work on?	How well have I done? What have I done well? How do I know?

FIGURE 9.9 Literacy targets: Key Stages 2: review

Targets may be written in terms of general literacy or may be divided into reading, writing, speaking and listening. Target books may be filled in whenever a child has completed an activity related to the target, or may be systematically reviewed on a weekly basis. Clearly, the nature of targets may vary, with some being long-term and some being short-term. The point, however, is that they should be relevant and appropriate to the child. The main aim of target setting, then, is to help bring children face to face with their own knowledge, skills and understanding; to enable them to be metacognitively aware of their own learning; and, as a result, to be in control of it.

The National Literacy Strategy

The specific methods for assessing literacy discussed earlier need to be used to inform planning of the Literacy Hour, as children will need to be placed in groups of similar ability during the focus group guided work time. Planning should be clear and specific in order to make the most of the limited time available.

Although assessment did not feature in the initial National Literacy Strategy (DfEE 1998) materials, subsequent documentation stressed the importance of setting targets for literacy.[18] Detailed assessment may be undertaken most easily during group guided work time, but there are also opportunities within shared whole-class work or at the plenary stage, as has been indicated.

Conclusion

Carrying out effective and systematic assessment provides teachers with an exciting challenge. Through it we can find out what children need to know, which, in turn, helps us plan for their learning more appropriately. Therefore, it is essential that secure and workable frameworks are in place to support the planning, teaching and assessment of learning. These frameworks are crucial for recording progress in literacy in a rigorous way. Children need to be partners in the process and to be given tools that enable them to gain understanding and control over their own learning. As Robena, aged 10, said after reviewing her work in a Literacy Hour,

> Talking about what I planned to write and putting it on my focus card has helped to fix in my mind what I had to do in my writing. Now I know what I've done well, I know what I need to do next time.

Notes

1. Handbooks of guidance for assessment are produced each year for each key stage, e.g. DfES (2005) *Assessment and Reporting Arrangements* (QCA).
2. Brief reference to assessment is made in DfES (2003) *Speaking, Listening, Learning: Working With Children in Key Stages 1 and 2* (QCA).
3. Research on assessment and learning by Paul Black and Dylan Wiliam is recorded in the following document: Assessment Reform Group (1999) *Assessment for Learning: Beyond the Black Box* (University of Cambridge, School of Education).
4. The document *Assessment for Learning: 10 Principles* is available for download at http://www.assessment-reform-group.org-uk/publications.html
5. *Assessment for Learning* materials produced by the QCA may be accessed from http://www.qca.org.uk/10009.html
6. The Task Group for Assessment and Testing (TGAT) Report (1987) emphasises the importance of formative assessment.
7. For more on conferencing see J. Graham and A. Kelly (2000) *Reading Under Control* (David Fulton Publishers), in their chapter on 'monitoring and assessing' reading, and in *The*

Primary Language Record (Barrs *et. al.* 1988).

8. Criteria for assessment may be found as level descriptions within the *English in the National Curriculum* (DfEE 1999).

9. See the following for recording formats: DfES (2003) *Speaking, Listening, Learning: Working With Children in Key Stages 1 and 2* (QCA).

10. For example, the developmental continua included in the *First Steps* (Raison 1996) published by Longman.

11. From *The Richmond English Record* (London Borough of Richmond 1989), as published by Richmond (Surrey) Education Authority.

12. Further information on miscue analysis may be derived from Y. Goodman and C. Burke (1973) *Reading Miscue Inventory* (Macmillan). A. Browne (1998) gives a comprehensive explanation and examples of miscue analysis in practice.

13. A. Pollard (2005) highlights the importance of reflective practice within the primary school context.

14. V. Koshy and C. Mitchell (1993) usefully describe the place of assessment within a cycle of teaching and learning.

15. S. Clarke (2004) underscores the importance of sharing specific learning intentions with children in a language that is accessible to them.

16. See DfEE (2000) *Grammar for Writing* (London, NLS) for a useful breakdown of non-fiction text-types.

17. The role of metacognition in children's learning is explored by R. Fisher (1998) and in M. Williams, (ed.) (2002) *Unlocking Writing*. London: David Fulton Publishers.

18. For example, the importance of setting targets for literacy was endorsed in QCA (1999) *Target Setting and Assessment in the National Literacy Strategy*. London: QCA.

References

Barrs, M., Ellis, S., Hester, H. and Thomas, A. (1988) *The Primary Language Record.* London: CLPE.

Black, P. and Wiliam, D. (1999) *Assessment for Learning: Beyond the Black Box. Cambridge:* University of Cambridge, School of Education.

Browne, A. (1998) *Teaching Reading in the Early Years.* London: Paul Chapman.

Clarke, S. (2004) *Unlocking Formative Assessment.* London: Hodder & Stoughton.

DfEE (1998) *National Literacy Strategy: Framework for Teaching.* London: HMSO.

DFEE (1999) *English in the National Curriculum.* London: HMSO.

DfEE (2000) *Grammar for Writing.* London: NLS.

DfES (2003) *Primary National Strategy: Speaking, Listening and Learning: Working with Children in Key Stages 1 and 2.* London: QCA.

DfES (2005) *Assessment and Reporting Arrangements.* London: QCA.

Fisher, R. (1998) 'Thinking about thinking: developing metacognition in children'. *Early Child Development and Care,* **141**, 1–13.

Goodman, Y. and Burke, C. (1973) *Reading Miscue Inventory.* New York: Macmillan.

Graham, J. and Kelly, A. (2000) *Reading Under Control* (2nd edn). London: David Fulton Publishers.

Graham, J. and Kelly, A. (2003) *Writing Under Control* (2nd edn). London: David Fulton Publishers.

Jones, D. (2002) 'Keeping track: assessment in writing', in Williams, M. (ed.) *Unlocking Writing.* London: David Fulton Publishers.

Koshy, V. and Mitchell C. (1993) *Effective Assessment.* London: Hodder & Stoughton.

London Borough of Richmond (1989) *The Richmond English Record.* Richmond: Richmond Education Authority.

Pollard, A. (2005) *Reflective Teaching: Evidence Informed Professional Practice.* London: Continuum.

QCA (1999) *Target Setting and Assessment in the National Literacy Strategy.* London: QCA.

Raison, G. (1996) *First Steps.* Harlow: Longman.

Task Group for Assessment and Testing (1987) *National Curriculum Report.* London: DES.

Williams, M. (ed.) (2002) *Unlocking Writing.* London: David Fulton Publishers.

Further reading

Black, P. Harrison, D., Lee, C., Marshall, B. and Wiliam, D. (2003) *Assessment for Learning.* Buckingham: Open University Press.

Drummond, M.J. (2003) *Assessing Children's Learning* (2nd edn). London: David Fulton Publishers.

Hall, K. and Burke, W.M. (2003) *Making Formative Assessment Work.* Milton Keynes: Open University Press.

Headington, R. (2003) *Monitoring, Assessment, Recording, Reporting and Accountability.* London: David Fulton Publishers.

Torrance, H. and Pryor, J. (2002) *Investigating Formative Assessment.* Milton Keynes: Open University Press

Useful websites

Assessment for Learning: 10 Principles –
http://www.assessment-reform-group.org.uk/publications.html

Assessment for Learning materials – http://www.qca.org.uk/10009.html

Teaching children with special educational needs (SEN) in the mainstream classroom

Paula Frew

'I do not have "a position" or a safe haven where what is "right" exists. Pragmatism precludes idealism. I search for questions which need answers...'

(Clay 2001:3)

Introduction

Every September most classroom teachers are faced with a new class. This is both an exciting and nerve-wracking event. A lot of the children in that class will be able to move easily onto the next stages of literacy. However, some children will not be achieving as much as they should or could. It is not the intention here to deal with children with severe learning difficulties but instead the type of problems teachers may encounter with some of the children in their classes. In this case the term 'special needs' refers to a child whose learning rate in literacy is noticeably slower than that of an average child at the same stage. It will be impossible to supply answers to all the questions that occur to us when faced with children who are finding the path to literacy long and difficult. There are ways in which the teacher can find out who these particular children with special needs are, and what their difficulties might be. It is possible to use the classroom environment to support them, and there are methods of teaching that will assist them. There are also specific interventions that will work effectively with most children. A child who has English as an additional language (EAL) should not necessarily be considered as having special needs. However, methods used to support children with SEN can also be of assistance to them. These ways and methods will be considered.

Our ideas as to how to define 'literacy' have changed over time, and while some might see it as a rather 'reductionist' view[1] this chapter uses the definition of literacy given in the introduction to the National Literacy Strategy (NLS) *Framework for Teaching*:

Literacy unites the important skills of reading and writing...It also involves speaking and listening...Good oral work enhances pupils' understanding of language in both oral and written forms and the way language can be used to communicate. It is also an important part of the process through which pupils read and compose texts.

(DfEE 1998:3)

Information about children

The teacher who is fortunate will have a 'provision map' of her new class showing her which children have special educational needs and what type of support has been organised for them. Information about provision which the child may have had in the past can be obtained from the school's Special Educational Needs Co-ordinator (SENCO) who will also be able to advise as to which level of the SEN Code of Practice (DfES 2001) the child might be on (School Action, School Action Plus or Statutory Assessment). See below for alignment with the 'three waves' of support. More quantitative data can be obtained from many sources, including the Foundation Stage Profile, end-of-key-stage data, other tests, P-scales and Individual Education Plans (IEPs).[2] However, while data can help form our judgement about attainment levels it is only a snapshot of what the child could do at a certain time. Do not be discouraged if this data throws up more questions than answers.

There are 'three waves' of support identified in the National Strategies. These are:

Table 10.1 The 'three waves' of support identified in the National Strategies

Wave 1	Quality first teaching	Aligned with the code of practice as the usual differentiated curriculum of the school
Wave 2	Small group intervention	School Action or could be School Action Plus
Wave 3	Specific, targeted intervention for pupils on the SEN register	School Action, School Action Plus or Statutory Assessment

'Quality first' teaching is teaching that draws on age-appropriate objectives from the *Framework for Teaching* with a balance of shared reading and writing during the week, regular phonics or spelling sessions with the planning and essential elements of the Literacy Hour carried out in the manner intended by the Strategy.[3] It may include differentiated activities for children with special needs, but these will be in the context of the whole class. The type of provision at Wave 2 could be one making use of the catch-up programmes designed by the Literacy Strategy, for example Early Literacy Support in Year 1 or Further Literacy Support in Year 5, both delivered by teaching assistants, or one of many other small group programmes. Provision at Wave 3 is more specific and may be targeted at individual children, such as the Reading Recovery programme. This provision may also be delivered by a teaching assistant or teacher.

Many children with SEN will also have an Individual Education Plan (IEP) which will record any provision that is *additional* to or *different* from the differentiated curriculum plan that is in place as part of provision for all children in the class. The IEP should be concisely written and focus on three or four individual targets that match the child's needs. Examples of targets from an IEP might be:

'This term, during independent writing, Anna will use her personal spellchecker to check her spelling.'

'By the end of term Leon will be able to stay on task for 10 minutes.'

'By half-term Jason will have learnt to spell, and use in his writing, the following six frequently recurring words – come, their, said, went, was, because.'

These targets should be time-related and measurable. These will normally be written by the SENCO and class teacher and should be shared with any other adult working with the child. It may be helpful if the child is made aware of these targets, albeit in appropriate language.[4]

The National Curriculum describes three circles that cover areas seen as necessary to be in place for inclusion to be effective (see Figure 10.1).

The first circle focuses on learning objectives and the necessity of getting these right for each child. This does not mean that the objectives will be the same for all children, but that teachers are able, when necessary, to track back through objectives in the Literacy Framework in order to identify appropriate levels for those children who are out of step. For example, a Year 3 class might be working on writing instructions for playing a game while the child with SEN produces a simple flow chart to explain the procedure. The process of differentiation which is an aspect of setting suitable learning challenges will be discussed later.

The second circle is concerned with overcoming the barriers to learning using appropriate access strategies. For instance, if the barrier to learning is written

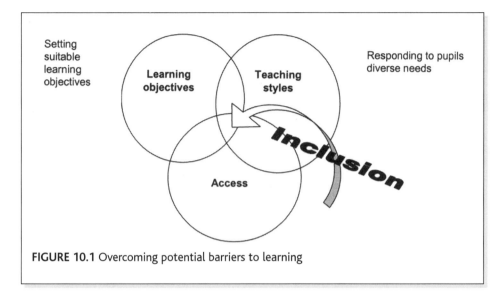

FIGURE 10.1 Overcoming potential barriers to learning

recording, the child might use an ICT program to help record, or work with a partner who scribes, or use another method of recording, for example using tape, video or diagrams. One way of overcoming barriers to learning is by making the classroom environment and organisation as supportive as possible. Ways of doing this are outlined below.

The third circle concentrates on responding to pupils' diverse needs, which means choosing appropriate teaching styles and approaches to take account of the different ways that children learn. Examples of this would be to use pictures and sound to support teaching points. These also can be very helpful for children with EAL.

When the three circles or elements are correctly balanced, the teacher will have maximised the opportunities for the whole class and all pupils will be included in learning. This sounds straightforward, but is a complex and challenging target for us all.

Wave 1, including quality first teaching, is probably the starting point for most teachers when they consider supporting the child with SEN. Good teaching ensures that optimal conditions for learning are in place for all children. Classroom organisation is one area where the teacher can ensure that maximum use is made of the learning environment.

Classroom organisation

Children with SEN need to be able to see any teacher demonstration clearly and without turning in their seat. They should be seated where the teacher can make eye contact easily. Any children who are left-handed must have room on their left-hand side to manipulate paper and pencil and should be seated on the left side of right-handed children. It is important to ensure that the chair and table the child is using are at the appropriate height and angle, using a writing wedge for the child to rest on if necessary. If the children are sitting on the floor for whole-class work, ensure that the child with SEN sits near the front to give a clear view of visual material and prompts. If big books, OHPs or interactive whiteboards are used, texts should be large enough for children to read comfortably from a distance. If in doubt, children with SEN can be given their own copy of the text, but in this case they may need help to focus their attention to the correct place.

Commonly used words, instructions and prompts can be on posters on the wall for children to use. Topic words can be on different coloured paper, for example red for history and blue for science. The class teacher needs to regularly remind children about these. Without this reminder, the child with SEN may forget to use the help available. Children with SEN might need a word list, prompts or personal spellings on their table to be available. These should be specific to whatever is being taught, and changed as required. An example of the sort of word mat that might be used is shown below:

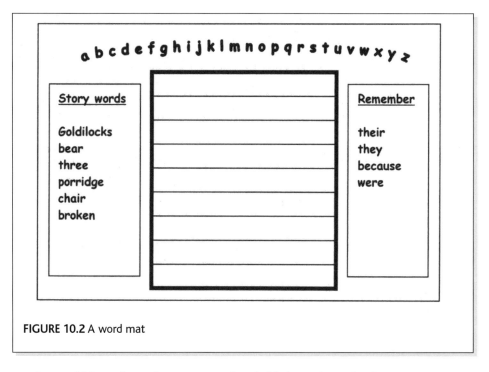

FIGURE 10.2 A word mat

This could be enlarged to A3 size. The child then places his/her writing paper over the central lined section as a writing guide. It might be necessary to add small pictures beside the story words to help selection of the correct word.

It is useful to have all equipment and resources clearly labelled with pictures and words made accessible when necessary. Children's own books, tables and drawers should also be labelled plainly and kept tidy. Teachers who show that they respect and value classroom materials and books will encourage children to do the same. A visual timetable can be helpful to show the structure of the day and week and the teacher can go through this with the class so that children are prepared for any changes that might be unsettling. All of these techniques will help children with SEN find their way through the school day so that they can participate and learn while at the same time supporting quality first teaching for the whole class.

There are many published materials to support children with SEN. Equipment such as magnetic letters for making and changing words, whiteboards and pens to practise spellings, sentences etc., and pencil grips to support handwriting should be part of every classroom. A supply of puppets is also useful. These can be for children to act out stories, both familiar and invented, helping to build story language and imaginative play. Teachers can also use hand puppets themselves to help demonstrate how to use letter fans, say words, etc. (A letter fan is an individual fan made of no more than six leaves of card with individual letters or blends on each card. These can be arranged and rearranged to make different words or parts of words which the child can hold up to show the teacher.) Children can be asked to explain to the puppet how words can be spelt or how activities are carried out correctly. They are often more keen to explain to the puppet what they are going to be doing during their independent activities than they would to simply repeat the instructions back to the teacher. Talking to the puppet about their learning helps children build a language to use to reflect on this learning. Children with difficulties in becoming literate frequently lack this reflective ability. The puppet is also less threatening for shy children to interact with than speaking directly to the teacher would be. These points should also be borne in mind by the teacher working with children with EAL.

One of the teacher's biggest aids when teaching children who are having difficulty learning to read is a wide range of both individual and guided reading books. Clay states:

A curriculum which allows the teacher to go to where the child is and help the individual child to apply whatever strengths he [sic] brings to school to literacy learning will allow for different paths to reading or writing acquisition even in the same classroom. This calls for organization and ingenuity from the teachers...' (Clay 1991:171)

While books should be enjoyable, there is also a need for the child to be able to read increasingly difficult texts with independence. The use of Reading Recovery Book Bands gives the teacher a quick guide to the level of difficulty of each book.[5] This enables them to select texts that the child can attempt to read at a level where they can apply the knowledge they already have to the text, while at the same time building up the strategies they need to become fluent readers.

When the child moves from primary to secondary school, it is useful if a teacher from the primary school visits the secondary and obtains as much information about the school as possible – for example a map of the school, outline timetable, school rules etc. These can be looked at with the child and then included in a resource wallet along with spellings of subject names, teachers' names and other spellings the child needs frequently. Children can then take this wallet to their new school and this helps them to feel more confident in their ability to cope.

However, it is the emotional climate of the classroom which can make the most difference to how the child with SEN approaches and enjoys learning. This brings us to the next section.

Teaching styles

The focus of this section will be on teaching styles that are particularly effective for children with SEN but are, at the same time, good practice for all children. We should ensure that the classroom is a place where it is acceptable to be wrong. Many children do not see that making mistakes is part of the learning process and it is understanding where we have gone wrong which helps us to get something right the next time. The child with SEN may have a history of failure and may not be willing to take risks or feel safe doing so. They need to believe that they can achieve and are valued. Some children arrive in school without a sense of self-worth, and in this case part of the teacher's role will be to support the child by respecting his/her uniqueness and valuing his/her contributions in class. When praising children with SEN, the teacher should be specific, not simply say 'good' but indicating clearly what the child has done that is correct.

Questioning

During whole class sessions, it is important to use the child's name and make any questions clear, ensuring that they are not included in the middle of a string of talk. We should not only use closed questions with children with SEN in literacy; it is their reading and writing that they are having trouble with, not necessarily their thinking. However, at the same time, we must try not to expose weaknesses in front of peers. If the child answers incorrectly we should concentrate on why they answered the way they did, rather than on the wrong answer. It helps to move from open questions to closed or forced alternative questions. For example:

- What do you remember about the book we were reading yesterday?
- What was its title?
- Who was the main character?
- Was it Mog or Rascal?

When a child responds to a question with a linguistic error, the teacher can repeat the child's answer in the correct form without any criticism. For example, the teacher might ask what happened next in the story, to which the child could reply: *'The three bears goes for a walk'*, and the teacher would respond: 'The three bears went for a walk; good, you remembered what happened next'.

During whole-class sessions that are a basis for writing, children should be encouraged to verbally prepare their initial sentence or the initial part of their plan. Once they have voiced their thoughts they will be ready to start work as soon as the independent session starts. If the child is unable to say their sentence aloud they will be very unlikely to be able to write it. When assessing written work, we should try to look at the content and creativity rather than the spelling and handwriting, unless that is the specific focus.

Multi-sensory teaching and learning

Multi-sensory teaching and learning, using all the senses, is of great value to children with SEN. Learning can be made visual by using mind mapping, concept maps, key visuals and images (using different colours, arrows, labels and drawings) as tools for presenting and showing children how to plan and revise their work.[6] Below is an example of a mind map for teaching spelling to children with special educational needs. The teacher would need to demonstrate to the class how to make mind maps to support the planning of stories, writing instructional text, and organising and sequencing ideas.

Different colours can be used for different branches and children could use images as well as words. Post-it notes can help children arrange and rearrange ideas. These can then be used to support either written or oral presentations. However, they may be an end-product in themselves and not necessarily used as a source from which to write. Not every piece of work needs to have a written outcome. The outcome could be the plan itself.

During whole-class and guided sessions, visual support such as pictures, concrete objects, gestures and facial expressions can be used to enhance teaching and keep children's attention.

Auditory methods such as using a range of speaking and listening strategies should also be employed. Children can be encouraged to repeat key facts, spellings and instructions and to clap out syllables and rhythms to support writing. We can have children tell others things they have learnt as an aid to

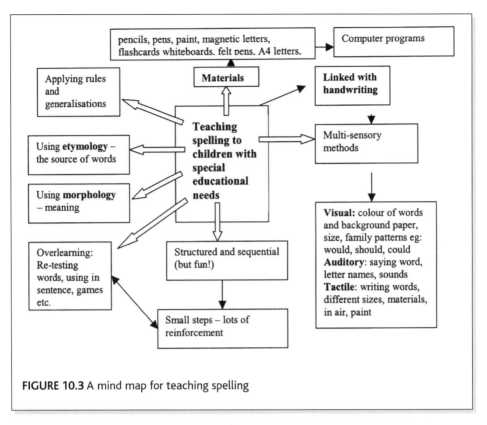

FIGURE 10.3 A mind map for teaching spelling

embedding memory and understanding. Learning can be made tactile by employing movement. Children can hold letters or words and physically arrange themselves to spell a word or make a sentence. They can make letter shapes in the air, in sand, on each others' backs, in the playground with their bodies.

Phonics and spelling

Phonics teaching should be structured and sequential so that each step is revised and revisited frequently. This does not mean that it has to be dull or slow. There are many ways of teaching phonics that actively involve children and will have much more impact than a worksheet. There are some good published schemes for teaching phonics and a lot of useful ideas in the National Strategy's 'Playing with Sounds' file.[7] The teacher will need to help the children understand why they are learning phonics and its use. Children having difficulties may well enjoy the games and activities yet not realise that they are learning these to help support them in their reading and writing.

When teaching spelling we need to be clear about what is meant by 'Look, Cover, Think, Write, Check'.[8] For instance, a Year 3 boy, Jason, who was continually getting spellings wrong was asked how he tried to learn them: 'I do Look, Cover, Think, Write, Check,' he replied. However, on further investigation it was discovered that he did not know what he was looking at, why he covered the word or how to check it once he had written it. Jason was then shown how to:

- look at the word – to ask himself what letters it started with, ended with, whether there were any tricky bits and how he would remember them, whether the word had any tall letters, double letters, to try and remember what the word looked like, whether he knew any other words like it?;
- say the letter names or sounds aloud to support his memory;
- cover the word so that he couldn't see it;
- think about how it looked, the letters in it, any tricky bits;
- write it down;
- uncover the first word and look to see if both words were the same; if not, to highlight in the original word the different bit and try the whole procedure again.

'Oh, I see what to do now,' said Jason 'it's like a memory game.' His spelling improved rapidly after this.

Drama techniques

The use of drama techniques such as frozen tableaux, where the teacher encourages children to ask questions with the characters in role will support recall and promote discussion. For example, starting to read *Goodnight Mr Tom* (Magorian 1998), children could make a tableaux of evacuees leaving their parents. Asking children in the tableaux about their hopes and fears, and 'parents' about their concerns at sending their children away would be an interesting method of enabling them to understand William's feelings when he first goes to live with Tom (for more on drama see Chapter 8).

Shared and guided reading and writing

During shared and guided reading and writing, we can try to give children thinking time as well as talk partners before asking for the answers to questions. We should model what is expected in 'thinking time'. Children with SEN need to know that this is not time to look out of the window and day-dream but to ask themselves specific questions about, for example, their response to the text. We should be similarly explicit when setting up talk partners and demonstrate the type of discussion that will develop critical readers. It is not fair on either child to always pair the child with SEN with the same partner; they need experience of discussion with peers who are working at their level and those who may be working above it. We must be very clear what we are expecting the children to learn from each session or sequence of work and these expectations should be shared with them.

It is crucial to motivate all children, but children who are having difficulties becoming literate need to be persuaded that it is worth doing. Whole-class reading should be enjoyable, and as well as using high quality texts during the Literacy Hour, teachers should ensure that whole class-novels, stories, poems etc. are read to the children outside the Literacy Hour, without the follow-up 'hard work'. This will give all children the opportunity to experience the pleasure to be gained from texts they might not be able to tackle alone.

ICT

ICT can be used to develop reading skills and motivate reluctant readers to become involved in developing the whole range of reading skills. Text manipulation software, such as that described in Chapter 11, can help the child to learn good reading strategies. Their motivation is equally important for writing. This can stem from exciting stimuli, use of drama, IT, real experiences, writing for a purpose and an actual audience. The use of e-mail and computer software writing packages, such as *2Create A Story* are very easy to use and allow children to make their own multimedia stories mixing text, sound and animation.[9] They allow children to experience making appropriate choices from a repertoire of approaches to communicate effectively.

Video can also be used to stimulate writing and materials from the British Film Institute (Starting Stories and Story Shorts) can be adapted to use with any age to encourage discussion, develop language skills and motivate children to write.[10]

Giving feedback

Having encouraged the children to write, the way in which feedback is given to them has an impact on their achievements, motivation for future work and self-esteem. Feedback should be linked to the lesson objective. Not too much time should be spent on correcting spelling, if it was not included in the objective. Positive feedback is a powerful motivator so we should ensure that we point out to children what has been successful about their work, this also gives them a model to use in the future. Only one or two areas to work on should be identified; more than this and the child may attend to none of them. The child can be given suggestions for improving work or avoiding making the same mistakes again. We should involve them in a discussion and ask for their ideas for improving their own practice. Marking when the child is present or as soon after the writing takes place is particularly important for children with SEN. They can be reminded before they embark on their next piece of work how they were going to try to improve it next time.

Differentiation

Matching work to the needs of children of different ability is a complex task. The teacher is required to keep a balance between high expectations and support. Almost any task can be made simple enough for children with SEN with extensive differentiation but the teacher needs to be aware that the learning must remain meaningful in terms of meeting the learning needs of the pupil. Differentiation can be carried out in various ways:

- by making use of an extra adult – the task itself might remain the same, but adult intervention and support provides the differentiation. The use of teaching assistants will be considered later;
- by use of resources – some children may need to have different levels of support by having access to word banks, writing frames, dictionaries, etc.;
- by outcome – in this case, the learning objective may be the same for all children, but it will be achieved at a different level for some. For example, the learning objective may be to join sentences in more complex ways through using a widening range of conjunctions (Year 3, Term 3). Some children may be doing this by collecting lists of conjunctions and using them in their writing, some children might have two sentences and think of different conjunctions to join them and some children might have words and conjunctions on cards which they can manipulate to make the best sentences; and
- by time – during independent activities children with SEN may need to have more time to tackle their work. They may need the 20 minutes, during which most children are expected to work without teacher support, broken into shorter sessions to help maintain their concentration. These children frequently have difficulty understanding how long 10 or 20 minutes is. The teacher could use a timer which visually displays how much time has gone and how much is left to help develop this sense of time.

Other adults

Two other groups of adults who may work with children are parents or carers and teaching assistants.

Parents of children who are having problems sometimes ask to be shown methods of supporting their children at home. Suggestions for helping children with reading, writing and spelling can be given and parents can be invited into school to watch how different aspects of literacy are taught. However, it is often more difficult for a parent who has a close emotional involvement with a child to keep the necessary detached patience that is needed to work with these children. The parent who comes to school saying that they find reading with their child difficult, too time-consuming or frustrating, can be encouraged to tell children the words that they struggle over or to take over the reading themselves. The main object is that the reading sessions at home are enjoyable for both parent and child and not a point of argument or dissatisfaction. The hard work of teaching the child can be left to the teacher.

Most teachers will have the help of a teaching assistant at some point during the week and this will frequently be to support children having difficulties with their acquisition of literacy. Different parts of the Literacy Hour can be supported in different ways. Before the teacher uses a specific text with the class, the teaching assistant might prepare a group of children for it by reading it through with them and explaining any unusual or new words, vocabulary or ideas. During whole-class shared reading or writing, the teaching assistant can sit with a child or group and encourage participation or focus children's attention. They could act as a partner during thinking or discussion time, asking questions to help the child formulate ideas. They can be helping with props and resources or observing and recording the strategies pupils use. During group or individual work, the teaching assistant might work with a group using a specific catch-up programme. They could work with the group on the task set by the teacher, reminding children of the learning objective and supporting them in their attempts to achieve it. They might work with a specific child on IEP targets or re-read the shared text with him/her.

Small group support

The NLS intervention programmes (Wave 2) specifically designed to help children catch up with their peers are:

- Early Literacy Support (ELS), which is aimed at children in Year 1 and is delivered in the second and third terms. The programme is delivered by teaching assistants with groups of six children outside the Literacy Hour.

- Additional Literacy Support (ALS) for children in Year 3/4, either during the independent time of the Literacy Hour or outside it. The programme is delivered by a teaching assistant with the class teacher doing some guided reading and writing sessions.

- Year 3 Literacy Support is a new programme which can also be timetabled for outside the Literacy Hour with teacher and teaching assistant delivering different sessions.

- Further Literacy Support (FLS) is designed for Year 5 children and is delivered mainly by a teaching assistant but with the class teacher starting each week's sessions.
- Year 6 Booster Units are specific units of work that cover writing objectives and can be carried out by either teacher or teaching assistant.
- Literacy Progress Units (LPU) are for children in Year 7 at secondary school and can be delivered by teachers or teaching assistants.

Further details of these intervention programmes are on the NLS website (www.standards.dfes.gov.uk).

It is important to note that the class teacher has some responsibilities in all of these interventions and they are more effective when carried out as planned in the programmes. While it may be difficult for teachers to timetable their sessions with the group, the responsibility should not be passed entirely to the teaching assistant. The class teacher can support the group and teaching assistant by keeping involved and being in a position to monitor progress. For example, in the ELS programme, teachers are expected to carry out progress checks at four-weekly intervals and there are notes designed to help them ask questions and prompt involvement from members of the ELS group in whole-class sessions. It is important that these are followed up because children with SEN do not always make the links between what they learn in one area and another. For instance, they do not recognise that the letter sounds learnt during the ELS session can be used during shared writing in the classroom. The teacher can help the child to make this link. All of these interventions are more successful if they are run as intended and not adapted too far from the original design.

Most local authorities offer training for these programmes and it is useful if the class teacher and teaching assistant can attend together. It is also expected that the teacher and teaching assistant will make time to liaise about the progress of children on the various programmes.

These suggestions should also be borne in mind if other small group support programmes are used. If the programme is to be delivered by a teaching assistant or a teacher, they will require training, and the management and monitoring of it should be carried out by the teacher.

Specific support programmes

Some children will require specific targeted approaches (Wave 3 or School Action, School Action Plus or have a statement of SEN). This intervention needs to be carefully matched to the needs of the individual. The progress of these children should be monitored carefully. The NLS has commissioned an independent research study to give an overview of the evidence from 40 different types of Wave 3 interventions. The main conclusions from the research were that:

- if the children in a school on a Wave 3 programme are not, on average, achieving at least twice the normal rate of progress it may be necessary to re-evaluate what is being offered;
- long interventions do not necessarily produce greater benefits, some of the most effective schemes were those that operated intensively over a short, focused period of up to 20 weeks;
- the largest number of studies were focused on phonological skills for reading; it was found that for greatest impact with struggling readers these need to be embedded in a broad approach; and
- spelling programmes were found to be more effective when they were highly structured and systematic.

Reading Recovery is a Wave 3 intervention for children in Year 1 where a teacher trained in the methods works with a child for 30 minutes a day on reading and writing activities.[11] Teachers who are lucky enough to have a Reading Recovery teacher in their school should observe a session. The Reading Recovery teacher could provide ideas for all staff as to how different facets of the session can be adapted for use in the classroom. For example how to:

- be an active listener when hearing children read, which is very useful during guided reading as it helps the teacher to make the right prompts at the correct time;
- cut up sentences for the child to rearrange, helping to support the development of word and sentence level skills; and
- take and analyse a Running Record as a valuable way of seeing what strategies a child is using when reading, and which need to be built on further.

Conclusion

There are no easy answers as to how we best support those children who are not keeping up with their peers in the classroom. The implementation of these strategies and ideas mean more work for busy teachers. However, by putting into place good practice for children with SEN, a class teacher will find they have 'quality first teaching' in their classroom and offer the best practice for all children. To support children who can easily become fearful and demotivated about literacy so that they look forward to and enjoy their literacy sessions in school will be rewarding and satisfying for all teachers and set the child on the road to successful reading, writing and language skills.

Notes

1. For another view of literacy see Street, B. (1994) *Language and Literacy in Social Practice* (Clevedon: Multilingual Matters).
2. The Foundation Stage Profile is completed for each child in the Foundation Stage and shows the child's attainment or progress towards the Early Learning Goals. End-of-key-stage data include SATs results in reading, writing and spelling. P-scales are eight levels used to assess progress in children working below National Curriculum Level 1. Individual Education Plans (IEPs) are working documents that show an individual programme of teaching that is additional to the main teaching and learning activities in class for specific children.
3. See the NLS website (www.standards.dfes.gov.uk/literacy).
4. For more details about sharing targets with children see Chapter 9.
5. To support book selection and for advice on guided and independent reading the following are recommended: Bickler, S., Baker, S., Hobsbaum, A. (ed.) (2000) *Book Bands for Guided Reading* (London: Reading Recovery National Network); Bickler, S., Baker, S., Hobsbaum, A. (2003) *Bridging Bands for Guided Reading* (London, Institute of Education).
6. More information on mind mapping can be found on the CD-ROM *Learning and Teaching for Dyslexic Children* from the DfES (Ref: DfES 1184-2005-CD). Information, templates and links about using key visuals and graphic organisers to support understanding are available from www.graphic.org.
7. While this is designed for early learning, children in Y1 onwards who are having difficulty learning phonics will benefit from the activities. For further information see the NLS website.
8. See Chapter 4 for more information on spelling.
9. Available from www.2simple.com
10. Available from www.bfi.org.uk/education
11. More on Reading Recovery can be found on the Reading Recovery National Network at www.ioe.ac.uk

References

Clay, M. (1991) *Becoming Literate*. Auckland: Heinemann Education.

Clay, M. (2001) *Change Over Time in Children's Literacy Development*. Auckland. Heinemann.

DfEE (1998) *National Literacy Strategy, Framework for Teaching*. London. HMSO.

DfES (2001) *SEN Code of Practice*. London. HMSO.

Magorian, M (1998) *Goodnight Mr Tom*. London. Longman.

Further reading

Brooks, G. (2002) *What Works for Children with Literacy Difficulties?* Nottingham: DfES Publications.

Clay, M. (1979) *Reading– The Patterning of Complex Behaviour*. London: Heinemann Educational Books.

Clay, M. (1991) *Becoming Literate – The Construction of Inner Control*. London. Heinemann Educational Books.

Cowne, E.A. (2003) *The SENCO Handbook* (4th edn). London: David Fulton Publishers.

DfEE (2000) *Supporting Pupils with Special Educational Needs in the Literacy Hour*. London: HMSO.

DfES (2005) *Learning and Teaching for Dyslexic Children*. Norwich: HMSO.

DfES (2005) *Speaking, Listening, Learning: Working with Children who Have Special Educational Needs*. Norwich: HMSO.

Reid, G. and Wearmouth, J. (eds) (2003) *Dyslexia and Literacy*. Chichester: Wiley.

Safford, K., O'Sullivan, O. and Barrs, M. (2004) *Boys on the Margin – Promoting Boys' Literacy at Key Stage 2*. London: CLPE.

Using the interactive whiteboard for whole-class teaching of reading and writing

John Garvey

'It's so obvious when I see it on screen...I can see what the teacher is trying to teach us...and I can show what I know to the whole class - that's really good.'

(James, aged 9)

Introduction

James's comment seems to personify the reaction of many children and teachers to the interactive whiteboard. While it may be invidious to suggest that children hardly need the presence of another big screen in their lives, research[1] indicates that the judicious use of the interactive whiteboard can have a positive effect on the teaching and learning of literacy. The National Whiteboard Network[2] have noted the following benefits:

> ICT can assist the modelling of literacy processes, encourage interaction with text and help to focus the study of objectives at text, sentence and word level. It provides the teacher with alternative ways of sharing enlarged texts with the whole class and can help the teacher to model the skills of reading and writing more clearly.

The key ideas here are the modelling of processes and skills and the concept of literacy as a shared endeavour. These will be explored throughout this chapter.

For many teachers new to the interactive whiteboard, the question is often 'Where do I start?'. Training in the technical aspects of whiteboard use is obviously critical,[3] but much can be achieved initially through point and click techniques that form the basis of everyday internet use. These can be complemented by the use of the whiteboard highlighter pen. The use of electronic texts is based on such simple techniques and can provide a relatively painless, but very effective starting point for the computer-wary teacher in the use of the interactive whiteboard.

Electronic texts

Electronic texts enable the sharing of texts with the whole class and groups of children. For many classrooms in Key Stage 1, *Sebastian Swan*[4] can serve as an ideal starting point. This has been designed as a comprehensive literacy resource for children, geared to promoting reading and writing on cross-curricular themes. A series of simple, enjoyable and attractively presented stories and rhymes based upon the environmental issues of the Australian rain forest, the life-cycle of swans and the arrival of spring can be shared with children. The texts are clearly designed for use with an interactive whiteboard, allowing the teacher scope to focus on specific issues pertaining to the development of key reading and writing skills. Appropriate sections of texts can be highlighted and analysed – for example in relation to developing an understanding of simple parts of speech or punctuation within texts. Plot lines and content can be discussed with a view to developing the young child's emerging sense of how fiction and non-fiction texts might be structured.

One text in the series, 'Pond Web', is particularly interesting in that it is written by Year 5 and 6 children for an audience of Year 1 and 2 children. The text can be analysed on a whole-class basis, with the teacher using the interactive whiteboard to model how children might be encouraged to write in similar vein, with the needs of a young audience in mind. The website is interactive, allowing children the opportunity to explore answers to questions posed in the text:

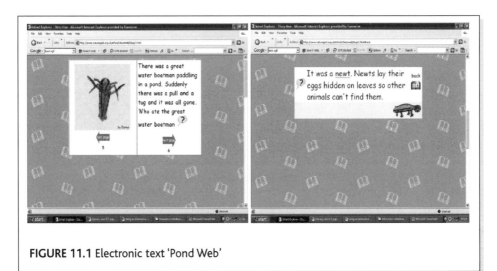

FIGURE 11.1 Electronic text 'Pond Web'

The interactive whiteboard can be used to share individual children's responses with the whole class, enabling the teacher to identify key learning points for future work. The option of saving particular annotated screens for future use can be of particular value here. Within one web page, children are encouraged to e-mail the website and share their thoughts on the texts:

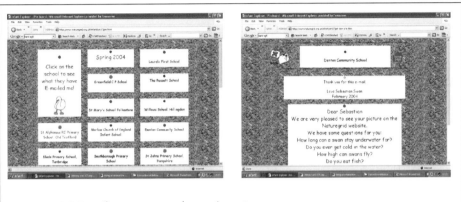

FIGURE 11.2 E-mail responses to electronic texts

Newly arrived e-mails can be reviewed by the whole class and used as a stimulus for communicating with children across the world. The prospect of a swift reply from an exotic place (or even from a neighbouring school) can be highly motivating as a reason for writing. The message might be a short informal greeting or an extended and highly structured response in relation to a topic of particular interest. Different genres of writing can be explored with audience and purpose fundamental to the whole exercise. E-mail has tended to be the Cinderella of the ICT revolution, but is of enormous and, as yet, unrealised potential in terms of a motivational resource for writing because of its simplicity, ease of use and potential for rapid feedback. Millum (1998)[5] has reported on an exciting shared writing project between primary schools in Sheffield and Scotland that succeeded in motivating boys to write extended collaborative narratives based on the book *Carrie's War*. Such work is particularly interesting in the light of McFarlane's[6] observation (1997) that in one primary school experimenting with e-mail, 'boys acted as technicians - happily logging on and downloading namesakes – but it was the girls who engaged with the content and substance of the messages. The boys liked the toys, the girls liked to communicate'.

Many classrooms, however, may have an interactive whiteboard without an internet connection. Teachers need not despair; there are many software packages and applications that can be used with stand-alone computers and whiteboards. Talking Books are an obvious case in point.

Talking Books

There is evidence that Talking Books (computer-based stories presented on screen through a combination of text, speech and animation) can provide a valuable resource for the teaching of reading. Talking books lend themselves particularly well to the use of interactive whiteboards – the attractive animations and limited number of words on screen means that children's attention can be focused on key teaching points in the analysis of texts.

When Talking Books first appeared on the market in the early 1990s, they generated a great deal of enthusiasm and interest from teachers who recognised a novel and original use of the computer with the potential to interest children in the idea of reading. However, this enthusiasm was quickly tempered by a more sceptical stance regarding the value of Talking Books as a stimulus for children to read traditional printed texts, best summarised by Burrell and Trushell's (1997) derogatory description of electronic books as 'interactive eye candy'.[7] This term was largely aimed at highly Americanised versions of stories featuring teachers who would turn into Elvis Presley impersonators at the click of a mouse button and animal characters displaying stereotypical sexist behaviour – the girls would get on with cooking or cleaning their homes, leaving the boys to engage in athletic, outdoor pursuits.

This stimulated a variety of small-scale research projects such as those of Medwell (1995, 1996,1998)[8] which suggested that electronic Talking Books can help Key Stage 1 children to read traditional printed texts, when used as a complement to those strategies normally employed in the teaching of reading. She found that sessions where small groups of children used Talking Books displayed many of the positive characteristics of teacher–child shared reading sessions, including enjoyment of stories, talking about characters, identifying with events and making predictions – all essential elements of the process of learning to read. The greatest benefits accrued when the teacher used a combined strategy of hearing children read in the traditional manner and allowing small groups to interact with Talking Books. The current state of research (Taylor 1994; Chu 1995; Adam and Wild 1997)[9] indicates that Talking Books have genuine potential in:

- helping children gain meaning from texts;
- teaching elements such as word recognition and phonemic awareness in an enjoyable and lively context (see Chapter 4);
- providing independent access to enjoyment of words for non-readers;
- teaching children about features of text (e.g. spaces and pauses can be highlighted on screen and related to the role of punctuation in clarifying meaning);

- promoting reading as an active rather than a passive process;
- generating a positive attitude towards traditional reading materials, particularly in relation to boys and reluctant readers;
- providing opportunities for peer tutoring;
- developing an understanding of the link between speech and written text; and
- facilitating group discussion away from the computer and in particular during review sessions within the Literacy Hour.

Only limited research has been carried out into the efficacy of Talking Books as a vehicle for promoting reading of traditional texts. However, the early indications are that this resource can be a useful complement to the range of teaching strategies that might be employed within Literacy Hour reading sessions and beyond.

Text manipulation software

As a group of 11-year-old children were trying to reconstruct a non-fiction passage on screen using the computer program *Sherlock* in which the challenge was to predict the content of a passage from punctuation, grammar and semantic cues, the following interaction occurred:

Sue: *It's 'Stephen started to cross the road to see what he could...'*

Teacher: *If it is this, what might happen next?*

Gareth: *He might get run over.*

Teacher: *Can we say what it's all about?*

Sue: *It's about a boy.*

Nicola: *He's eighteen.*

Sue: *It's about road rage – someone's saying something. Look, there's speech marks.*

Nicola: *Someone could be yelling something, to warn him.*

Sue: *Yelling at someone driving a car.*

After the activity Sue was heard to comment further:

'When I work with my friends on this it helps me to talk about what I already know about reading. The interactive whiteboard really helps because we can all see the screen and talk about our ideas.'

The comments above demonstrate some of the potential of the computer in helping children to share their own thinking and understanding about the structure of language, or to put it another way, engage in an intuitive but informed 'metalinguistic dialogue' about their understanding of the rules of grammar and punctuation and the way in which these might be used to derive meaning from texts. It reflects a key aspect of the National Literacy Strategy (DfEE 1998) Termly Objectives in relation to children developing an understanding of the way in which language is organised at sentence level:

> to use awareness of grammar to decipher new or unfamiliar words, e.g. to predict from the text, read on, leave a gap and return: to use these strategies in conjunction with knowledge of phonemes, word recognition, graphic knowledge and context when reading.[10]

The concept behind text manipulation software is remarkably simple. Initially, the teacher types in or uses a pre-loaded text which the computer presents as a blank screen with only punctuation and dashes to show the placing of letters. Children are then invited to reconstruct the text through 'buying' individual letters that then appear on screen and, from this, predict the meaning of words in context. For example, in work involving the use of *Sherlock*, Year 6 children had been studying a text on the murder of Stephen Lawrence, derived from the 'Newswise' website[11] and had studied contemporary newspaper accounts surrounding the tragedy. In a whole-class session using the interactive whiteboard, they began with a traditional strategy of 'buying' all the instances of the common vowels 'e', 'i' and 'a' and the consonants 't' and 'h'.

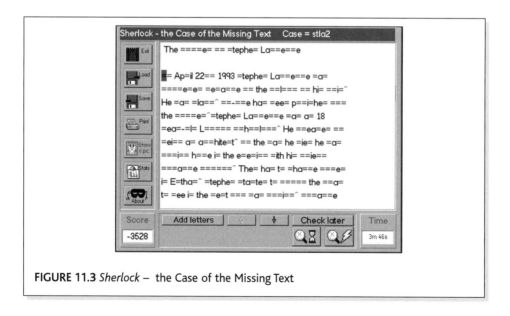

FIGURE 11.3 *Sherlock* – the Case of the Missing Text

This led to a pupil seeing a pattern emerging that indicated that the name 'Stephen' might be in the text, leading to the prediction that a letter 'p' would appear between 'e' and 'h.' This prediction showed the pupil's knowledge of the phoneme pattern 'ph' inside the name Stephen. From this the children predicted that the surname was 'Lawrence', that the date was April 22 and the place name (indicated by a capital letter in the second to last line) was 'Eltham'. Thus semantic cues were used, derived from the pupil's knowledge of the events leading up to the murder.

The marriage of the interactive whiteboard and text manipulation software can be particularly beneficial. Emerging texts can be shared on a whole-class basis with the full range of ideas from individuals made available for consideration. Through a collaborative process of discussion, guesswork, inference, prediction and hypothesis testing, based upon their own knowledge of how texts are written or presented, children can slowly reconstruct the text on screen through the context of an absorbing 'game' which is motivating and satisfying, drawing upon some of the addictive power of computer software in a positive manner. Govier (1997)[12] has commented perceptively that 'the simplest software can foster the most sophisticated thinking'. Despite the simplicity of text revelation software, it has the capacity to develop a wide range of skills that are key characteristics of the literate pupil as defined by the National Literacy Strategy (DfEE 1998:3):

- be able to orchestrate a full range of reading cues (phonic, graphic, syntactic, contextual) to monitor their reading and correct their own mistakes
- understand the sound and spelling system and use this to read and spell accurately
- have an interest in words and their meanings and a growing vocabulary
- understand a range of non-fiction texts
- have a suitable technical vocabulary through which to understand and discuss their reading and writing
- be interested in books, read with enjoyment and evaluate and justify their preferences through reading and writing, develop their powers of imagination, inventiveness and critical awareness.[13]

Text revelations tend to work best with large groups in a community of enquiry in which children can discuss how texts are structured at word, sentence and text level. Teacher questioning is critical in extending children development of skills of inference, prediction and hypothesis testing. The interactive whiteboard has a key role to play in this endeavour in making the text available to a wide audience.

Reading non-fiction texts: CD-ROM encyclopaedias and the internet

The unparalleled recent growth of the use of the computer as a resource for accessing information through multimedia CD-ROMs and the internet provides a particular challenge for the primary teacher. Despite Anthony Burgess's caustic observation (1992) that 'The transference of the *Oxford English Dictionary* to a metallic beer mat is one of the major technological achievements of this century',[14] CD-ROM encyclopaedias represent a widely available and accessible medium for children to explore the world around them. They are now inexpensive (respectable and well-designed versions are frequently given away on the covers of computer magazines) and allow access to a wide range of information in a variety of media including text, video and sound. What would traditionally have been stored on a full set of encyclopaedia volumes can now be stored on a single compact disc.

The growth of the internet and availability of multimedia CD-ROMs has highlighted the need for children to interact effectively with non-fiction texts. This challenge has been recognised for many years with regard to the effective reading of non-fiction texts. Wray and Lewis (1997:1) have commented that:

> Concern about this area is not, of course, new. In their 1978 survey of primary schools...HMI found little evidence that more advanced skills were being taught...Their 1990 report on the teaching of reading in primary schools makes almost the identical statement.

The interactive whiteboard can be a powerful resource for whole-class teaching and modelling of these advanced skills. In using non-fiction resources it is critical that children should be clear about what they are trying to find out, and have a range of strategies for understanding, evaluating and presenting information. The work of the University of Exeter EXEL project[15] has shed light on the strategies needed to become effective in interacting with non-fiction, resulting in the EXIT (EXtending Interactions with Texts) model shown in Table 11.1.

In relation to the skills of the EXIT model the following strategies have proved to be beneficial:

- *Activation of previous knowledge:* the teacher can use a word processor to produce KWL grids. A KWL grid is a frame which allows children to record what they already **K**now about a subject, what they **W**ish to find out, how they will find it out and what they have **L**earnt from the process. The pupil can use a word processor to brainstorm and record ideas – key ideas can be highlighted, presented in tabular form and edited for future reference.

- *Establishing purpose:* children can use the word processor to brainstorm, draft and edit key questions concerning what they wish to find out. Such work can inform the generation of KWL grids.

Table 11.1 The EXIT model

Process stages	Questions
Activation of previous knowledge	What do I already know about this subject?
Establishing purposes	What do I need to find out and what will I do with the information?
Locating information	Where and how will I get this information?
Adopting an appropriate strategy	How should I use this source of information to get what I need?
Interacting with text	What can I do to help me understand this better?
Monitoring understanding	What can I do if there are parts I do not understand?
Making a record	What should I make a note of from this information?
Evaluating information	Which items of information should I believe and which should I keep an open mind about?
Assisting memory	How can I help myself remember the important parts?
Communicating information	How should I let other people know about this?

- *Locating information:* children can be encouraged to research a range of resources including traditional printed texts. If they are accessing information using CD-ROM encyclopaedias they need to be taught specific search strategies. These tend to rely on an understanding of a few specific terms that help to pinpoint articles that are immediately relevant to the enquiry.

- *Adopting an appropriate strategy*: children can be encouraged to cut and paste passages from CD-ROMs or the internet into a word processor. This allows the copying of hard texts with a view to skimming, scanning and intensive reading of texts. The word processor can be used as a device for on-screen work using cut, paste and highlighting functions. This can be complemented by off-screen work on hard copy with groups of children – under sensitive guidance from their teacher – working on editing the writing of peers. A good strategy here is to ensure a positive, constructive critique of work through the teacher posing the question, 'Can we say two things we like about this work and give one suggestion to improve it?' Comparisons can be made between on-screen and hard-copy editing of work.

- *Interaction with text:* text manipulation software such as *Sherlock* (as evaluated above) can be particularly powerful in constructing meaning from texts. In addition to this, the teacher can use a word processor to alter the sequence passages of text derived from CD-ROM encyclopaedia or the internet and challenge children to re-order and make sense of it. Teachers can model the highlighting of key words in texts through the use of a word processor and interactive whiteboard and then invite children to develop their own expertise in this area.

- *Making a record*: teachers can develop writing frames to scaffold children's writing in a range of genres. A writing frame is a template that helps children to structure their writing according to genre and purpose. Modelling of the use of writing frames through the use of an interactive whiteboard can be a particularly powerful teaching strategy.

- *Evaluating information*: one useful initial strategy is to evaluate newspapers with regard to recognising bias in printed material. Children can be encouraged to compare how tabloid and broadsheet papers approach the same news stories and be invited to compose their own versions of the same stories from differing points of view – an example of this is presented in the section on word processing.

- *Communicating information*: children can use word processing and desktop publishing software to draft and edit work with a view to publishing texts in a variety of genres such as leaflets, posters or newspapers. The computer can be valuable in terms of making books for sharing with peers or perhaps to read to younger members of the school community. There is also considerable scope for multimedia authoring, explored in more depth below.

Word processing and desktop publishing

The main ICT tools for developing writing skills are word processors and desktop publishing software. The Nobel Prize-winning author Gabriel Garcia Marquez has given testimony to the liberating power of the word processor, claiming that writing had become much easier 'since I made the greatest discovery of my life: the word processor'. From an average of writing one page a day, 'now I can do 20, 30 even 40 pages a day. If I'd had this machine 20 years ago, I'd have published two to three times as many books' (Hamil 1988:50).[16] It would be folly to ignore the educational potential of such a tool, particularly with regard to promoting writing of quality from children.

In the early years, children can quickly learn that they can produce marks on the screen by typing on keyboards or using overlay keyboards. This can be rapidly refined by asking them to talk about aspects of their own experience with an adult (e.g. a parent) who can act as a scribe on the word processor. The contributions of the whole class can be compiled to make a book to be placed in the book corner or library for other children to read, or used as a shared text within the Literacy Hour on the interactive whiteboard. This is one of the major benefits of using the word processor – multiple copies of work can be produced and shared with others, be it family, friends or people who are unknown to the child. The personal can be made public (with the pupil's consent) through the publication and display of word processed posters, stories, reports or books. The interactive whiteboard can play a key role in making the personal endeavours of children available for all to share. Children can quickly realise that the sharing of written work is pleasurable, thus promoting the move to composing their own writing on the computer. Short pieces such as poems, menus, jokes, invitations, labels or greetings cards can be an ideal context for small group work for children who have not yet got to grips with using the keyboard quickly and accurately and who thus might struggle with writing longer pieces. Such work can also help children to begin to understand that writing serves a purpose, which will influence content, style and presentation.

Children as young as 6 or 7 can be taught to redraft their own work (Durkin 1997)[17] – the major reason for using a word processor. Thus children can overcome the obstacle of the third of the 'three R's: 'Reading, wRiting and Rubbing out', and gain an understanding of writing as a process rather than a rush towards an end-product. The redrafting of work involves considerable technical skills on the part of the writer – skills that can be modelled by the teacher via the medium of the interactive whiteboard.

As children become more proficient in their writing, keyboard skills and understanding of genre, they can be challenged to write for a specific purpose and audience. A class of Year 4 children were invited to collaborate on producing *Tudor Times* newspapers after having considered the contrasting styles and intended audience of broadsheet and tabloid newspapers (see Figure 11.4).

The computer, allied to the interactive whiteboard, enables the publication of work for public consumption and helps give writing a sense of credibility. As Lauren, one of the Year 4 children, was heard to comment, 'When it's on the large screen for everyone to see you feel like real writer'. An awareness of audience is critical in promoting writing of quality. Work of this nature can be given authenticity by a preliminary visit to a local newspaper office. One interesting feature that has been observed has been the intense motivational effect of children working to a deadline for the publication of their newspapers (Wray and Medwell 1996).[18]

FIGURE 11.4 Contrasting newspaper styles

The level of challenge is important as children may be routinely using software at home that is far more sophisticated than that which is available at school. As a case in point, desktop publishing software such as Microsoft Publisher has become far more user friendly with the result that functions such as altering size of text to create headlines and insertion of dates or issue numbers are carried out automatically, leaving the writer free to focus on telling his or her own story. Consider the following vivid newspaper report on a school trip produced by a six-year-old boy who had been taught the rudiments of writing text and inserting clipart by his mother. It is interesting to note (in Figure 11.5)the memorable incidents of the day as seen through the eyes of Joe (which are perhaps not what the teacher intended!).

Desktop publishing software is particularly valuable in terms of promoting an understanding of genre in that it employs templates or 'wizards' designed to support the writing of different types of texts, e.g. postcards, newsletters, leaflets, business cards, invitations and greetings cards. This can be profitably combined with CD-ROM software such as Dorling Kindersley's *The Jolly Postman* which includes templates for children to communicate through letters or e-mail to characters from nursery rhymes and fairy tales.

Multimedia authoring

Multimedia authoring software allows children to construct their own computer presentations using a combination of words, video, animation, pictures and sound. It is analogous to children producing their own CD-ROM resource which can be shared with others on the computer and can vary in scale from a simple

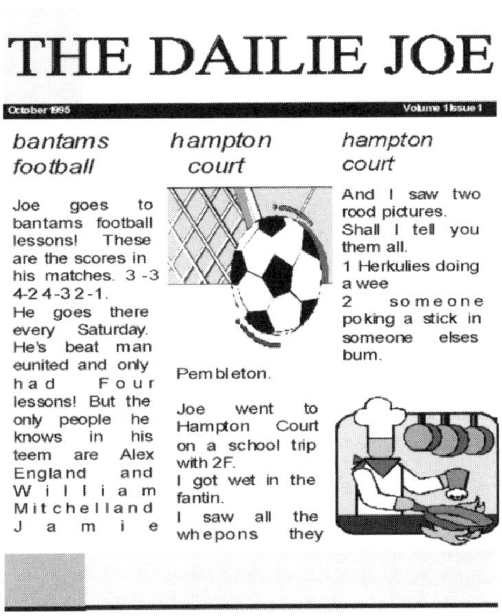

THE DAILIE JOE

October 1995 — Volume 1 Issue 1

bantams football

Joe goes to bantams football lessons! These are the scores in his matches. 3 -3 4-2 4-3 2-1.
He goes there every Saturday. He's beat man eunited and only had Four lessons! But the only people he knows in his teem are Alex England and William Mitchell and Jamie

hampton court

Pembleton.

Joe went to Hampton Court on a school trip with 2F.
I got wet in the fantin.
I saw all the whepons they

hampton court

And I saw two rood pictures. Shall I tell you them all.
1 Herkulies doing a wee
2 someone poking a stick in someone elses bum.

FIGURE 11.5 The *Dailie Joe*

page on the screen which includes text and pictures to a series of linked screens which can tell the particular 'story' (which can be fiction or non-fiction) that the children wish to relate. The process of constructing a multimedia presentation is similar to that of web page design in that it requires planning of the whole resource in terms of the 'hyperlinks' that guide the user through linked items of information on different pages. This requires some technical competence in using the computer on the behalf of children – key skills that need to be taught and modelled by the teacher. An interactive whiteboard within an ICT suite can be a very efficient means for teaching large groups computer skills.

The simplest starting point can be extremely effective – children at Key Stage 1 can be encouraged to use a digital camera. The digital photographs can be immediately transferred to the computer and used as a basis for the children writing simple sentences with each page representing an individual pupil's efforts, which can be linked by computer screen 'buttons' which guide the reader on to the next page. Multimedia software such as *Hyperstudio* can be used to add video clips and sound, which add enormously to the motivational effect of the use of the computer. As children move into Key Stage 2 more thought needs to be put into the initial planning of the multimedia presentation. This is best achieved in small groups away from the computer using pencil and paper to decide the content of each page and the mapping out of the links between each page. An accessible tool for planning can be 'Microsoft Powerpoint', a business orientated tool for designing slide presentations, which is user friendly enough to use with children at Key Stage 2, as is evident from the simple plan below produced by a group of keen Year 5 football fans:

AFC Wimbledon are the Greatest!

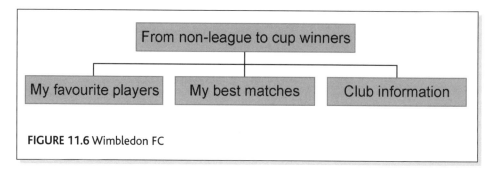

FIGURE 11.6 Wimbledon FC

Conclusion

In conclusion, a cautionary note - there is anecdotal evidence emerging that the interactive whiteboard can be used as a 'large screen pacifier' for children, lending itself well for use as a didactic teaching tool – little more than a traditional 'animated blackboard'. It is critical that not only are key skills and processes modelled, but also that the interactive nature of the medium is realised – a tool for children to share and take delight in demonstrating their skills to the whole class. On such foundations can the teaching and learning of literacy become akin to a genuine shared enterprise.

Notes

1. A summary of research into the introduction of interactive whiteboards into primary classrooms can be found on http://www.kented.org.uk/ngfl/ict/IWB/whiteboards/index.html
2. The National Whiteboard Network's website http://www.nwnet.org.uk./pages/literacy.html is a fund of valuable information on the use of interactive whiteboards.
3. The National Whiteboard Network (2004) report that 'experience from two pilot projects into the use of interactive whiteboards in primary schools tells us that it is important to see the installation of whiteboards as the beginning rather than the end of a process. Good quality support, training and resources are all important if the investment in whiteboards is to have a positive effect on the quality of learning and teaching'.
    http://www. nwnet.org.uk./pages/downloads/faqs_teachers.doc
4. The resource *Sebastian Swan* (and a host of other excellent resources for interactive whiteboard use, with useful teachers' notes) can be found on
    http://www. naturegrid.org.uk/infant/bigbook.html
5. See Trevor Millum (1998) 'Making the most of email: the virtual writer in residence'. *MAPE Focus on Literacy* (Autumn).
6. See page 170 of McFarlane A. (ed.) (1997) *Information Technology and Authentic Learning*. London: Routledge.

7. Burrell, C. and Trushell, J. (1997) take a critical stance on the use of talking books in their paper 'Eye candy in interactive books - a wholesome diet?' *Reading*, **31**, 3–6 July.

8. Jane Medwell has carried out extensive research into the value of talking books that is summarised in the following papers: Medwell, J. (1995) 'Talking books for teaching reading'. *Microscope*, **46**, 22–4; Medwell, J. (1996) 'Talking books and reading'. *Reading*, **30**, 41–6; and Medwell, J. (1998) 'The Talking Books Project: some further insights into the use of talking books to develop reading'. *Reading*, **32**, 3–7 April.

9. For a full analysis of research into the value of talking books refer to Adam, N. and Wild, M. (1997) 'Applying CD Rom interactive storybooks to learning to read'. *Journal of Computer Assisted Learning*, **13**, 119–32; Chu, M. (1995) 'Reader response to interactive computer books: examining literary responses in non traditional reading sessions'. *Reading Research and Instruction*, **34**, 352–66 and Taylor, C. (1994) 'Teaching reading with talking story books'. *Computer Education*, **84**, 25–6.

10. See page 32 of the National Literacy Strategy (DfEE 1998) for work at sentence level in Year 3 Term 1.

11. The 'Newswise' website (http://www.dialogueworks.co.uk/newswise/) is a valuable subscription-based on-line teaching resource for enabling children to analyse contemporary news stories.

12. This quote is from an interesting analysis of the information handling skills that can be developed through using the computer, written by Heather Govier (1997) in Microscope's *Information Handling Special*, pp. 2–8. Refer also to the MAPE website on www.mape.org.uk

13. A full description of the 'Literate Pupil' can be found on page 3 of the National Literacy Strategy (1998).

14. Anthony Burgess (1992) 'The electronic revolution', *The Observer*, August 17.

15. This quote is taken from page 1 of Wray, D. and Lewis, M. (1997) *Extending Literacy: Children Reading and Writing Non-fiction* (London: Routledge) which also describes the EXIT model of extending reading skills in detail.

16. This description, taken from Peter Hamill's (1988) *A Romantic in Cuba*, appears on page 50 of a comprehensive summary of research into word processing by Ilana Snyder entitled 'Writing with word processors: a research overview' in the journal *Educational Research*, **35**, 49–68, Spring 1993.

17. The paper by Kathy Durkin (1997) 'Redrafting at Key Stage 1', *Reading*, **31**, 47–50, contains numerous examples of children editing and redrafting their work.

18. Refer to Wray, D. and Medwell, J. (1996) 'Newspapers in education and children's writing'. *Reading*, **30**, 38–43, July.

References

Adam, N. and Wild, M. (1997) 'Applying CD Rom interactive storybooks to learning to read'. *Journal of Computer Assisted learning*, **13**, 119–32.

Burgess, A. (1992) *The Observer*, August 17.

Burrell, C. and Trushell, J. (1997) 'Eye candy in interactive books – a wholesome diet?' *Reading*, **31**, 3–6, July.

Chu, M. (1995) 'Reader response to interactive computer books: examining literary responses in non-traditional reading sessions'. *Reading Research and Instruction*, **34**, 352–66.

DfEE (1998) *National Literacy Strategy: Framework for Teaching*. London: HMSO.

Durkin, K. (1997) 'Redrafting at Key Stage 1'. *Reading*, **31**, 47–50, July.

Govier, H. (1997) 'Making sense of information', in *Microscope Information Handling Special*.

Hamil, P. (1988) 'A romantic in Cuba', cited in Snyder, I. (1993) 'Writing with word processors: a research overview'. *Educational Research*, **35**, 49–68, Spring.

McFarlane, A. (ed.) (1997) *Information Technology and Authentic Learning*. London: Routledge.

Medwell, J. (1995) 'Talking books for teaching reading'. *Microscope*, **46**, 22–4.

Medwell, J. (1996) 'Talking books and reading'. *Reading*, **30**, 41–6, April.

Medwell, J. (1998) 'The Talking Books Project: some further insights into the use of talking books to develop reading'. *Reading*, **32**, 3–7, April.

Millum, T. (1998) 'Making the most of email: the virtual writer in residence'. *MAPE Focus on Literacy*, Autumn.

Taylor, C. (1994) 'Teaching reading with talking story books'. *Computer Education*, **84**, 25–6.

Wray, D. and Medwell, J. (1996) 'Newspapers in education and children's writing'. *Reading*, 30, 38–43, July.

Wray, D. and Lewis, M. (1997) *Extending Literacy: Children Reading and Writing Non-fiction*. London: Routledge.

Further reading

Ager, R. (1998) *Information and Communications Technology in Primary Schools*. London:David Fulton Publishers.

Bennett, R., Hamil, A. and Pickford, T. (2005) *Learning ICT with English*. London: David Fulton Publishers.

Canterbury Christ Church University College (2001) *Talking about information and Communications Technology in Subject Teaching KS1 and 2*. Canterbury: Canterbury Christ Church University College.

Gage, J. (2004) *How to Use an Interactive Whiteboard Really Effectively in your Primary Classroom*. London: David Fulton Publishers.

Gage, J. (2005) *How to Use an Interactive Whiteboard Really Effectively in Your Secondary Classroom*. London: David Fulton Publishers.

McBride, P. (1998) *The Schools' Guide to The Internet*. London: Heinneman.

National Association for the Teaching of English (1993) *Developing English: Approaches with IT*. Sheffield: NATE.

National Council for Educational Technology (1995) *IT Helps: Using IT to Support Basic Literacy and Numeracy Skills*. NCET.

Useful websites

BECTA – www.becta.org.uk

Easiteach – http://www.easiteach.com/visitors/examples/users/lessonlist.htm

The Electronic Classroom – http://www.readingonline.org/electronic/elec_indexasp

Interactive whiteboard resources index – http://www.kented.org.uk/ngfl/ict/IWB/ index.htm

Literacy and ICT – http://www.kented.org.uk/ngfl/subjects/literacy/index.htm

Literacy Trust – www.literacytrust.org.uk

NAACE (formerly MAPE) – www.mape.org.uk

National Grid for Learning – www.ngfl.gov.uk

National Whiteboard network – http://www.nwnet.org.uk./pages/downloads/ faqs_teachers.doc

Newswise – http://www.dialogueworks.co.uk/newswise/

Nature grid – http://www.naturegrid.org.uk/infant/bigbook.html

Promethean Whiteboards – http://www.prometheanworld.com/home.html

Smart Board Resources – http://smarteducation.canterbury.ac.uk/home.asp

Literacy for life: the world of signs and symbols

Julie Scanlon

'They don't write like this in books, only on phones!'

(Harry, Year 4)

Introduction

We live in a visual world of developing communications and technologies and it is our responsibility, as teachers, to equip children with the skills needed to read and interpret texts that belong to this new age. After all 'what was basic literacy two decades ago is not compatible with current needs' (Craggs 1992:3). This chapter will explore two aspects of visual literacy, symbols and colour, by focusing on two areas of techno- and media-literacy:

- the use of text messaging; and
- children's understanding and perceptions of the news through pictures and colour.

It will consider how it is possible to use these areas to develop, motivate and challenge children's existing knowledge and values.

What is visual literacy?

The term visual literacy refers to the skill of being able to understand how meanings are written into a symbol or image. This is done by, first, identifying the particular symbol or sign and then interpreting its meaning. From an early age children are aware of the visual impact of environmental print in the form of signs, symbols and logos. This was evident in my own son (now aged 11), who at the age of two-and-a-half, would shout 'Ah, someone cares!' each time we drove past a Boots lorry on the motorway. What he was shouting was, of course, the 'Boots the Chemist' TV advertising slogan at the time, thus suggesting his ability to both recognise and link a logo with a product despite a lack of understanding of meaning. Now he is older he is able to think about and discuss possible reasons as to why a company chooses particular colours and logos for advertising purposes, therefore applying a meaning.

The run up to the 2005 General Election provided an excellent opportunity to explore this area further at home. This has been due mainly to my son's sudden interest in politics. His enthusiasm is linked to his enfranchisement, in a mock election at school. He has been very keen to find out about what each party represents - the three main parties and the fringe parties as well. One of the first questions he posed was 'Why is each of the parties represented by a particular colour?' I asked him what each of the colours meant to him and his responses were interesting. The red of Labour made him think of 'blood'. He went on to elaborate how this would be the blood of men who worked hard 'after all, the Labour Party does support the workers'. The yellow of the Liberal Democrats made him think of the sun and spring. We explored this idea further with the result of spring being a time of new life and therefore the Party's ideas may also be new. The sun, he suggested 'makes you feel happy, so the Party must want its policies to make people feel happy'. The blue of the Conservatives posed more of a problem, as he was only able to relate the colour to the sea and sky that he thought were 'everywhere'. However, after considering the colour alongside the Conservative logo of the torch his response was much more considered. The logo he likened to pictures he had seen in his Latin textbook and images from the Olympic Games. Therefore, because Romans and Greeks were ancient civilisations, he felt that the Conservatives must have 'been around for ages and must have lots of experience of running the country'. Their policies and ideas he felt would be 'traditional' and maybe 'old fashioned'.

This exercise really did focus on the idea of colour and symbols in visual literacy and highlighted how interpretations are rooted in personal, social and cultural experiences, through associations. It also showed the importance of questioning initial thoughts and meanings in order to think more critically about the images and 'reveal deeper cultural, sociological and ideological messages' (Craggs 1992:25).

Why teach visual literacy?

The National Curriculum (DfEE 1999:55) recognises the fact that children need to be prepared to live in a rapidly changing world and that part of this preparation is the ability to both read and interpret a range of media texts. In fact, it is a requirement for the knowledge, skills and understanding to be taught through a range of 'literature...non-fiction and non-literary texts'. The ability to make sense of the vast array of media text genres requires an understanding of visual literacy, as the reader learns to deconstruct the text in order to interpret a correct meaning. In deconstructing a text the reader also learns to interpret a set of codes and conventions which are often common among media texts, for example, the use of colour, choice of font style and size, choice of image etc. Because perception of pictorial images always involves interpretation it is important that children's interpretive powers are developed by setting them 'divergent tasks that encourage them to speculate imaginatively about pictorial images' (Allford 2000:51) It is the role of the teacher to select appropriate tasks, based on the children's interests, ages and abilities, in order to enhance children's understanding of the world around them. Taking this idea further I developed two activities with my own Key Stage 2 class consisting of Years 4, 5 and 6. The focus of the activities was based on the children's own interests.

Techno-literacy and text messaging

As more people, including children have access to mobile phones, text messaging is an increasingly popular form of communication. It is essentially note writing with the additional restriction of using the least possible amount of characters and spaces between words. This ensures that the message meets its purpose of being 'speedier and less expensive' (Mander 2001) while also meeting its prime aim of communicating. This communicating requires sender and receiver to understand the conventions of text messaging.

The brevity of the text message makes it an incredibly attractive form of communication for the reluctant writer. My own recent experiences within a Year 4/5/6 class have seen abbreviations, based on a phonic system, and symbols which would be acceptable in a text message being used increasingly in more formal styles of writing. One child, in particular, insists on writing 'u' instead of 'you' and 'plz' instead of 'please', and has even resorted to a smiley face for 'happy'. She struggles with the syntax of conventional writing but appears to have mastered that of the text message. This highlights the fact that 'the works of contemporary young adolescents who write fiction also show evidence of other media influences' (McClay 2002:47). This can be construed as problematic in relation to basic skills acquisition as 'text messaging is often blamed for bad spelling, bad grammar and a general dumbing down of the English language' (Attewell 2003). However, *The Guardian* recently published the findings of a small-scale research project,[1] which has shown that children seem able to 'code switch...and have an ability to switch between two forms of language when texting or writing Standard English' (Ward 2004).

My concerns are that as phones advance and make available more symbols such as 'emoticons' to express emotions or feelings, then the attraction of text messaging language will increase. Should this be the case then it is more important than ever that children are made aware of its intended purpose alongside other reasonable possibilities such as, for example, making notes rather than in formal writing. They also need to be made aware of the fact that the sender and receiver both need to be able to interpret the symbols to make meanings. Therefore, it should be considered a generic form in its own right.

Text messaging in the classroom

In my class of 21 children, whose ages range from 8 to 12, five possessed their own mobile phone and regularly sent messages to friends. Of the remainder, ten had access to either a parent's or older sibling's phone and they, too, sent and received messages. I knew that numbers of primary aged children with access to mobile phones was increasing, but was still surprised that almost 75 per cent of my class were texting regularly. It was clear from discussions, and from the slips into text-speak in their written work, that they enjoyed writing in this format and I felt that I should use this interest to create activities based on text messaging syntax. Interestingly, when I showed them my rather outdated mobile phone, which has no capacity to write symbols, they were not impressed. One Year 6 boy commented, 'It's not possible to send a real message with that [phone], you need pictures'. An important point to bear in mind!

Poetry activities using text messaging

Reading poetry

There had been a poetry focus during the term and so the children had been exposed to a range of poetry styles. I managed to find a short poem written in text message language (Winch. *et al.* 2002:23) and adapted this to use as the starting point (Figure 12.1). I wanted to establish the children's existing knowledge about texting conventions and so asked them to 'translate' it into conventional English. This enabled me to gain an understanding of their approach to the decoding process and to compare the results of those who were regular text messagers with those who had little or no experience of the language form.

The children were quick to ask if I had sent this poem on my phone as there were no pictures! This was interesting as they assumed that I had written it from the type of symbols used. The symbols in this poem are mainly a mix of numbers and letters but it proved to be a good starting point. When I suggested it was

---

OIC

ImInA10derMood2day

&FeelPoetic2

4FunIJust-OffALine

&Send ItOff2U.

ImSorryUvBn6OLong,

DontBDisconsol8

BtBerYrIIsWth42de

&TheyWontSeemSoGr8

FIGURE 12.1 Text message poem

---

similar to a poem I had found in a book they showed some surprise because as one younger member of the group pointed out, 'They don't write like this in books, only on phones!' – a point I was quick to pick up on when I spotted similar abbreviations in a formal story the following week. However, it does show an awareness of purpose and appropriateness.

The poem has a good rhythm and rhyme, which I felt would aid the younger children. However, it also contains some challenging vocabulary, such as disconsolate and fortitude, and I was particularly interested in the approach the children took in decoding and making sense of these two particular words. All of the children were able to rewrite the first two lines without any problems. The '–' depicting the word 'run' in the third line did not prove to be a problem to the experienced users. Two of the more able children guessed the word 'run' correctly because, as one of the children commented, it 'kept the rhythm of the poem. You had to put something there'. It was refreshing to think that this activity had prompted a discussion into the metre of the poem.

The word 'fortitude' in line seven (represented as '42de') posed more of a problem. I encouraged the children to discuss possibilities which ranged from 'fourtwodee', to 'fortytwoder'. It proved a real stumbling block until a Year 6 boy suddenly said 'I think it's fortidude, you know fortytwo**de**, but I havn't got a clue what it means!' There was then a race for the dictionaries to find a definition. This was ground breaking! The majority of children in the class, when asked to use a dictionary to find a definition or check a spelling, usually groan and say, 'Do I have to, can't you write it for me!'. Therefore, this activity had generated a real enthusiasm, a desire to learn among all of the children.

Writing poetry

The next stage in the process was to encourage the children to write a short poem themselves, in a similar format. They were asked to think about their friends and what it is like to have friends. What would it be like to have no friends, etc.? They were also told that their poem did not have to rhyme. Interestingly they were happier carrying out this activity on paper, rather than in their books because it '...wasn't like real work' (Clemmy, aged 10).

The poems produced were fairly simple but all included pictorial symbols or 'emoticons'. The children left spaces between words as in conventional writing, unlike a standard text message in which a new word is demarcated by a capital letter. In the first example (Figure 12.2) by an 11-year-old, the word happy is used in the title and is shortened to 'appy'. However, in the main body of the text an emoticon is used to represent the same word. Despite the inconsistency, this shows a degree of experimentation in the child's work and a lack of fear of trying new approaches.

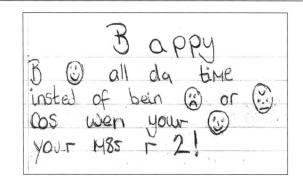

FIGURE 12.2 A child's text message poem

Another of the poems (Figure 12.3) produced by a regular sender of text messages (aged 10), began by addressing the receiver directly. She later told me she always begins text messages to her friends in this way. It is more complex with a rap-like rhythm and uses a variety of text messaging language and syntax, for example she omits the spacing between words. She combines both letters and numbers and letters and emoticons although she uses the symbol '@' incorrectly to represent 'and'. Incidentally, this style never appears in her formal writing, thus showing the ability of a confident writer to switch between codes.

The children who produced the poems both agreed that it 'felt less like real work' because it was 'fun, less tiring and you don't have to worry about spellings'.

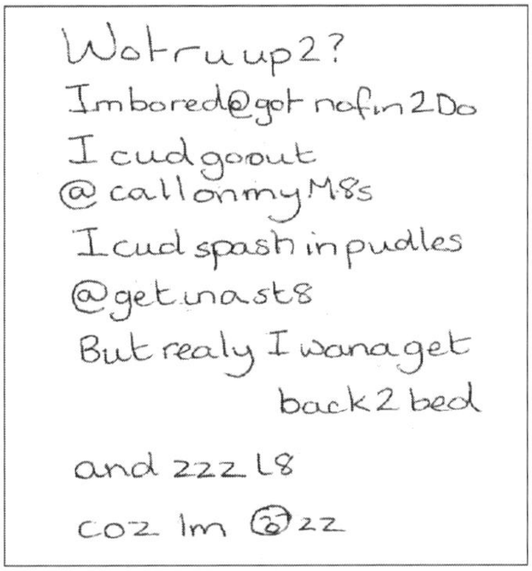

Wot r u up 2?
Im bored@ got nofin 2 Do
I cud go out
@ call on my M8s
I cud spash in pudles
@ get in a st8
But realy I wana get
back 2 bed
and zzz L8
coz Im @zz

FIGURE 12.3 A child's text message poem

Getting over the hurdle of spelling can be a real problem and this is often the underlying cause of reluctance to write. There is no doubt that tapping into the child's enthusiasm and encouraging an understanding of techno-literacy can encourage creativity as well as an understanding of the practical use of language, despite reservations about its use encouraging poor spelling and grammar. In fact, I would suggest that the use of techno-literacy activities should be encouraged as part of the English curriculum, as positive endorsement will serve to dispel fears by breaking with formal writing syntax. In addition, it may well engage boys and improve their literacy levels, as there is no doubt that they were enthused by these activities. They particularly enjoyed rewriting the poem and saw it as a code-breaking mission.

Tapping in to texting

If teachers feel uncomfortable about teaching 'texting', it is probably because they feel like the children in the activities described above; that is it is not really a legitimate school activity. However, I would argue that it is possible to use the genre within a language lesson without feeling guilty. I have previously mentioned note making which is an activity recognised in the National Literacy Strategy (1998) objectives from Year 3. The concept of identifying key points and 'noting' them can be difficult. Various methods can be used such as underlining, bullet points, key words and graphic representations.[2] Text messaging abbreviations and symbols can also be used, after all texting is simply a modern day form of shorthand. Begin with abbreviations that are familiar to the children and a text containing a small number of key points about a subject the children will find interesting (I used a paragraph about sharks with Year 5 to conduct this activity). My children identified the key points under bullet points and for issues that needed expansion, texting abbreviations and symbols were used. This activity has two benefits in that it prepares children for modern technologies and, perhaps more importantly, it offers alternatives for *taking* notes as opposed to *making* notes in lessons and lectures as they progress through the education system. From a teaching perspective, it is a gentle way in to the subject area without straying from government objectives. For example, it can be explored across the three strands of the National Literacy Strategy:

- Year 4 Term 2 text level work: *'To make short notes, e.g. by abbreviating ideas...'* (41)

- Year 5 Term 3 Sentence level work: *'To understand how writing can be adapted for different audiences and purposes...'* (48)

- Year 6 Term 3 word level work: *'To experiment with language, e.g. by creating new words...'* (54)

Media-literacy and children's perceptions of the news

In order to understand how news is manufactured, children need to develop the skill of critical awareness. This is not an easy process, as even the youngest primary aged children have begun to attach individual personalised meanings to symbols and pictorial representations, based on social and cultural values. For example, a five-year-old boy commented that my car, a Nissan, was 'rubbish' and that a good car was 'a Mercedes'. He went on to draw a car shape with a huge star at the front and back. He was making a connection between the Mercedes logo and quality.

More recently, I took my Year 6 children on a residential Welsh language course. One of the activities was media based, provided by the BBC in conjunction with Bangor University and the Welsh Language Association. The children were invited to dress up in a wig and spectacles of their choice. One boy chose a blonde wig and sunglasses. His friend, a keen footballer, shouted 'You look like a footballer's wife'. I asked him why he thought this and he replied 'Because he has blonde curly hair and is wearing sunglasses'. He was adamant that all footballers were married to women with blonde hair. I asked him what ladies with blonde hair were like and the response was 'not very clever but very rich'. I went on to ask him what ladies with blonde hair and sunglasses liked to do in their spare time. 'Shopping' was the response, 'Definitely shopping – oh, and getting their hair done. They'd always be doing that.' At the age of 11 this child had made certain stereotypical assumptions that were rooted in his own interest in football. He could not be persuaded that such women may have different attributes. This failure to be able to question his preconceived views concerned me and I went back to the classroom with the intention of exploring symbols and colour in news stories in order to encourage critical analysis of the visual image.

Seeing is believing

There is an old saying, 'Seeing is believing'. This idea obviously influences the newspaper editor's choice of photograph to enhance a written article. I wanted the children to begin to understand how a visual image can coax a reader into a preferred interpretation and that pictures in newspapers do not simply illustrate written words. As many newspapers use both black-and-white and colour photographs, the activities were intended to allow the children to think about symbolism in colour and the impact of its use, in addition to the actual image itself. My overall intention was for the children to think about how people are portrayed in the news, as this would expose any preconceptions and offer the opportunity for the children to take part in critical analysis and discussion.

Symbolism in colour

Different colours will signify different meanings to different people. Some, however, may generate similar connotations. In this preliminary exercise I wanted to establish the children's perceptions and ideas on what a range of colours meant to them and to find out what meanings were most common. I hoped, eventually, to examine how these personal perceptions transferred into generating an understanding of a pictorial image. I began by offering the children a colour and asking them to write down the first thing that came to mind; that is, what the colour made them think about. Out of the 21 children taking part there were some interesting results.

Table 12.1 shows the overall consensus of opinion. As a class, the children discussed which of the colours were happy and which were sad or bad. Yellow, green and pink were deemed to be happy and the remainder, with the exception of blue, evil. Blue was the cause of much interesting debate as it was likened to a 'stormy sea' that was bad. The contrary argument was that it could represent the Caribbean Sea, suggesting holidays and happiness. They finally agreed that a dark blue would represent evil and a light blue happiness. This demonstrates how the children were able to move on from allocating an actual item to a colour to the more abstract idea of using colour to suggest feelings.

However, it was the alternative responses to those in the table that proved most interesting. This was because they included a personal perspective. The colour

Table 12.1 Colour connotations

Colour	Connotation	% in agreement
red	blood	45
pink	pig	40
blue	sea	40
black	darkness	60
green	grass	100
grey	clouds	40
yellow	sun	80

grey was particularly interesting as a number of the children likened it to 'old people's hair like Granny's' (three suggested Granddad), Dad's moustache, and one girl responded with 'Lucky my rabbit'. Pink was also interesting as although 40 per cent responded with pig, the remaining 60 per cent all made a feminine link to the colour in that all those children with a sister made either a direct reference to her, for example her name, or to her clothes, for example 'dress'. Other ideas included lips, lipstick and flowers. A number of boys are keen followers of football and the colour red conjured up images of Wrexham AFC for 15 per cent of them. For another 10 per cent, red was the trigger for homework as it is the colour of their homework book. These individual responses suggest that strong personal interests, thoughts, ideas and worries can influence what we see.

As a class we looked at two pictures, one of a man in a white suit and one of a woman in a white dress. Their initial feelings about the characters were that the lady concerned was young and happy and was probably getting married. 'Old ladies don't wear white dresses', commented one Year 4 girl. The male character provided more interesting and contradictory responses. The class were divided. One group considered him to be 'a bit soft' like a character 'in *Mary Poppins*'. One Year 6 boy commented, 'He must be gay; all gays dress like that'. I was taken aback at such a stereotypical comment from such a young child. The other group thought he would be 'a dodgy dealer' and a bit 'hard, you know scary'. They likened him, first to a boy they had met on their recent residential trip, and secondly, to a celebrity footballer 'who is a dirty player on the field and not kind to his wife because he has other girlfriends'. This group offered a more personally related response. As a class these initial responses were discussed and the children began to comment about matters that had affected their opinion and how their opinions might be changed. For example, 'You wouldn't think he [footballer] was bad if you supported his team' and 'a man in a white suit would look smart if he was getting married'. Also they began to think about other issues such as hairstyle and facial expression and concluded that these would have an affect on their opinion.

Working with photographs and headlines

I extended the colour activity using a suggestion from Carol Craggs (1992) in which the children worked in pairs and selected a picture from a newspaper along with its headline. In this case they worked from a range of local newspapers along with a national tabloid and broadsheet. They then mounted their chosen picture on card and went on to devise a headline to support the picture. On one side of the picture they wrote the original headline; on the other they wrote their own headline. The next stage of the activity was for the children to present their work to the class who had to guess which of the headlines was the original, and which was the children's own work. Each pair then had to justify their choice of headline by discussing the detail in the picture and what they had seen. In doing this they began to both deconstruct the image and to consider its impact more critically. One pair chose a picture of an old lady. It was actually an artist's drawing, although it was very much like a photograph. I was intrigued to know why they had chosen it. They felt her 'crinkly skin made her look kind'. This also suggested age. She had been drawn with a bookshelf behind her although this was not prominent. On the shelves were books and photographs. The three Year 5 boys examined the photograph closely to look for clues for a suitable headline. The headline eventually read 'Famous Ourther Celebrates her 100th Birthday'. Note the phonetic spelling of author which shows that they felt comfortable and were not afraid to make mistakes. Although a literal headline, the children had thought hard and used the picture to simply illustrate the headline.

Another group worked with a photograph of the Prime Minister, Tony Blair, holding two ice-creams (a much publicised incident during the 2005 election campaign when he bought one for himself and one for Gordon Brown, the Chancellor of the Exchequer). They immediately recognised him and their initial response was that he was buying the ice-creams for his family. At that point a Year 4 girl exclaimed 'The election! That's what it is about'. From this point the girl took control and acted as 'editor', listening to and reasoning about the other children's arguments. One child commented that he looked tired in the photograph. This made them agree that they 'felt sorry for him'. Our editor suggested that this might make people vote for him. 'That's what this picture should do. Make people vote for him. Now what sort of people would he buy ice-cream for to make people say 'ah, he's kind?' After a few seconds of thought she said, 'The homeless, that's our headline – "Blair buys ice cream for the homeless".'

'What about "Blair buys ice cream for beggars",' suggested another child, 'then we've got alliteration.' This group had moved on from the literal to think about the powers of suggestion that are contained within the visual image. The exercise also demonstrated how collaborative discussion and sharing ideas can encourage children to redraft responses and use metalanguage comfortably with peers in the classroom setting.

Good guy, bad guy

It was time to take this idea of the power of the editor in choosing photographs further. I created a discussion board on which I had a headline, the story, its accompanying photograph and an alternative photograph. The headline, from the *Chester Chronicle* read 'Teen Held on Head Stamping Charge'. The supporting story contained details of the incident. The supporting photograph displayed a youth with shaven head wearing a white tracksuit looking at the floor. The alternative photograph displayed a youth wearing a dark suit and tie sporting a short-back-and-sides haircut, smiling at the camera. Both photographs were cropped to size and would fit the cut out in the text. The headline was read to the class who then shared opinions and ideas relating to who was the guilty party from the headline. All but three children suggested the correct photograph. Some of the reasons given were, 'He's not dressed very well', 'He's got a skinhead and looks like he takes drugs and smokes' and 'He's got a guilty face... and looks like he's hiding from the camera'. The majority of the children felt that the youth in the suit looked 'civilised' and 'important' and just 'wouldn't do that sort of thing'. However, three children argued that the man in the suit was guilty because he 'looks like he's dressed to go to court'. They explained that it was important to look smart if you had to go to court because then the 'judge thinks you are good'. I asked if they knew anybody who had been to court and two of them, who are brothers, said, in unison 'Yes, my Dad'. Again this highlights how personal experience can influence our interpretations of what we see.

After agreeing that the responses had been carefully considered I read the article to the class and the children went on to think about how the choice of picture enhanced the story. They agreed that the picture made you think, 'He's an awful lad, must be guilty' before reading the article. They decided that the editor must have chosen it to 'make him look really bad so you would think that'.

Working with newspapers

It is very easy to focus on writing reports but understanding how the package of photograph, headline and article work together is vital if our children are able to question what they read and see in the news. After all, the news we are exposed to is selected and manufactured for us. Therefore it is vital that children begin to understand that from an early age. The activities used in this chapter would be suitable for use in language or citizenship sessions, as they have proved to be fantastic tools for generating critical discussion and encouraging the use of new and technical vocabulary.

Upper Key Stage 1 children could begin work on visual literacy in media texts by considering characters in familiar comic strips and how they are represented, for example Dennis the Menace. Lower and middle Key Stage 2 could then move on to local newspapers that are jam-packed with a variety of issues such as environmental campaigns and crime to local flower show winners. This can then be extended to national papers and more abstract photographs along with staging photographs for a given headline.

Conclusion

It remains the case that the teaching of techno- and media-literacy is considered to be of little importance especially when teachers have so many targets and objectives to meet in the classroom. It is not only teachers that may be reluctant to teach, research[3] has found that parents also see such areas of language as being 'utilitarian and not of much relevance' (Wyse 1998). However, from my own experiences in the classroom I have seen children develop a confidence and enthusiasm that transcends all four Programmes of Study of the National Curriculum for English, especially the often undervalued skills of speaking and listening. In order to prepare our children for the future we need to provide enjoyable learning opportunities that our children can relate to. In so doing we will nurture young people who 'are keen to communicate with each other and learn collaboratively' (Attewell 2003) and create the team players of the future.

Notes

1. The comparative study was conducted by the City University, London. It found that there were no significant differences in spelling and punctuation ability between 11- and 12-year-olds who text messaged regularly and those who did not. However, it did find that children familiar with text messaging wrote considerably less when asked to describe a picture. This highlights concerns over the expressiveness of children's writing.
2. Bobbie Neate offers a range of interesting ways to introduce and develop note-making skills in her chapter in Evans, J. (ed.) (2001) *The Writing Classroom*. London: David Fulton Publishers.
3. Domimic Wyse's book *Primary Writing* combines theoretical research and practice. The findings mentioned in this chapter are taken from the responses of parents to the reading process. The school concerned was keen to empower parents in the process of co-operation in language learning.

References

Allford, D. (2000) 'Pictoral images, lexical phrases and culture'. *Language Learning Journal*, 22, 45–51.

Attewell, J. (2003) 'Mobile Learning'. *Literacy Today*, 36, September (www.literacytrust.org.uk).

Craggs, C. (1992) *Media Education in the Primary School*. London: Routledge.

DfEE (1998) *The National Literacy Strategy*. Suffolk: DfEE Publications.

DfEE (1999) *The National Curriculum Key Stages 1 and 2: England*. London: DfEE/QCA.

Evans, J. (ed.) (2001) *The Writing Classroom*. London: David Fulton Publishers.

McClay, J.K. (2002) 'Hidden treasure: new genres, new media and the teaching of writing'. *English in Education*, 36, 1, 46–55, Spring.

Mander, G. (2001) *ltl bk of pwr txt*. London: Michael O'Mara.

Ward, L. (2004) '"Texting" is no bar to literacy'. *The Guardian*. 23 December.

Winch, G., Blaxwell, G. and Rigby, H. (2002) *Comprehension Ages 10–11*. Leamington Spa: Scholastic.

Wyse, D. (1998) *Primary Writing*. Buckingham: Open University Press.

Further Reading

DfES (2003) *Speaking, Listening, Learning: Working with Children in Key Stages 1 and 2*. London: QCA

Useful websites

National Literacy Trust – www.literacytrust.org.uk

The Guardian – www.guardian.co.uk

Index